"[An] absorbing memoir . . . Schwartz's book is revealing about the criminal mind and its thought processes and thus contains valuable lessons for those at risk of incarceration and for those close to them."

—*The New York Review of Books*

"A gritty, unflinching book."

—*The Nation*

"Intimate memoir and impassioned call to arms for prison reform from a respected criminal-justice advocate . . . inspiring idealism refreshingly free of jargon or fluff."

—*Kirkus Reviews*

"Lucid, gritty and penetrating."

—*Publishers Weekly*

"Effectively told . . . eye-opening."

—*Library Journal*

"Sunny Schwartz understands accountability, kindness and forgiveness. In her brave and empowering book about people's ability to change, she tells the story of her life and her work with people who are often detested, feared or forgotten and explains how restorative justice can transform these criminals, their victims and our communities."

—Sister Helen Prejean, author of *Dead Man Walking*

"*Dreams from the Monster Factory* is as gritty as the halls of the San Francisco jail in which it takes place. But rather than being filled with despair and violence, Sunny Schwartz's story is marked by hope and respect. It is truly breathtaking to read about the transformation of the jails that Sunny has led. Putting the principles of restorative justice to work at ground zero of the crime culture, Sunny and her team have created a space where hardened criminals can realize their better selves and begin giving back to the community that they have heretofore only taken from."

—Pat Nolan, vice president of Prison Fellowship

"I couldn't put this book down. This is to the world of prisons and rehabilitation what *Dead Man Walking* is to the death penalty. It's gritty and real, simple yet revolutionary, hopeful but realistic. It isn't all happy endings, but there is vision combined with experience that suggests a way out of the morass our society is in. Dreams, yes, but not fantasies."

—Howard Zehr, professor of restorative justice at the Center for Justice and Peacebuilding, Eastern Mennonite University, and author of *Changing Lenses*

"A powerfully honest and revealing glimpse into a little-known world. Ms. Schwartz captivates the reader with her clear-eyed belief that even violent offenders can change. Her work shows that violent behavior is a choice and our communities can be stronger if each of us—victims, offenders, citizens—better understands why we act the way we do. As a survivor of violent crime, I respect Ms. Schwartz's insistence that the penal system is not working. I admire her willingness to follow her heart toward a vision that will make a difference."

—Trisha Meili, author of
I Am the Central Park Jogger: A Story of Hope and Possibility

"Personal and provocative, Sunny Schwartz's book demanded my wide-eyed attention. Schwartz confronts our skepticism of the prison system and its ability to prevent violence with gripping and authentic stories from her life and her work on a visionary program in San Francisco jails that has actually reduced recidivism rates for violent crimes. *Dreams from the Monster Factory* is an inspiring story about justice and forgiveness."

—Terrie M. Williams, author of
Black Pain: It Just Looks Like We're Not Hurting

DREAMS

from the

MONSTER FACTORY

A TALE OF PRISON, REDEMPTION AND
ONE WOMAN'S FIGHT TO RESTORE JUSTICE TO ALL

Sunny Schwartz

with David Boodell

SCRIBNER

New York   London   Toronto   Sydney

SCRIBNER
A Division of Simon & Schuster, Inc.
1230 Avenue of the Americas
New York, NY 10020

First Scribner trade paperback edition February 2010

SCRIBNER and design are registered trademarks of
The Gale Group, Inc. used under license by Simon & Schuster, Inc.,
the publisher of this work.

For information about special discounts for bulk purchases, please contact
Simon & Schuster Special Sales at
1-866-506-1949 or business@simonandschuster.com.

The Simon & Schuster Speakers Bureau can bring authors to your live event.
For more information or to book an event contact the Simon & Schuster Speakers
Bureau at 1-866-248-3049 or visit our website at www.simonspeakers.com.

Designed by Kyoko Watanabe
Text set in Aldine 401

Manufactured in the United States of America

3 5 7 9 10 8 6 4 2

Library of Congress Control Number: 2008020441

ISBN 978-1-4165-6981-7
ISBN 978-1-4165-6982-4 (pbk)
ISBN 978-1-4165-7010-3 (ebook)

For Frieda, Lauren, Ella and the Chicago Cubs

The future belongs to those who believe in the beauty of their dreams.

—ELEANOR ROOSEVELT

You don't need to wait for a roof to collapse on your head to fix something.

—FRIEDA SCHWARTZ, MY MOTHER

DREAMS

from the

MONSTER FACTORY

INTRODUCTION

by James Gilligan

I first met Sunny Schwartz in 1996 when I was invited to address the Commonwealth Club in San Francisco. My talk was on crime, punishment and the most effective ways to facilitate violent offenders' motivation and ability to renounce violence as a strategy for living and problem solving. It was based on my experience over several decades as a psychiatrist at Harvard Medical School, directing mental-health and violence-prevention programs in the prisons and prison mental hospital in Massachusetts. Some of Sunny's remarkable and very impressive coworkers, Hamish Sinclair and Michael Marcum among them, were there and realized that they and I were on the same wavelength. So they asked me if I would be willing to conduct a research project for them, to ascertain whether the violence-prevention program, RSVP (Resolve to Stop the Violence Project), that Sunny had put together in the San Francisco jails was succeeding in enabling its participants to discontinue committing acts of violence.

With Sinclair's and Marcum's cooperation, and that of their boss, Michael Hennessey, the politically courageous and public-spirited sheriff of San Francisco, my main research partner, Dr. Bandy Lee, who did the lion's share of the work in this very labor-intensive project, and I were able to redesign some of the administrative procedures by which they assigned prisoners to the RSVP unit so that there was in effect a random assignment to the program. We also established a "control group" of prisoners in a conventional jail who were statistically indistinguishable from the experimental group with respect to the major demographic variables that are predictors of violent behavior (such as age, education, ethnicity, past criminal history and substance abuse) and who would have been admitted to RSVP except for the fact that there were no free beds at the time they were admitted to jail. That made it possible for us to create a quasi-experimental research design, which we could then use to compare the differences in rates of violence between the experimental group (RSVP) and the control group.

What we found, as we reported in two journal articles,[1] was that the rate of in-house violence dropped literally to zero in the RSVP unit for the entire first year of its existence (as compared with about three violent incidents a month in the control population during the same time period, and about the same number of violent incidents a month in the RSVP dorm during the year before RSVP was started). And we found that after they were released from jail, the rate of rearrests for new violent crimes was 83 percent lower among those prisoners who had been in RSVP for at least four months than it was among those who had been in the conventional jail for the same length of time (with a proportionately smaller decrease in the violent rearrest rate among RSVP graduates who had been in the program for shorter lengths of time, such as two or three months). In other words, we observed what in medicine would be called a "dose-response curve": the longer the men were in the RSVP program, the more sharply their rate of violent recidivism decreased, compared to the control group. And it was significantly lower even in those who had been in the program for shorter time periods.

In other words, Sunny and her colleagues had created living evidence that, despite the skepticism (or "therapeutic nihilism," as we call it in medicine) of many people on this subject, violence actually can be prevented. It takes time, energy, dedication, courage (against both physical and political harm) and money, but it can be done. With respect to the latter, we found through a cost-benefit analysis that, although having a program of this sort in the jails slightly increased

---

1. James Gilligan and Bandy Lee, "The Resolve to Stop the Violence Project: Reducing Violence in the Community through a Jail-Based Initiative," *Journal of Public Health* 27, no. 2 (June 2005), 143–48; Bandy Lee and James Gilligan, "The Resolve to Stop the Violence Project: Transforming an In-House Culture of Violence Through a Jail-Based Programme," *Journal of Public Health* 27, no. 2 (June 2005),149–55.

their overall running costs, the program was actually saving the tax-payers $4 for every $1 spent on it, because the program was so success-ful in lowering the rate of reincarceration. The costs of incarceration even in the most pared-down jails and prisons is so great (as they say, quite correctly, "a year in jail costs as much as a year in Yale") that the only question we should be asking is not "Can we afford programs such as this?" but rather "Can we afford not to have programs such as this?" The costs of the unprecedentedly bloated penal system in this country, which now houses seven times as many prisoners (per capita) as it did thirty-five years ago, are forcing many states, counties and cities to the verge of bankruptcy.

The book you are now holding in your hands is Sunny's vivid description of how this extraordinary project came into being and what we need to learn from it. It is a book about what is arguably the most important unsolved problem in American life: namely, the uniquely high rate of lethal violence in the United States, a rate that is far higher than in any other economically developed nation. It is also a brilliant and passionately argued analysis of some of the reasons that our overpopulated and expensive penal system has not only failed to solve the problem of violence on a national scale, it has actually exac-erbated it. And it gives a detailed, perceptive and very moving descrip-tion of the methods that Sunny and her colleagues employed in their work with violent criminals in the San Francisco jails, showing that we can reverse the self-defeating policies and practices that have been fol-lowed in our criminal justice system up to now, and actually prevent violence far more effectively.

This book is not an academic study. I do not say that as a criti-cism—quite the contrary. It would diminish its importance and value to relegate it merely to the reference shelves of university libraries, or the reading lists of social scientists. Whatever else you can say about it, this book is not pedantic. Rather, it is like Sunny herself—bold and articulate, gutsy and honest, tough but also compassionate, knowl-edgeable (because it is based on decades of firsthand experience) but unpretentious and, above all, wise. It is Sunny, in the sense that it is a revelation and expression of her personality, her mind and her heart. And even though she wrote it with a coauthor who is a skilled writer, her own voice comes through so loud and clear that there is no paradox in saying that this is a book that only she could have written. Sunny's voice enables the book to reach out to anyone who is interested in what actually works in preventing violence, as opposed to what some ideology or other says should work.

This is a book for conservatives and liberals, Republicans and Democrats, legislators and voters, the punitive and the compassionate. And I guarantee it will knock your socks off, if you approach it with an open mind and an open heart. That does not mean an empty mind and heart but, rather, a willingness to reexamine and, when the evidence is compelling, discard many of the most widely held assumptions, practices and emotional responses to violent crime and adopt new ones—as Sunny shows herself doing in this book.

Sunny's descriptions of the work she and her colleagues did in the jails are vivid and compelling and specific, and the reasons for the program's success may seem so self-evident that the attempt to identify the underlying principles of its success may seem at first like creating a set of bloodless abstractions that are hardly needed to understand why her approach to violence prevention worked as well as it did. Nevertheless, I think it is worth engaging in this exercise, since no demonstration of a set of successful interventions is in fact self-explanatory. For example, when I present the results of my evaluation of Sunny's multidimensional program to my professional colleagues in psychiatry and the other behavioral and social sciences, one of the first questions I am often asked is "Which particular intervention was the most effective in preventing violence?" They ask this because one of the primary methods of all science is to isolate all the variables involved in any given experiment from one another, in order to learn what effect each individual variable had on the overall outcome. For example, if a given jail or prison—or school or court clinic or domestic violence program—had only enough money to implement one of the components of Sunny's RSVP program, which one should it be? My answer would be that that approach would miss the point and the significance of this particular study, which is that it was precisely the combination of all the components, the comprehensiveness of the approach to preventing violence and the mutually reinforcing interactions between the different components, that led to its success. That is, the whole was greater than the parts.

I say this for several reasons. First, because one of the first things I learned when I began to work with violent criminals some forty years ago was that the degree of deprivation and neglect and abuse that they had suffered was in almost all cases so great—so much greater than I had ever imagined or thought possible, especially in our supposedly wealthy society—that almost any intervention was helpful and effective, and the more interventions one could offer, the more effective they all were. This group had been deprived of almost every source of human development and thriving—education, nutrition, housing, medical care, dental care, physical safety and protection, emotional support (respect, love, praise, attention)—and almost any form or combination of those and other sources of psychological well-being were eagerly absorbed and utilized.

For example, when I first began my violence-prevention work in prison as part of my clinical training in psychiatry at Harvard Medical School, I was stunned to realize that many of the incoming inmates were having all their teeth removed by the prison's dental service. At first I thought, is this a horrendous example of institutionalized sadism? Then I learned that these men had never seen a dentist before in their lives, and their teeth were so rotten that they were forming abscesses that could become deadly. The thought that in our society today there could be so many children who are never taken to a dentist had simply never occurred to me.

Another example: When one of the psychiatrists I was supervising brought in a cupcake and lit a candle on it in order to celebrate the birthday of the prisoner with whom she was meeting, he burst into tears. Never before in his life had anyone given a birthday party for him. I realize that this is the kind of example that drives "tough on crime" nuts crazy. We should be giving birthday parties for criminals? What they fail to recognize is that it is precisely the deprivation of these rituals of everyday life—that most of us take for granted so automatically, it never occurs to us that there might be some children who are raised in an environment without them—that turns them into criminals in the first place. Children need birthday parties primarily for their own sakes, to celebrate their existence, but we need to make sure that no child in our society grows up without birthday parties for our own sakes as well; that is, for the sake of our own moral integrity, and also of our own physical safety. No one should have to commit a violent crime in order to have his first birthday party. But those who have never had a birthday party are precisely those who commit violent crimes. Concern for others, for *all* others, is the only form of being "tough on crime" that actually *is* tough on crime.

The second reason that the RSVP program works better as a whole than in parts is that, because RSVP involved all of the prisoners in the experimental housing unit, not just some of them, and engaged them in the program six days a week, twelve hours a day, the program was able to prevent the splitting into antagonistic subgroups that could otherwise occur. That is, RSVP succeeded in changing the whole subculture of the jail system and by involving everyone all the time made it impossible for one group to undermine or ridicule or punish the participation of another group. For example, I remember seeing one of the prisoners who had been involved in the RSVP program for some time greet a new prisoner on the RSVP unit. The new man was pumped full of adrenaline, and it was clear that he was prepared to hit anyone who even looked at him in the wrong way. The old-timer came up to him and said, "Look, man, I know where you be at. I been there myself. But you don't need to be that way here, brother, we don't treat each other that way here." The new man looked doubtful at first, and it was at least two or three days before he began to relax. But when he realized that no one was threatening or disrespecting him, he dropped his offensive stance (which to him was defensive) and joined the group.

Third, the human psyche, like Caesar's Gaul, is divided into three parts, different psychological functions—cognition, emotion and action. All of these functions are equally important and necessary for healthy and normal adaptation, and they must be integrated with one another for successful functioning to be possible. What RSVP did was come up with programs, each of which, while useful with respect to all of these functions, was particularly useful in strengthening one of them at a time—rather in the way that a comprehensive and integrated fitness program will include a variety of different physical exercises, each of which is useful to the whole body while also focusing on a specific muscle group or a specific component of physical well-being, such as flexibility, strength or endurance.

From that point of view, one can understand three of RSVP's component parts as equally necessary but different. The Manalive program, with its emphasis on deconstructing and reconstructing the "male role belief system," concentrated on correcting the cognitive distortions that predispose people to violent behavior. These include the belief that all human groups are divided into the superior and the inferior, and that to be an adequate male one must control and dominate other people (women and men), by means of violence if necessary, whenever one's superiority is questioned and one is cast instead into the role of the inferior (by being disrespected or humiliated).

The Victim Impact program focused on enabling these violent men to strengthen their underdeveloped capacity for empathy, sympathy and compassion for the suffering of others, for being able to love and care for others and for feeling remorse and guilt over hurting others. These are among the emotional capacities that prevent most of us from engaging in violence but that are notably missing in those who are most violent. Indeed, how could it be otherwise? How could anyone injure other people as grievously as many of these men had done unless they were almost totally lacking in the capacity for feeling empathy and remorse and for caring about others? The more egregious and heinous the crime, the more totally lacking the perpetrator was in these emotions. Freud once said that no one feels guiltier than the saints (which is true—that is one reason they are saints, because they would feel guilty about harming a fly or failing to help anyone in need), but I would add—referring to a population that Freud did not study—that no one feels more innocent than the criminals.

The drama program, in which prisoners were requested to write a one-act play based on the incident in their lives that they could identify as the turning-point that directed them toward a life of violence— we called it the "loss of innocence" moment—and then act themselves in the play, while other inmates or volunteers from the community played the other roles in the drama, was able to give them practice in learning that they could control their actions. It is no mere verbal coincidence that the word "acting" refers both to real actions in real life and to the dramatic enactment or reenactment of similar actions in a controlled, consciously symbolic milieu, which we call "play-acting," or "plays," because it is actually the controlled acting out of a conscious fantasy rather than the uncontrolled acting out in real life of a script that is written only in one's unconscious mind. By writing and then acting in these plays, the men can see that they could have acted differently; that is, they could have written a different script. The increase in their self-control, their ability to become consciously aware of and able to control their actions, resulting from their acting in these dramatic exercises, was almost palpable.

What has to be recognized in any enterprise of this sort, of course, is that total success is an unattainable goal, whether we are trying to prevent violence (toward others or the self) and heal those who have become violent or to prevent cancer or heart disease and heal those who have become ill with those diseases. Even the most successful program can never be more than relatively successful. Every death that occurs despite the program is an irretrievable loss. But every fewer death that occurs because of the program is an immeasurable gain. And by that criterion, the program that Sunny Schwartz and her colleagues created in the San Francisco jails has proven to be a major success to the degree that it is vitally important now to replicate it, to adopt and adapt it, in as many correctional settings as possible, in this country and around the world.

PROLOGUE

I don't think my truant officer ever knew where I went. I'd ditch class and ride the El to Chicago's north side, jump off at Belmont and plant myself in the Wrigley Field bleachers. I'd soak up the squawk of the beer man, the steam coming from the bins of the Vienna Beef hot dog vendors, the gentle slapping sound of a ball dropping into a mitt in the outfield and the emerald green expanse of the diamond. Wrigley was my sanctuary when I was a gawky teenager stumbling through adolescence. Even if school gave me palpitations and my family drove me nuts, I still had the ballpark and the dream that bound all of us fans together: the dream that this year the Cubs would go all the way.

I was raised on the south side and by rights should have pledged allegiance to the White Sox, but my heart has always been with the underdogs and so it was the Cubs for me. Later, when I moved to San Francisco, I gave myself with equal passion to the Giants, who have validated my devotion by failing to win the big one year after year. I am like this in the rest of my life, too: I root for underdogs.

I work in the jails of San Francisco County, and my clients are thieves and wife beaters, gangbangers and murderers—underdogs, every one of them. They have hurt their victims, their families and their communities and are now paying the price, abandoned to society's scrap heap. There are lots of names for this scrap heap: the big house, the slammer, the joint, lockup. I think the best name is monster factory. In these factories, men exist in cells on long tiers, where they have nothing to do. They sleep in their bunks, play dominoes and cards, watch the *Jerry Springer* show on TV and scheme. They scheme about how to steal someone's lunch, how to pull one over on the DA, how to score black market cigarettes for five bucks a smoke and how to get even with whoever crossed them. They make shanks out of mops, pens and metal shards broken off their bunks. These are places where the strongest thugs are allowed to terrorize the weakest. In most of our nation's jails and prisons, violence in the form of beatings, racial threats and rapes is normal. The most predictable product of this system is rage, which builds and builds in each prisoner until he is set free—and about 90 percent are set free someday, released back into our communities.

It's no news flash to say that traditional criminal justice is in chaos. One out of every hundred adults in the United States is behind bars. This is the highest incarceration rate in the world. Recidivism rates—which are difficult to track since no one keeps comprehensive statistics—hover somewhere around 70 percent, despite state budgets for corrections that have been climbing for years now. "There is no other business in the world," one coporate attorney told me, "that gets an increase in their budget when they have a seventy percent failure rate."

I was trained as an attorney, and always thought I'd spend my life as a defense attorney, but have instead worked on what I call "true defense." True defense is working for the good of all: the victims of crime *and* the perpetrators as well as the community. It has been my life's work to fight the monster factories, to reject the presumption people make that nothing can ever change. It hasn't been a simple fight. The question I get most often is "Why should I care?" I've found there is no more persuasive way to answer this question than by taking people to see the monsters. I first show people the traditional jail. Then I take them to the jails I've helped set up. I take them to RSVP (Resolve to Stop the Violence Program), the program I'm most proud of, where we work with violent men to make them less violent. I tell people about the evaluation of our program, done by psychiatrist James Gilligan, who directed the Center for the Study of Violence at Harvard Medical School and now works at NYU. He is one of the country's leading experts on violence. His study showed an 80 percent drop in violent recidivism for inmates who had spent more than four months in our program. I take people to see the charter high school (the first charter school for incarcerated adults in this country) and the college classes, and show them what a jail can be like in a place where there are high standards, and where the presumption exists that despicable men and women can change for the better and rejoin the human race. One venture capitalist I took around with me came away thunderstruck. "Sunny," he exclaimed, "those programs for violent men. They could help me! They could help any man." The stories I tell in this book will take you on the same journey, to see both the worst the system has to offer, and the best.

Everyone has a stake in this, Republican or Democrat, liberal or conservative; this isn't a partisan issue, it is a human one. What do we do with the people who get out of jail and come back to our communities? I know that we can actually use the prisons to make us safer and our communities better. I know it because I've seen it happen. I've seen men who have committed horrible crimes defy all predictions, take responsibility for their lives and begin to make amends. Every time that happens, for me, it's like the Cubs have won the World Series. If RSVP stops just one person from committing a murder, that's an entire community of family and friends saved from devastation. Now imagine if across the country, every jail and prison challenged criminals to stop their violence, to stop using drugs, to get a job, to become responsible citizens, to become, as one friend described it, "taxpayers instead of tax drainers." If that happened, we wouldn't just change the prisons and jails; we would remake the face of American society. That's the dream I've had. That's what has sustained me in the monster factory.

CHAPTER 1

1980

Jails are about doors. You wait for them to open. You wait for them to close. There is nothing subtle about a jail door. It rumbles and clangs like a death knell. You don't open them yourself. Others decide whether you come in or go out.

I was waiting at Post 5, outside Mainline, the processing center for anyone arrested in San Francisco County. I was shoving my ID up to a window so that the annoyed-looking deputy sheriff could flip the switch and let me in. I was beginning to grow angry at how long the deputy was taking when an electrical buzzing shriek cut through my thoughts and the door shuddered open.

A wave of noise crashed over me, quickly followed by a rancid smell of ammonia and body odor. I stepped out onto the tier. Mainline was like a zoo, except uglier than any zoo I'd ever been to. Huge cages framed the long corridor in front of me, which stretched out the length of a football field. Every cage was filled with men wearing jail-issue orange—orange pants, orange T-shirts, orange sweatshirts, orange flip-flops or canvas shoes. A few prisoners wandered the corridor. They were workers with special privileges, allowed to be out of the tanks when going to or from their jobs. Half the cages were open dormitories filled with bunk beds; the other half were lined with two-man cells. The echoing of angry voices was deafening. There was nothing to absorb or interrupt the noise. Shouts and shrieks banged off bulletproof glass, steel bars and cinder blocks. There were probably four hundred prisoners in the jail that day. I was the only woman in sight. This was my first day of work.

I'd been hired as a legal intern for the San Francisco Prisoner Legal Services unit. There were eight of us: five men and three women. The interns handled legal issues for prisoners for everything but the crimes that had brought them to jail in the first place. They had their public defender for that. My colleagues and I spread out through the jails every day, going wherever we were assigned or needed. If a prisoner was accused of a rule violation in the jail, or if he wanted to accuse a deputy sheriff of harassment, or if he was getting evicted from the apartment where he lived, or if he was losing custody of his children, he talked to me or one of my colleagues. The legal interns were the catchall. I wasn't a lawyer, none of us were, but I was supposed to function like one.

I was twenty-six years old, had barely made it through high school and didn't have a college degree. I'd never been in a jail before, and had one day of training, which consisted of being told how to use the phones and how to file paperwork. I was told repeatedly not to give the prisoners gum because they'd use it to jam the locks, but I received no training on what to do if someone turned violent. I was handed a box of pens and a legal pad and told, in essence, to go save lives. "Wildly unprepared" would be the polite way of describing how I felt.

I'd been warned about walking Mainline my first day. Rita, a colleague I'd met during training, compared it to being a sheep in a pack of wolves. She'd recommended that I present my request at the front office and meet the prisoner in an interview room, at least until I got the hang of things. But I wanted to prove that I was strong enough to stare down the monsters without flinching. I was curious, too, wondering if the men were as scary as I'd heard.

The men crowded to the front of their tanks to watch me when I stepped onto the tier. The few inmate workers in the hall stopped in place and turned toward me, as if they were a compass and I was due north. The noise receded for a second, then there was an explosion of voices.

"Oooh baby, come over here. I won't hurt you."

"Hey, baby. What's the matter, you get lost?"

"Come here, I need some smokes."

"Hey, little girl, I got something you could smoke."

Some of the men smiled, some made a meal of me with their eyes, a few just stood there with pitiful looks, like little children trapped in men's bodies.

With each step, a jolt of fear coursed through me. But I was also growing angry. I singled out a jeering kid on my left, walked up to him and barked, "Are you addressing me? Do you need something?"

I surprised him. His face went blank. I went up to the bars. "If you whistle at me again, I will hurt you like a dog. How would you feel if your mother was walking down these tiers and she was treated like this?"

The guy's voice barely slipped out of him. "Uh, um, I dunno." His eyes were wide. The others were watching. I could see some were smiling, taking my measure.

I was there to interview my first client. His name was Martin Aguerro. I'd been handed his file with a pile of others that morning. His seemed like the most interesting case and so here I was, ready to work. I returned to Post 5 and told the deputy I wanted to interview Aguerro. He rolled his eyes at me. This was the second deputy sheriff I'd talked to and the second set of rolled eyes, and it was pissing me off. Moving at a glacial pace, he checked his books, got on the phone, and after a few grunts, hung up and said, unceremoniously, "No."

"What do you mean no?"

"Just what I said. No." He crossed his arms.

I expected to fight with the prisoners, but I hadn't expected to fight the deputies, too. "First of all, he filed a claim," I said through clenched teeth. "The only way to follow up on the claim is to meet the guy. Why can't I see him?"

"I'm just doing what I'm told, lady. They tell me he's too dangerous. You can't see him without a two-deputy security complement and I don't have the staff right now."

I knew the deputy was giving me the "weak girl" assessment. I didn't look older than my twenty-six years, but I was no Twiggy. I was five feet nine, solid and could handle myself. After all, I had two older brothers whose idea of nurturing was an unceasing flurry of full nelsons and charley horses. I liked to think that had made me tough.

"Listen," I said, "I don't care if he's the biggest gangbanger ya got. He has a right to see me and I am not leaving until I meet with him."

I got a tired stare. I stared back until finally, with a shake of his head, the deputy reached for the phone and called the chief. Twenty minutes later the chief deputy sauntered up with a smirk on his face. At six feet five and three hundred pounds, he towered over me. "You know your so-called client is a shot caller in the Mexican Mafia?" he said.

I was too green to know that the Mexican Mafia was one of the most powerful gangs operating behind bars in California, and they controlled large portions of the drug traffic coming up from Central and South America. What I did know was what any child of Chicago knew: anybody who came from *the* mafia, *any* mafia, was probably a tough SOB. I pushed on, breathing through my teeth. "I couldn't care less; this is my job."

"Well, Miss Schwartz, I want you to know, I can't guarantee your safety."

I rolled my eyes, told him I understood and sat down to wait and bring my heart rate down. I was sitting right outside the deputy's station. Prisoners periodically came up asking for things. They needed to get to the next tier for work detail. Someone's toilet was stopped up. Somebody else was complaining about his mail delivery. I caught pieces of conversations I didn't understand—the guys on D block were freaking out because they missed their commissary delivery, a sergeant was twitching because two code 3s had been called yesterday and he was buried under paperwork. (A code 3 was radio shorthand for a deputy needing assistance because a situation had turned violent, meaning the prisoners were fighting or there was an attack on a deputy.)

As I sat there, I was struck by the most unexpected thought. Even though this was my first time inside a jail, and I was far away from Chicago, where I'd grown up, and far from Tucson, where I'd spent the last eight years of my life, I felt like I was home. In the eyes of the inmates, in the cold stares of the men trying to be hard, in their vulnerability, in all the pathetic, twisted, mangled personalities on display on the walk down Mainline, I'd seen shadows of myself.

I could do something for these men.

I certainly felt more at home on Mainline than I did in a law school classroom. I'd been a first-year law student at this point for exactly three weeks. (How I managed to scam my way into law school without a college degree is a story I'll get to later.) The world of books and notes and tests and number-two pencils had always been a place of shame for me. My school transcripts were a minefield of truant reports, failing grades and discipline problems. I thought about the class I had that night—it was about contracts—and, honestly, I felt more comfortable in the jail.

Half an hour went by and there was still no sign of my client. Martin Aguerro had filed a claim accusing the San Francisco Police Department of shooting him in the back. The allegation was serious and could end up in court one day, but the rules said he had to file an administrative claim against the city first and exhaust that route, so that's where I came in. Out of the mountain of files I'd been handed that morning, his sparked my interest. Most claims were from inmates needing a defense after they'd broken some jail rule. They'd gotten into a fight or had refused to obey an order from the deputies. Penny-ante crap that might add a day or a week onto their sentence. This was different, something I could sink my teeth into.

Finally, I heard the echo of a gate opening and closing, and I saw a man in red who I presumed was my client at the end of the tier with two deputies flanking him. The color red was for the most dangerous inmates and escape risks. I watched Martin Aguerro come toward me. He was moving slowly, as if he were underwater, and it looked like he was pushing a cart. As he and the deputies came closer, I realized that this violent, dangerous prisoner, the man around whom they could not guarantee my safety, was dragging his legs behind a walker. He was trussed up in full belly chains that kept his hands secured at his waist so he could barely hold the walker. Martin Aguerro was a skinny Latino man with greasy hair that hung into his eyes. His file said he was my age, twenty-six, but he looked eighteen. He was no taller than I was and had to be a good twenty pounds lighter. When he got closer, I could see he had the trappings of toughness. He had *hate* tattooed on the fingers of one hand and *love* on the other. On his left arm, he had a Sacred Heart of Jesus, on his right, a half-naked woman. But yapping poodles have frightened me more. I suppose he could've whacked me with his walker, if he'd been able to lift his arms.

I introduced myself as we sat down at a table. He was polite, didn't bring any attitude. His voice was slight, his speech a little lispy. We talked about his claim. He said that there'd been a warrant for his arrest and the cops came for him. They surprised him at his apartment and he didn't know what was happening. He'd tried to run, and before anyone said anything, a cop had shot him in the back.

"They didn't say 'You're under arrest'?" I asked. "They didn't announce themselves, identify themselves as cops?"

"Nah, man, they just started firing. I get hit. The next thing I know, I'm in the fucking hospital. Man, I can't piss right. Can't walk. They really fucked me up."

Good, I was thinking, good. It was a miserable story, but if what he was saying was true, I had a case. I'd barely started law school, but I did know that the police had to announce themselves. They couldn't just come in firing.

I pushed on. I didn't know anything about Martin, didn't know his rap sheet and had no way of assessing if he was being truthful with me. Someone had told me during training that I didn't need to worry about what crime they'd committed. Our job was to deal with their grievances, not with the reason they were locked up. But I felt like I needed to know.

"What was the warrant for?" I asked.

"Oral copulation on a child and rape." He said it like he was wanted for traffic tickets. Here I'd been feeling sorry for the guy, ready to jump into his corner and fight it out. But in an instant that feeling was replaced with disgust. After a few more questions, I was shaking with rage. The girl he was accused of molesting was nine years old.

"I gotta tell you something." I coughed, my fist clenched. "I want to hurt you for committing such a horrible act of violence. So we're gonna have to talk about this 'cause I'm sickened."

Martin's eyebrows shot up. But he didn't say anything except "Yeah?"

I paused for a second, trying to find my words. "It's really unpleasant for me to be in the same room with someone who's done that to a child. So actually working on this complaint is going to be difficult for me."

Martin stared at me during my explanation, nursing his silence. He didn't try to defend himself. He didn't tell me he'd "been framed" or that there were "extenuating circumstances" or that everything was consensual. He just looked at me and answered my questions, as I tried to figure out how I was going to live with myself and work with him.

I was making it up as I went along. I made sure he knew how to read and assigned him a book report on Susan Brownmiller's *Against Our Will: Men, Women, and Rape.* I'd read Brownmiller's book a year earlier. It was a comprehensive history of rape and its place in Western culture. It wasn't full of academic jargon—*I* got through it, for God's sake— but it clocked in at around five hundred pages, and I was pretty sure Martin was never going to finish it, which worked for me. If he didn't do the assignment, then I wouldn't have to deal with him. He said he'd try and we set a time to meet.

A week later, when I sat down with him again, he'd made it through the first chapter. He'd even produced a book report. His writing was pathetic, looking like mine did in the fifth grade, full of misspellings, bad grammar and incomplete sentences, so his report didn't reveal much. But we talked about his insights, such as they were. He'd read the "Personal Statement," and chapter 1, "The Mass Psychology of Rape," which contained references to Freud and Marx. He didn't know who they were, but he did get the basic point of the chapter, which was that throughout history, women have had to contend with men defining what rape is. "It's like, these ladies came along and they said, rape ain't right, right?" he said, which was pretty close to the gist of the first chapter. I wanted to believe he was taking something away from our discussion, but honestly, I couldn't read the guy.

We met every week. He reported on the chapter he'd read and I learned about his case. He was so unguarded in everything he said to me. I didn't have any reason to disbelieve his story of the night of the arrest. But his account—that he received no warning, that he was unarmed, that he was running away scared when he was shot—was contradicted by the arresting officers and some of the physical evidence. The arrest reports said all the proper protocols were followed: officers had clearly identified themselves when they came through his door and he was shot going for a handgun found at the scene. Was he telling me the truth, or just trying to game the system? Eventually I decided I wasn't going to figure it out. If the cops were as disgusted as I was, I could picture them going in with guns drawn ready to fire.

The third time we met, he said to me, "Can you believe it, they're shackling me when I'm paralyzed. Where the hell am I going to go?" He complained all the time. "It's a jungle in here," he'd say. "I wanted to do the book report but they don't even let me have a pen to write with." Other times he told me, "I can't take a shower because they don't have any facilities for guys like me." They were all garden-variety complaints, and I couldn't disagree with him. The food sucked? Yup, no argument there. The doctors didn't care? True as well. He *was* being treated like an animal; who wouldn't complain? But eventually I just wanted to shake him, knock some sense into him. "You've got to be kidding me!" I wanted to tell him. "Whose fault is it that you raped a little girl?"

He read the book dutifully. Finally, after two months, even though he hadn't finished the book, I told him he'd done enough and I'd file his complaint. But I had him sign a contract, a contract I made up, that said if he heard someone joking about rape or objectifying women in any way, he would confront the man and tell him to knock it off. We'd been talking for weeks now, and when I asked him to do that, it was the first time I heard any interest from him, any sense that he was thinking about the ideas I'd been trying to put into his head.

"I can do that," he said over and over. "Man, I will do that." Either he was hustling me, or he really thought it was a good idea, or maybe he just liked the idea of telling other men what to do. Whatever the reason, he signed the contract and agreed to confront other men if they made women-hating jokes. He also agreed to try to start a study group in prison to figure out ways to help women and children who'd been raped.

Then and only then did I file his complaint. Even as I did, I pictured Martin back in his cell spouting off, "Get this—this bitch is crazy," and laughing with the other predators. I had no time to do follow-up with him, no way to call him out if he did go back to his cell to form a predator support group for his hideous views.

His complaint was summarily dismissed. Given the evidence against him, it didn't matter if he was right or wrong. He was a child predator resisting arrest and it was his word against the cops'. There wasn't much more to it than that. By the time the decision came down, I'd had at least sixty clients, and I'd realized that Aguerro's complaint was a fool's mission. Complaints from inmates passed through my hands every day, some about the quality of the food, others about the high phone bills inmates' families had to pay. Some were assault charges against deputy sheriffs. Some had merit, some didn't. There were a few I could actually win, many more I couldn't.

Martin's case was never anything but a long shot. But Martin himself was unique. He didn't excuse his crimes with me or claim he'd been framed or claim that there was a good explanation for what happened. Most other prisoners did that. But Martin *was* like the other prisoners in a specific way.

He had no remorse. He complained about jail conditions, complained about his lawyer, felt bad for himself, but never offered me one word of sorrow for the people he'd hurt, the pain he'd caused.

Oh brother, the child rapist doesn't like jail. That's how I felt most of the time. But his attitude nagged at me.

"How you live is how you die" is what my mother, Frieda, always said. She was a woman of sayings. This one was always declared with a sigh whenever someone's failings were on display. Every day in the jails, as the doors were opened onto a new set of problems, my mom's words rang in my ears as if they were on a loop. I heard them every time the doors clanged shut behind me on Mainline. Every week there were new faces staring out from the bars, faces showing the barest hints of beards. And standing beside them were men I recognized. Men who'd been released only to return for their third or fourth or tenth visit. Martin Aguerro soon was gone. He was offered a deal of ten years and went off to follow his walker around San Quentin before I lost track of him. There he probably still got shoddy medical care and filed complaints to fill his time and maybe, just maybe, he held court and told men to knock off the women-hating crap. But I doubt it.

Martin Aguerro didn't defeat me. I didn't give up on the prisoners because of him, but he did educate me on the limits of what I could do. I went on to meet murderers and petty thieves and everyone in between. Almost all of them hid behind an excuse. After six months on the job as a law intern, I'd heard them all. After a year I could recite them chapter and verse. I didn't stop asking prisoners why they were in jail. But I learned not to be surprised when very few could answer with the simple truth: they were in jail because they made the choice to commit a crime.

Many convicts used their past to justify their crimes. It was infuriating to listen to. But the past did matter. There are plenty of people with sad stories to tell who end up as good citizens, but I never met anyone behind bars who went through childhood unscathed. There are reasons why people end up behind bars. It's no coincidence, not for any of the inmates I've worked with, and not for me, either.

CHAPTER 2

1966

"Don't trust rich folks, Sunny," my dad, Seymour, said, wagging his finger at me. "You can't. They're full of shit."

He said this to me all the time. But in this particular instance, my dad was referring to Cindy's new in-laws, the Millers, whom my sister was bringing over for Passover seder. Seymour imparted this nugget of wisdom while banging the vacuum through the living room. He was a handsome, cranky piece of work, whom all my friends were afraid of. But my parents really loved each other despite all their problems, and that day he helped clean the living room so my mom wouldn't have a conniption. She had been wandering through the house for days, mumbling nonstop to herself.

"Look at this dreck!" Frieda pointed to the worn carpet. "It's dreck! And look at the stains on the furniture. *Oy vey,* I hate this peanut house," she said as she tried to rub the stains off the pink hand-me-down couch. I normally loved my mother's voice, the way it revved up and went bouncing along like an accordion. She was a talker. Everywhere she went, she had friends and confidants. I'd listen to her on the phone, kibitzing with her girlfriends, her voice breaking into peals of laughter. But as we prepared for Passover, she was a dark cloud, scowling at me if I dared tell her to relax. "Dolly," she'd bark, "go clean your room."

Our family lived in Marionette Manor, in the shadow of the South Works steel plant on Chicago's south side, in a roiling stew of working-class Jews and Catholics, Polish, Irish and African Americans. Cindy was my half sister and, since she was fourteen years older than me, more like a favorite aunt. She came from a mysterious time in my father's life, his short-lived first marriage to an alcoholic woman who was evidently so unfit that my father had been granted custody of Cindy. Where my two older brothers, Jerry and Stevie, were full of my father's bullying energy, Cindy was nurturing. When she still lived with us, her room was all lace and pillows and delicate things, a refuge from the tough-guy atmosphere in the rest of the house. Cindy had married a boy from a wealthy family and now lived in Hyde Park. And to my mother's ever-lasting embarrassment, had invited his parents to our Passover seder.

My mom had a rich, earthy family legacy, which suited her like an old housedress. She would have traded up for a more sophisticated model if only she could have. Frieda's mother lived with us. She was a lumbering old tank of a babushka who had fled a Russian pogrom. We called her Bubba. Bubba had never bothered to learn English beyond the basics, and I could barely understand what she said half the time because her dentures were the wrong size and wandered around her mouth. Bubba charred pieces of toast and saved them in the drawers of our kitchen to crush into her borscht. My mother would find the crusts and grit her teeth.

Uncle Harry, my mom's brother, lived nearby. He arrived that afternoon and parked himself in front of the chopped-liver appetizer. Uncle Harry was "touched," according to Frieda. "He got goofy from the war," she'd say with a sigh. "Ya know, war wound." And she'd look at me knowingly and tap her head. Illness seemed to be leaking out of his fingers where they were stained brown from his unfiltered Lucky Strikes. Frieda lovingly yelled at Harry a few times while waiting for the Millers to arrive. "Stop eating! Leave some for the company!" she'd beg. Liver was smeared all over Harry's fingers.

My father just nodded at Harry and snorted. He was on his best behavior that day. Seymour had an edge—a gruff, volcanic spirit that was always on the verge of erupting. On days when his temper did flare up, my mother would retreat to the kitchen to defrost the refrigerator, her mouth pressed into a thin line. The rest of us worked out our own methods to avoid him. Jerry would go do his homework. Stevie would go out to play baseball. I would mope in my room. Seymour was an orphan whose parents came from Eastern Europe, one from Russia, the other, we think, from Latvia. I'm not sure he really knew.

He never talked about it, except to say that he could remember that his mother was beautiful and that she had a voice like a nightingale. I'd catch him sometimes in his basement room going through old photos, his eyes misty. The photos were the only remnants of his mom and dad that he had. Whenever he talked about them, he seemed hurt, then quickly grew grumpy. If my mother's family was an embarrassment, my father's family was missing in action. But, in general, Seymour tried to make my mother happy, even if it meant being polite to some full-of-shit in-laws.

My sister and her husband, Bob, arrived in their Porsche. Bob's parents came in a chauffeur-driven Cadillac. They spoke so quietly, I can remember sitting in the living room, my mother shushing everyone, straining to make out what Mrs. Miller was saying.

"Frieda," she said, smiling, "you have such a warm home." My mother smiled back, desperate to be the perfect hostess, glaring at Stevie and me because we kept cracking up at Bubba's wandering dentures.

Jerry rarely laughed along with Stevie and me. We called him the Alderman. He was the oldest boy. He behaved. He did well in school. Stevie was two years behind him and trouble—trouble for the girls, who all loved him, and trouble for my father. Stevie just wouldn't fall into line with Seymour. It helped make us allies.

I was the kid sister, two years behind Stevie, and he and Jerry ganged up on me. There were the names—Dumbass, Fat Pig, Loser and Chubs (Stevie gave me that last one; I had a spare tire at age eight). There were also the attacks—being pinned down and sat on while one or both slapped my face until I went nuts; them spitting in my butterscotch pudding; being locked out of the house in winter while I shivered and pleaded with them to open the door. But when Jerry wasn't looking, Stevie would ask me what I was thinking. He sometimes even took my side against Jerry, and he taught me how to throw a curveball, too. When Harry started mumbling incoherently during the lighting of the candles, it was Stevie who got me laughing uncontrollably by mimicking it under his breath. I was always his best, easiest audience.

We got through it. My mother shushed us and smiled uncomfortably and the Millers seemed kind, not at all what my dad led me to expect. Seymour blessed the wine and we all got a sip. Stevie slipped some to Bubba, and by the end of the meal, she was smiling a little too broadly and spitting out her water. We washed our hands and ate the parsley dipped in salt water, my father intoning the prayers as a reminder, as if we needed any with the Millers sitting there, of our lowly origins and how we'd all been slaves in Egypt. Matzoh was passed. Bubba yelled out non sequiturs in quiet moments and my mother leaned over, finally giving up appearances, and stage-whispered "Ma—shhhh." Uncle Harry interrupted to ask my mom, "Fritzy, where's the chopped liver?" and everyone laughed, even the Millers. Finally we sang the Dayanu that concludes the Passover story. We were liberated from the seder and got down to eating my mom's amazing meal.

Those were the good times in our house. They were few and far between.

If there's one memory from my childhood that stands out, it's of my dad stretched out in the backseat of our Buick with the windows rolled down, fingering the stops on his cornet. Seymour Schwartz was a self-taught jazz cornet player and songwriter. My mother would say he'd gotten lost again when he'd retreat to the car. He played "God Bless the Child" slowly, mournfully, the notes expanding along the quiet residential streets. The old Billie Holiday standard was one of his favorites. Mine, too. I'd sit alone at the window, singing along with the melody.

> Mama may have, Papa may have,
> But God bless the child that's got his own

My dad was always scrambling for his big break but never quite making it. The closest he got was when he worked with Mahalia Jackson. They became friends in the early 1950s and our family went to her house for fried chicken dinners on a few Sunday nights. Seymour wrote a song for Mahalia called "The Holy Bible" and they performed it on the Studs Terkel radio show. My heart swelled with pride every time my mom cued up the reel-to-reel recording. But Mahalia moved on and my father's career stalled. His style was too schmaltzy, not original enough. He didn't have many live gigs, either. He fought with the other players. At some point it seemed, he always marched through the kitchen door referring to his bandleader as a "fucking Nazi bastard," and then he'd stalk off to the basement to write.

With Seymour you were either his enemy or you were his friend. There was no in between. His kids could fall into either category. I can remember poking around in the garage when I was nine. It was filled with milk crates of records and sheet music, my dad's work, along with junk that should've been thrown out, old broken chairs, a broken radio, tools for the garden. The garage was my father's domain. I spied some dusty records that had fallen behind a filing cabinet and on top of the pile was a 45-rpm recording I knew he'd been looking for. It was one of his schmaltz-soaked ballads, "No One Seems to Care." That evening, when I heard the car drive up, I ran out to meet him with the record in my hand.

"Daddy, look what I found!" I was all giddy energy.

He left the car with a scowl and wheeled on me. The 45 was there in my hand one second, and the next it was like a magic trick, my hand was empty.

He broke the record over his knee and threw it to the ground. "This is shit," he bellowed at me. "I never want to see this or any other record again. Fuck it!"

My mom saw the whole thing from the front porch and tried to stand up for me. "She didn't mean anything by it."

My dad huffed away, grumbling to himself, "Everything's bullshit."

I looked at my mother, my little fists clenching. She looked so powerless and sad in that moment. I ran off down the street, sobbing.

My father periodically would climb into bed with my brothers and me. He didn't molest us, he just needed us near him, needed the comfort of another body. I guess he did it when my mom got tired of him. He usually came around when he'd been moping in the basement over one of his songs. Jerry or Stevie would shout out from their room, "Don't Greek me, Dad! Jesus!" and I knew he would make his way to my room. When I got old enough to stand up for myself, I gave him the same line and kicked him out. I knew even then that he wasn't there to comfort me.

Truth be told, I didn't feel safe in my house. Between my dad and the torment of my two older brothers, I didn't feel safe. When we first moved into the house, I was around four, and my next-door neighbor, a chain-smoking Irish Catholic with the remarkable name of Laverne Liberty encountered me in the yard.

"I heard this tiny voice screaming bloody murder." Laverne would laugh as she recounted the story. "'Shit, goddamn, I'm gonna kick your ass!' And I came out into the driveway and it was you howling at your brothers, who were sitting on top of you and pummeling you. Just another day at the Schwartz house."

Laverne's house became my refuge after one too many charley horses or dead arms or taunts about how I was in the remedial classes with the retards. She'd make me Oscar Mayer hard-salami sandwiches with butter on white Silvercup bread. My dad would complain that I was spending too much time with the goyim.

The worst part about it was that I *was* in the remedial classes. I'd started to fall behind the other kids at the very beginning, sent home year after year with report cards burning a hole in my hand, never sure when I opened them if I had passed on to the next grade. In the sixth grade, I tested at a third-grade reading level. I yelled at the teachers, learning how to fight like my father, never learning how to deal with school, with the shame and fear I had that I might be a complete loser. The teachers liked to mark me for "Citizenship Failure" at Luella Elementary. I was mouthy. I came to know the principal's office intimately. Luella Elementary was two blocks from our house and every morning the walk felt like a death march. The torments of my father and brothers were well matched by the torments of geometry and the Battle of Hastings.

Those torments also competed with the Pulaski brothers, the scourge of the neighborhood. There were three of them and they were about the same ages as my brothers and me. I can't tell you how many times one of them and their punk friends chased me and cornered me up against the church that was between school and my street, taunting, "You killed Jesus! You killed our god! You killed Jesus! Go home, you dirty Jew!" The Pulaski brothers were greasers. They were big and tough. Each had slicked blond hair and wore green iridescent pants and pointy half boots. The Pulaskis were Polish Catholics, and I was too scared to shout back the Polack jokes I learned from my brothers.

Jerry stayed out of their way. He was a bookworm who walked around with black-rimmed glasses, oxford shirts, and kept to himself. He was no nerd, he was tough, but no one really knew who he was. Stevie was popular, and had a pair of iridescent pants, too, so was more of a target.

When I was ten, one of Stevie's girlfriends came running up to me after the last bell at school. She was out of breath, "Stevie's in a fight, and the guy has a knife." I ran to find Stevie cornered in the playground. Eddie Pulaski, the middle brother, was taunting him with a switchblade. A crowd of kids was watching. My brother was on the verge of tears, his eyes wide like a surprised rabbit. He was trying to keep it together, but tight short sobs kept spurting out. It was horrible.

I had a Trapper Keeper, one of those heavy, three-ring binders, in my hand. I sneaked up on Eddie and I brought it down on his head with a knee-buckling thwack. I grabbed Stevie and ran. He turned on me as soon as we were free, tears staining his checks. "Why did you do that? Why did you do that? Now they're gonna make fun of me because my kid sister protected me."

Summer was one of the only times I felt some freedom. I had my bicycle, a Schwinn with a white banana seat, and I had friends. I was mouthy after all, like my mother, a good talker, willing to walk up to almost anyone and give them a piece of my mind, or tell them to come riding with me to the beach.

I trailed after my brothers when I could but when they had no use for me, I took off with my girlfriends. There were no rules about where I could go or when. I just had to be back for dinner. My friends and I whirled like dervishes during the day—to the beach, to Pinzer's drugstore, where we'd hang out on the mechanical horse out front, or if it was hot enough and we had some money, to DeVito's bowling alley to roll a game—anywhere our bikes would take us.

July 1966 boiled. Biking on days that hovered in the nineties with ninety percent humidity felt like swimming through hot soup. The heat finally broke in the middle of the month, and when I went to bed on July 13, I didn't stick to the sheets. If I'd been paying attention to omens at age twelve, I might have thought good times were ahead, but then the morning came.

"Oh my God, oh my God, oh my God." A hysterical woman was yelling. It took me a minute to realize it was my mother. My eyes flicked open. I sat up in bed. It was early, I could tell by the light. There was another voice seeping in through my screen, our neighbor, Laverne Liberty. I felt disoriented, my stomach turned over.

My mother's voice scared me. She didn't say anything but "Oh my God." I could hear bits of what Laverne was saying, and her voice didn't sound much better. She kept whispering, "Keep the kids in the house. And keep them away from the town houses."

The town houses were six rental apartments two and a half blocks from the house, and right across the street from my school, Luella Elementary. I was just able to pick out a few phrases of the story Laverne was telling: "Just terrible . . . one tried to crawl out through a screen . . . they haven't caught the killer!"

My brothers and I all rushed to breakfast that morning, dying of curiosity. My mom, her face drained of color, wouldn't reveal anything.

"Hey, Mom, Mom," Stevie was begging. "What's going on?"

"Be quiet," she snapped. She never snapped at him. Stevie was her favorite. Jerry and I stopped moving.

"Stay near home today and don't you dare go near 100th Street. Don't go any further than the church." Our Lady Gate of Heaven was at the end of our block.

I tried to ask why and she shushed me. No one spoke much after that. The clinking of spoons in cereal bowls felt unnaturally loud. My brothers left me alone that morning. They kept to themselves, playing catch briefly in the backyard but giving up because a helicopter was hovering over the neighborhood. I watched it hang just over the tree outside the front window; I'd never seen a helicopter so close. I was antsy, watching the blades turn; I wanted to see everything for myself and was mad to be cooped up in the house. I told my mom I was going for a bike ride. She looked at me sideways. I'd never had to ask permission to go biking before, but she was preoccupied, so she just repeated her orders to stay away from 100th Street.

I went running out the back door and hopped onto my bike at a jog. Stevie was sitting on the front stoop as I peddled away. "Hey, Chubs, Chubs!" he yelled. "Where ya going?" I kept peddling. I wouldn't have known what to say if I'd stopped. Something had frightened my mother. I needed to see what had happened, needed to understand what had caused this sickening shudder down in the dark core of things. I couldn't have said this to Stevie. I was just going.

After a heartbeat, I passed the church. A block later, I was turning the corner onto 100th Street. A crowd of people was milling outside the town houses. Reporters and cops were still at the scene. I stopped at the edge of the crowd and stared up at a window on the second floor. People were talking around me and I picked out a few more awful details. Somebody had murdered the women in that apartment. They were all young student nurses. Somebody said three women had been killed; another person said there were over a dozen. A story was told of one woman trying and failing to escape through a window screen. I could see a screen torn back from its frame on the second floor. Every once in a while a figure, most likely a cop, would move behind it.

Just then, the front door opened and two men in white coats wheeled out a gurney. A bundle went by. I stopped breathing. A woman's arm had slipped out, as if its owner had fallen asleep. Everyone was quiet. The gurney wheels squeaked.

I looked at the people around me and suddenly wondered who had come out to watch. I realized (I don't know why I hadn't thought of it) that the killer could be there, too. The hair on the back of my neck prickled. I suddenly jerked my bike backward out of the crowd, knuckles white on the handlebars, afraid to look around me. I raced home, my legs working the pedals as hard as I could. I was scared for the first time, terrified of passing cars, of monsters lying in wait in our backyard. I went straight to my room and threw myself under the covers. I thought of the ripped screen and the night before, a woman tearing at the screen like a wild animal, her eyes glazed in terror, and then a man coming up behind her and catching her. My stomach kicked. I squeezed my eyes shut, trying to blot out the image.

I wished Cindy still lived with us. I could remember violent thunderstorms from when I was small and the sky would turn yellow, the color of death, and the leaves looked like they were standing upside down in the wind. I would run to my sister's bed to whimper under her covers. Cindy comforted me as the thunder crashed, saying, "Sunny, dear, there is nothing to be afraid of. The flowers need the rain." She'd put on a record, usually Rimsky-Korsakov's *Scheherazade*. She'd coax me out and we'd dance, and soon enough the rain and noise would stop.

But the storm that rolled through our neighborhood that summer night in 1966 did not end, and there was no one to make me feel better. The next day, I told my brothers that I'd gone to see the crime scene. I was half proud of myself for being brave, half needing to talk about it.

Jerry sneered, "That was stupid. What did you do that for?"

"Jesus, Sunny, you're crazy," Stevie chimed in. "I can't believe you did that." There was disapproval in his voice, but also a little admiration. I think he wished he'd done it himself.

"If that killer tried to come after us," Stevie confided, "you know I could take him. I bet I could beat him up. But Sun, you're crazy for going over there. You're an animal." He gave me a small nod. I grinned back.

That night, my mother lit the Shabbos candles as she did every Friday. I loved watching her do it. My brothers and my dad usually weren't interested but that night, everyone gathered around the kitchen table. Everyone knew the bare facts of what had happened. Eight women, all student nurses, had been murdered. Unspeakable things had been done to them, and the killer was still loose. My mother was more solemn than I'd ever seen her. She waved both hands over the flames three times as if she were lapping the light into her heart, her movements slow and deliberate, and then she covered her eyes for the blessing. My mom's little nose stuck out and turned bright red and her lips moved a little. The words of the prayer echoed in my head.

> *Baruch atah Adonai Eloheinu melech ha'olam*
> Blessed are you, Lord, our God, sovereign of the universe,
> *asher kideshanu bemitzvotav vetzivanu l'hadlik ner shel Shabbat.*
> who has sanctified us with His commandments and
>   commanded us to light the lights of Shabbat.

I knew my mom was praying for "those poor girls." It's what she'd been saying to herself the last two days. "Those poor girls, all they tried to do was help other people. What must their families be feeling?" She stood with her eyes covered for a long time. The house was quiet. Then she passed her hands over the candles a final time.

I was waiting for magic. If God, the sovereign of the universe, was ever going to demonstrate his power, I thought, it had to be now. I stared at the flames, waiting, hoping for something that would explain the horror committed against those women. The candles flickered. There were no signs, only an empty homesick feeling.

My mom opened her eyes. She sighed once, then said, mournfully, "May we all live and be well," and she kissed me on my forehead.

Within days we knew what to call what had happened—the Richard Speck murders. A troubled journeyman and carpenter, the product of an alcoholic, abusive family, Richard Speck followed a path from petty crimes to assaults and murder to the horror of July 13 and 14, 1966, when he had surprised nine student nurses in their apartment, then tortured and murdered eight of them over the course of the night. The ninth woman had managed to hide under a bed undetected, and later identified Speck at the trial. In its day, the Richard Speck case was called the "crime of the century."

For me, for my neighborhood, for Chicago, there was a before the Richard Speck murders, and an after. A shift happened at that moment in our behavior, in the way we saw the world. On my street, we locked our doors for the first time. We feared strangers. We were suspicious of our neighbors. Speck had been caught within days, put on trial and sent away to prison to live out the rest of his days. But the man had still tracked each of us into the deepest darkest recesses of our hearts, and settled there, a resident bogeyman, ready to jump out and come after us if we got too comfortable.

Richard Speck was the first true monster I can remember in my life. He was far from the last.

CHAPTER 3

1971–1980

Before he went crazy, Stevie saved me. Before his brain turned against him, he was the one who paved my way out of Chicago. He didn't know what he had done, and neither did I, but he saved me all the same.

Jerry, the obedient son, had already gone off to the University of Illinois as a pre-med major. Stevie had rushed out of high school a sports star, a passionate Roman candle of a kid, liable to go off at the least provocation. Ever since my Uncle Rolly gave him a set of golf clubs for his Bar Mitzvah, he'd obsessed over the game. If you could imagine golf as a ferocious game of blistering hits and violent tempers, that was how Stevie played. Always an indifferent student, he'd won a free ride to the University of Arizona in Tucson on a sports scholarship.

I brought up the rear in every sense of the word, ejected from high school with a pathetic whimper and an upraised middle finger. My sophomore year, my parents moved from the south side of Chicago to a small house in Glenview, Illinois, a white suburb with a growing Jewish population. My parents were following the crowds, joining the white flight of the time, complaining, in their sometimes narrow-minded way, how dangerous it had become since the "*shvartzes*" had taken over. *Shvartze* was the Yiddish derogatory term for a black person.

I'd gone from the back of the line at Bowen, the Chicago public high school where I was barely getting by in remedial classes, to the absolute bottom of New Trier West, a large, college preparatory powerhouse of a school. To the white well-to-do kids who were my new classmates, a mixed crowd of Catholics and Protestants and a few random Jews, I might as well have been a redneck from the hills of Appalachia, or a foreign-exchange student from India. And they seemed equally bizarre to me. They had chandeliers in their houses, maids who cleaned their bathrooms, and they took ski trips to Colorado over the Christmas break. The closest my friends and I got to downhill skiing was "skeeching," which was when we chased cars down the streets to grab their fenders and get dragged through the dirty slush. In Glenview, I learned phrases I'd never heard before: "I'm so depressed" and "I'm ambivalent about that." No one was ambivalent where I came from. They were either loyal to the ends of the earth or wanted to hit you upside the head with a two-by-four. What was there to be ambivalent about? I wasn't ambivalent about Glenview. I hated it every fucking second I lived there.

They tried to expel me a few weeks before graduation because I yelled at a teacher. (I did it so often I can't remember what I said.) I was sent home and told not to come back until my parents and I had a conference with the principal. My mother wouldn't come. She was mortified, afraid that I'd finally gone too far. My father put on a tie and jacket and I would've said he looked handsome, except the pulsing muscle at his jawline kept clenching with fearful regularity. He looked like he was chewing something unpleasant.

"Dammit, Sunny," he said as we drove to school. "You keep your trap shut today, you hear me! And you do whatever they tell you!" He slapped the steering wheel as he said it. He knew I was as liable to play the obedient daughter as he was to play the cool-headed dad, so he added, "You're almost done with this place, Sunny. I know you're miserable but it'll be over soon if you just follow the rules."

I'd been in the principal's office half a dozen times already but I couldn't pick the guy out of a lineup. He looked like one of those anonymous guys with a shit-eating grin from an Oldsmobile ad. He had on a suit and horn-rimmed glasses, and he told me I'd have to agree to behave and follow all the rules in order to return to school.

"I want you to come back, Sandra," he said, pouring salt in the wound by using my given name. No one called me that except my old truant officer from the south side. My father said that of course I'd behave, then they both looked at me. "Do we have your promise, young lady?" asked the principal. Behind him on his bookcase, I could see a photo of his smiling family skiing in some mountain paradise. In the photo he was wearing a hat with a pom-pom. I wish I could say I thought about my response, thought about what it would mean to go forward without a high school diploma, had some clue about what the phrase "the rest of my life" actually meant to the rest of my life, and come up with a reasoned, rational and engaged response. But I didn't.

"No, you'll have to throw me out. I'm not going to do it." My father groaned. I felt a sharp pain in my shin from where he kicked me with his wingtips. "God, Dad, what'd you do that for?" I yelped. He groaned again. The principal looked stunned, as if I'd plunked him on the head with a baseball.

"Of course she'll behave," my dad barked. "Don't listen to her; she's too dumb to know what she's saying. You tell him that you'll behave."

"No, I won't do it. I got a right to speak up when something is bull-shit."

My dad unloaded again on my shin. I gave a shout of pain. The principal looked scared, and then confused, and then just sad. He gave us both long, searching stares. I don't think he wanted me back for another year and I had enough credits to graduate. He finally gave a resigned shrug and said, "Get out of here. I'll expect you in class on Monday." I slammed the door on the way out. I refused to go to their damn graduation.

Two months later I was driving west. Stevie was entering his junior year at Arizona, and had grudgingly agreed to let me ride shotgun. I left Chicago with fifty dollars in my pocket and no plan beyond escape and Tucson seemed like as good a place to land as any.

Stevie had grown, to use my mother's words, "a little goofy" since going off to college. He used to be full of confidence, a joker and a fighter. But now he was a brooder, all dark thunderclouds, and when he came home he kept to himself. He didn't laugh as much; his temper had grown to resemble my father's. The most popular boy I knew now barely left the house except to play golf. Still, I was his failure of a kid sister with no cash and no friends in Tucson, and he was willing to take me with him, which earned him big points in my book.

Out in the Sonoran Desert, I swear I felt like Neil Armstrong taking one giant scary leap. The exotic landscape mesmerized me—the saguaro cactus with its long arms waving in all directions, the ocotillo with its spinelike vines speckled with bright red flowers at the tips, the Palo Verde trees and jumping cholla and Gila monsters and tarantulas and mountains. Chicago is flat as a pancake and to wake up and see mountains surrounding the small city, I was my own personal astronaut.

In Tucson I kissed a girl for the first time and it was heaven. I discovered the theater, finding a voice with friends and a community that didn't know me as the dumb kid in the remedial classes. I went to free classical concerts at the University of Arizona. I painted with watercolors. I read and read and read for the first time in my life. I took ceramics classes, making myself the shadow of my teacher, an old man named Fay. He had one hand. The other he'd lost in an industrial accident. He was quiet, his brown face cracked and lined like a catcher's mitt, often lost in a cloud of Pall Malls. I kept up with him cigarette for cigarette with my Tareytons. I'd punch the clay and swear when it didn't spin into shape. Fay laughed at my short temper. "Sunny, life's too short," he'd murmur, without looking up from his wheel. "Life's way too short."

I made a paycheck. I paid rent. I took lovers. I broke hearts. I fought Nixon and the Vietnam War and myself, and, eventually, after much coaxing, I held my nose and went back to school. The students at Pima Community College were my kind of people—diverse, working class, all trying to figure out how to catch a break and some dignity. I took English and drama and feminist theory classes.

I'd gone to Tucson with Stevie, but I barely saw him. He slipped away. I'd go visit him and he'd seem agitated, distracted. One time he was convinced his philosophy professor, who happened to be Catholic, was deliberately trying to fail him because he was Jewish. Another time he told me that his golf teammates were conspiring against him. He was kicked off the team for fighting. He started playing only in the early morning, barefoot. I began to think he was doing peyote. Then he was gone, graduated, back to Chicago where he moved in with my parents.

I can see now that we were traveling different paths. He was beginning to explore his nightmares; I was starting to explore my dreams.

Back in high school I'd always been stuck in the classes with the castaways. "Sunny and the *shvartzes* and poor kids," as Seymour would say. My classmates and I danced to the Temptations and never talked about our grades. And then, regular as clockwork, we'd lose someone. They'd get into trouble, sent to the Cook County juvenile detention center, known as the Audi Home. I felt so awful for them, knowing that they had no one to help them, that they'd skated along the brink for years, facing abusive parents, or the abuses of poverty, until they finally slipped into the abyss and into a life of crime. Every time someone disappeared there was that shock to the system. Could it have been me? Could I ever fall so low? I also had another thought, a crazy one, little more than a whisper in my ear. I wished I could help them, almost as fervently as I wished I could help myself. I knew it was stupid, an impossible hope. But even so, I had a dream. I wanted to become a lawyer.

In Chicago I was too stupid to be a lawyer. But in Tucson, I became the shoot-from-the-hip feminist/lesbian-in-training with a big heart. And I didn't have to be embarrassed about it. And hell, if there was anything I knew how to do, it was talk. I was a shouter, and a toughie, and if you tried to stick a finger in my chest, I'd stick mine in your eye. With each class I took at Pima Community College, that pipe dream began to seem more and more possible. When a friend of mine told me about a law school that didn't require a college degree, I jumped.

My girlfriend, Debby, practically wrote my application and miraculously, terrifyingly, unaccountably, it worked. In the fall of 1980, I drove to San Francisco to start classes at the New College of California School of Law in San Francisco. This happened even though the dean had told me during my interview that she couldn't allow me to attend, couldn't take my money in good conscience, because she knew I'd wash out. She said it to me with a kind look and a gravelly voice that exuded wisdom. I told her I was coming with or without her blessing. I was going to show her, just like I was going to show the anonymous principal who tried to throw me out of New Trier, that I was going to do it my way.

My way was defiance. In San Francisco, all I had left was my defiance. My parents had finally stopped trying to change me and we rarely spoke now. Neither of them could accept that I was a lesbian. I hadn't told them. My father had discovered some letters from a girl-friend of mine when I'd come home for a visit. He'd confronted me and told me I'd betrayed every article of the faith, and that he could not accept this "horrible sinful phase" I was going through. I told him that he'd have to get used to it. He threatened to have a funeral for me, sitting Shiva to let everyone know I was symbolically dead to him. He only gave up on the idea when I told him I'd show up. My father now spoke to me only when my mother forced him to take the phone. My brothers couldn't figure out why their idiot of a kid sister thought she had to be a fruit. My mother was more forgiving, but troubled, throwing up when she found out, wondering what she'd done wrong, wondering if it was her fault.

But I long ago ceased to be the greatest heartbreak for my parents. In 1975, Jerry and Stevie took a pilgrimage to Israel and came home strict Orthodox and had convinced my parents to join them. Then, in 1977, Stevie went on a second pilgrimage to Israel. My parents thought it would do him some good, get him out of the house and challenge him. But in the streets of Jerusalem, Stevie started an argument with an Israeli Arab. By the time it was over, he had the man on the ground, and was kicking him in the head, calling him a "dirty Arab" and a "fucking anti-Semite." Stevie was sent home babbling incomprehensibly and heavily dosed on antipsychotic drugs. This was his first breakdown. We were lucky he hadn't been thrown in prison. Back in Chicago, Stevie was diagnosed as a paranoid schizophrenic with depressive tendencies. He now maintained his equilibrium only if his meds were calibrated just right.

He and I still talked. He still asked me what I thought. I still sought his approval. I still thought of him first when I wanted some family in my life, especially when I wanted to talk to someone about law school. Sometimes he would cheer me on. "You can do it, Sunny. You are the only one in the family who will make it!" he'd say when his energy was peaking. But sometimes, if I caught him on the wrong day, he'd launch into a tirade. "You are such a loser," he'd yell. "Are you crazy? You can't pass shit. You were the worst student in high school. This is law school. You need a college degree for that but you were too dumb to get one." I'd have to put the phone down and let the tears come. Even though I knew he was crazy, he was repeating my inner monologue, the one I'd carried with me from Chicago, which whispered, ever so cruelly, "Who the fuck do you think you are?"

Half the week I worked with prisoners in San Francisco's jails. The other half I attended class. Walking Mainline and walking into a law school lecture were almost equally scary to me. I almost lived up to the dean's predictions in my first year, but after getting three tutors, and studying like it was my new religion, I was allowed to come back for the next year. I barely made it, but I did *not* wash out.

On the first day of my second year, I rushed in from work late as usual. I pushed through the door for Criminal Trial Skills and was relieved that the professor hadn't arrived yet. Professor Paul Harris was supposed to be an amazing trial lawyer, and I'd actually been looking forward to this class. I dreaded contracts, felt like a complete moron in torts and legal analysis, but I had a new notebook and set of pens that I stole from the jails, and I felt ready.

I climbed the stairs to the back of the vaulted classroom. There was nothing particularly majestic about my law school. It wasn't *The Paper Chase*. There were no gargoyles and limestone. The place was bare-bones, with furniture that looked like it had fallen off the back of a truck. I felt comfortable in the New College student body. As I made my way to my seat, I passed discussions about Reagan's right-wing policies and the need to divest from South Africa. Most of my fellow students came from the liberal fringe of America, and that suited me fine. I settled in with eight other regular smokers whom I knew well. Our packs came out, lighters flicked, and soon we were in a cloud of smoke.

Professor Harris walked in as rumpled as they come—wrinkled shirt untucked in the back, glasses sliding haywire off his nose. He started to tell us about himself, and the kind of assignments we should expect, the usual drill. Then all of a sudden, he stopped and turned to a student in the front row.

"Excuse me," he said, annoyed. "I'm talking here. Could you please keep it down?"

The class shifted uncomfortably. I couldn't see what was happening, didn't hear anyone talking, either. But the moment passed and Harris returned to his talk. Five minutes later, Harris stopped again.

"I'm gonna ask you another time, please have some respect." He was more annoyed this time. "Please keep it down."

I exhaled a column of smoke and craned my neck, trying to see what was going on. I couldn't figure out who the guilty party was. I whispered to the guy next to me, "What the fuck?" He shrugged his shoulders and Harris again resumed his lecture.

Finally, a third time, Harris stopped. He was angry now. "I've asked you a couple times to stop talking. I want you to leave." His voice was brittle. He pointed to the door.

I could see the student now for the first time. He hadn't said anything, from what I could tell. Neither had anyone else. Again, Harris, his voice rising, repeated his demand.

"Listen, how long is this going to go on? I asked you to leave."

No one said anything until, all of a sudden, my mouth opened. "What the fuck is going on up there, man? I didn't hear that guy say anything."

There was a sickening silence. Everyone turned to stare at me, then back at Harris, who grinned.

"I've done this lecture countless times, at Stanford, Berkeley, all over the place, and . . . I can't see you back there in the fog, what's your name?"

"I'm Sunny Schwartz."

"Well, Sunny, I think we need to work on your delivery. That kind of language would never work with a judge. But congratulations. You're the first person who ever challenged me."

The guy he singled out hadn't been talking out of turn. He hadn't been doing anything, just sitting there. Harris was teaching a lesson in the power of authority, and people's willingness to suffer injustice in silence. The message was loud and clear, at least for me. Just about every day I'd questioned whether I would make it in law school, and whether anyone would take me seriously. This was the first time I was sure I was in the right place.

CHAPTER 4

1983

I sucked in a lungful of smoke, felt the kick in my blood, then opened my eyes. Fog hung over the hills. If I squinted hard enough to block out the road cutting across the hillside, I could imagine the world without people, a world with only deer, raccoons and seagulls wheeling overhead trying to find the ocean. The cigarette burned to the filter and I tossed it as I walked back into one of the greatest scars I could imagine people carving into the hillside. County Jail 3 was south of San Francisco, in San Bruno, on seven acres of beautiful, rolling, forested land. The jail was built during the Depression and embodied everything the time had to offer. The exterior looked like a giant concrete bunker. It smelled of mildew, even in the administration section, where the law interns had their office. Paint peeled off the ceiling in large ribbons. The few windows we had were smudged and cracked.

I checked the assignment clipboard, picked up my notebook and a file full of complaints and grudgingly headed into the belly of the beast. To talk about the life I faced every day in the jails, it's probably best to start with the language. There was a unique slang I'd had to learn in order to communicate. First, there were terms that deputies and civilians, like me, had for the inmates.

Baby banger: a young gang member who looks like a child and is often covered in menacing tattoos

Badass or **Hard-core convict** or **Gangbanger**: a major thug, often covered in menacing tattoos

Poocasso: a crazy person who uses his feces to draw on the cell walls

Sack a nuts, Roof job, 800, or **5150**: crazy person, someone who needs holes patched in his head. The numbers *800* and *5150* came from the penal codes and the health and safety codes respectively. Anyone who earned any of these terms was usually destined for the psych ward.

Shit-thrower: an inmate who throws shit, usually at deputy sheriffs

Spitter: an inmate who spits, usually at deputy sheriffs. "Be careful on rounds, there's a spitter in the second tank."

Then there were the terms that inmates had for one another, or for us.

Fish: a new inmate, a rookie, usually someone who has never been to jail

Narc: informer or snitch

Pig or **Turn-key**: a deputy sheriff. *Pig* was used more universally. A *turn-key* was a lazy know-nothing, only good for opening and shutting doors.

Public pretender: a public defender. "I don't want no public pretender, I want a real lawyer."

Punk: This was the worst put-down there was and it was pretty universal. A punk behind bars specifically meant a submissive homosexual—the receiver of anal sex. The term could be directed at anyone as a put-down, as in, "That guy's just a punk," or "a punk-ass bitch."

After four years on the job, I'd run into spitters and poocassos, and had prisoners complain about "public pretenders" and the "fucking pigs who threw me to the ground." It was a violent language to match a violent place. And every day on the tiers required stamina.

"Another day in paradise, hey, Sun?" Deputy Richard Drocco nodded at me as he pulled out a dirty brass key to open the bar door.

"Another day in paradise, Ricky," I said and smiled back. In my job I didn't have much interaction with deputy sheriffs but I'd managed to befriend a few. They were protective of their turf, dismissive of any-one who was too soft on inmates, and that meant anyone who was a legal intern. Too many times to count, deputies had said to me, "I don't see why you bother. Bunch of liars, you can't do anything for them." But there was no way to avoid them. The deputies were the gatekeepers, in every sense of the word. If I wanted to do my rounds, they had to open the door. Deputy Richard Drocco and I had a mutual love affair with losers, both the Cubs and the San Francisco Giants, so we had friendly gripe fests when we saw each other. Drocco was a handsome bear of a man who could take a prisoner down in one sec-ond and in the next donate his paycheck to help get him back on track. He didn't look at the inmates as his enemy, but that didn't mean he loved them, either. He was fair, and he and I had a good relationship. He was one of the exceptions.

Many deputies would barely look at me, much less talk to me. But the law interns had a similarly dim view of deputies. We were like two rival cliques in high school. To them, we were the dope-smuggling hippie liberals, the prisoner lovers, the pillow fluffers. To us, they were the sadistic, mean-spirited, right-wing thugs.

In my experience, some deputies were assholes, to be sure. They talked to inmates as if they were cattle to be rounded up. A few seemed to take pride in antagonizing inmates as much as they could. During night rounds, they would take their keys and knock them against the bars to wake up anyone who was sleeping. The worst deputies would send inmates to lockdown for the most minor rule violation, and if a prisoner said something even slightly disrespecting, they would wres-tle the guy to the ground, stick a knee in his back and cold-cock him with a forearm for good measure. But most deputy sheriffs I'd met weren't like that. They were simply trying to survive an incredibly stressful job. They spent their whole day with prisoners, many of whom were infuriating, and some of whom were dangerous. They had to manage intake, where men were stripped of their personal belongings, given a number and a uniform, and had to squat and cough during the strip search. They had to manage the prisoners' complaints, search for contraband, confiscate weapons and drugs and cut down the "string-ups," which was the euphemism we had for sui-cides. Many deputies had short fuses but could be prevailed upon to do the right thing, even if they were cynical about the results. Deputy Drocco swung the door wide and I walked in.

As I moved through the gate, the quality of the noise changed. The decibel level rose as I climbed the stairs to the fourth floor. The central stairwell in County Jail 3 climbed up through ten different living quarters, stacked five high on the south and north sides of the building. There were no sound barriers of any kind, and only bars separated the stairwell and each tier. The noise was so bad I'd started to lose my hearing. Many older deputies needed hearing aids. As I got to the top of the stairwell, the echoing voices grew shrill. I could hear cackles and shrieks by the time I made it to the entrance to 4 North, my assigned tier for the next few weeks. Four North was more commonly referred to as the Queens' Tank.

"Hey, Sunny! Who's the finest advocate this side of the Mississippi?" Barbara's high-pitched yelp cut through the noise. The Queens' Tank was a men's dorm, but most of the men were in some stage of preoperative transition. I tried to refer to them by the female pronouns *she* or *her* out of deference to their emotional self-identification. If they thought of themselves as "she," who was I to disagree? Barbara was giving me a limp-wristed wave from in front of the television. She was one of the more recognizable queens in the Queens' Tank. Her hormone treatments had given her these amazingly firm, full breasts that would be the envy of any biological woman. On the day we met, she'd introduced herself as Mark Toms and I'd replied, "I know that's your birth name, honey, but what do you want to be called?" She smiled wide and said, "Barbara," a little coyly. I had won an ally.

Barbara, with her slim figure, plucked-thin eyebrows and practiced flounce to her walk, was also, remarkably, the father of three children. Inside, off smack, she couldn't be more generous. She spent her days making picture frames out of cigarette packs to give to her kids. But outside she was a holy terror with no impulse control, losing her mind in drugs and prostitution. She rarely made it three months before she returned for another stay with us. Barbara sat with a bunch of other queens around the television watching *All My Children*. The volume was turned all the way up to compete with a radio that was blasting a talk show on the other side of the tier.

Transvestites and preoperative transsexuals made up the bulk of the population in the Queens' Tank, which was the dumping ground for the most vulnerable inmates in the San Francisco jail system. Snitches were housed here, as well as any inmate who had been raped and filed a claim. Their willingness to testify made them open to reprisal— especially out on the yard, where a hundred men at a time roamed the dirt-covered, hundred-foot-square field. Child molesters were also housed in the Queens' Tank. They were considered, in the class system of the jails, the lowest of the low, and the most likely to be singled out for "jailhouse justice" by the gangbangers on the yard. But looking around, you barely noticed the men. The queens drew all the light.

The way these inmates passed as women was ingenious. Makeup wasn't allowed inside. Everyone had a standard-issue uniform. But looking at the ladies crowded around the television, you'd think we were somewhere in the Bahamas. Most everyone had their T-shirts tied in a knot at their belly button. Their hair was twisted into ponytails, Farrah Fawcett feathered curls, Afro puffs, Zulu knots and braids in every variation. For curlers they used toilet paper rolls. Stuck behind their ears were glinting flowers constructed out of potato chip bags from the commissary. In their cells, a homemade frame might hold family photos.

Dawn wandered over as I settled down at one of the metal picnic tables. "How ya been, Sunny?" she growled at me. Dawn was like Barbara, also a preop transgender, but not nearly as successful at passing. She was about six feet two, 230 pounds, with dark black skin and intense flashing brown eyes. She was also more prone to violence.

"I'm good, Dawn. Whaddya know?"

"I know I'm getting out in a month because of you, honey. That's what I know." I'd helped Dawn get a few months knocked off her sentence. Many of my cases came from the miscalculation of sentences. If the inmate couldn't make bail, the time he or she served before being convicted was supposed to be subtracted from the sentence. But often someone forgot to write it down, and I had to get inmates like Dawn their time back. "You just let me know if there's anything Dawn can do for you," she said.

I smiled. Offers of help from inmates always had to be viewed in the most skeptical light. Sometimes they came with requests for special favors. Often they came with questions like "Where do you live?"

"How long ya been there?" and then, eventually, "You got a special someone at home?" These were barriers to be protected. I'd heard plenty of cautionary tales about deputies or civilians who had started relationships with prisoners. The power dynamic was too stark. Some of those people who crossed the line got involved in the criminal lives of the prisoners, often to sell drugs. Whatever the motivation, even if the relationship was completely innocent, there was nothing consensual about a relationship between an individual and the person he or she had locked up. But neither Dawn nor Barbara had ever crossed the line with me, so I just smiled at Dawn's offer.

I spread my papers out. I almost always worked in the common areas. It was either that or call my clients out one by one, and that was time-consuming. In the common area, I could cycle through men quickly, despite how unpleasantly loud it was. As I sat down, my clients began to assemble. I could feel a headache starting up behind my left eye. I spent the next four hours holding court—going over claims with inmates who had already filed them, and filling out new complaints for the prisoners who were illiterate or too lazy to do it themselves. I heard stories that ran the gamut. Some were about how they were being evicted and needed help, or how their wives had run off with their kids, or how they'd been given an eight-month sentence but that they'd already spent nine months in jail awaiting trial and "why haven't I been released?" Some stories were from inmates who'd been written up by a deputy for having contraband and now needed a defense. Other stories were more serious, about deputy sheriffs who they said beat them up, or raped them.

I wrote up each one in an Action Request Form. If the inmate was being accused of a rule violation, then I would represent him at the hearing in front of the watch commander, who ran the jail. If the inmate was having trouble out in the world, I functioned more like a social worker. If someone was being evicted, I might contact his leasing agent and try to work out a deal for payment. If the complaint was serious and could involve criminal action, I would normally go straight to the chief deputy or his boss, the sheriff, and Internal Affairs would need to be brought in.

Lately, I had been finding it hard to stay patient. I listened to an inmate named Ramón ramble on for twenty minutes about how he was about to be evicted from his apartment, and how all of his earthly belongings were going to be tossed into the street, and how his drug dealer had stolen his last three hundred dollars and all I could think was, If you didn't want to get robbed, you putz, you shouldn't have given your dealer your keys.

I glanced at the clock. Finally, my shift was drawing to a close. I was trying to finish up with Ramón. His voice was grating on me but then it was drowned out by a rush of voices from around the television. Maybe Erica Kane was getting married again. A group of inmates started this high-pitched screaming, like teenage girls in a lunchroom. "Oh my God!" "Girl, you didn't just do that!"

I shot out of my chair. "Jesus Christ, folks. I'm trying to work over here. Show some respect and keep it down!"

The group fell silent. I saw some irritated, childish looks, but they'd received the message. Good, I thought, I hadn't expected it to be so easy. I returned to my table.

As soon as I was back in my seat, a flutter crawled up my neck. There was a subtle, barely noticeable shift on the tier, like the wind was changing direction. Then I heard a grumbling sound. I looked up, and a man was walking toward me. He had the standard uniform on, nothing "queened out" about his orange T-shirt and pants, but his eyes were wild, as if his lids had been yanked open. In his hands, he had the only thing on the tier that wasn't bolted down, a mop wringer that he had just pulled off a bucket of filthy water. As he walked toward me, he lifted it over his head.

"What'd you say, bitch?" he mumbled. It was almost like he wasn't talking to me but it was clear he was. "You can't tell me what to do. Who the fuck do you think you are?"

I was totally on my own in the Queens' Tank. I had no whistle, no radio, no keys, nothing. That was true for every civilian who worked the jails. When I first started, the communication issues had scared me. But I'd grown complacent. The nearest deputy wasn't physically far away, maybe about fifty feet, but he was behind a gate, and behind a wall of sound. I wouldn't be heard if I screamed. An inmate with a mop wringer could crush my skull, and I would be powerless to stop him. I stumbled off the bench, stepped back and tried to speak.

"Wait a minute, wait a minute!" For a brief moment, I thought of

Stevie. I'd seen the same look in his eyes; the glassy madness that I knew meant that he could do anything. I was paralyzed, watching the guy come at me. There was nowhere to run except deeper into the tier.

All of a sudden, there was a flash of orange, and my attacker was on his back. The mop wringer clattered up against a cell door. Dawn had tackled him, and now lifted herself up over him, cocked her meaty fist and started raining down blows.

"That is *our* girl," Dawn yelled. She repeated it over and over, using it as a backbeat to her punches, until her knuckles were stained red. "That is our girl! That is our girl! That is our girl! Leave her alone!"

I finally came to my senses and realized Dawn could kill the man. "Dawn!" I shouted. "That's enough. *That's enough!*" The world around me smeared. There were deputies rushing in, inmates looking on. Ramón was cowering a few feet away. Dawn and my attacker were flattened beneath a pack of green uniforms. Then I was gone, hustled out of the tier, down the stairs and into the staff area. My colleague Rita was in our office and was startled when I barreled in with two deputy sheriffs as escorts. She brought me a glass of water.

I'd seen violence in the jails before. I'd gone out into the yard after one especially brutal fight. An inmate had turned a softball bat on an enemy, cracking open his head, staining the dirt around third base. I'd seen the victim being wheeled away. I'd heard the deputy sheriffs in the break room, talking about fights they'd broken up, beatings they'd had to dole out, or riots they'd been caught in. But it had never happened to me.

I sat there numb for a few minutes in the intern's office until I thought to take a sip of water. Deputy Drocco wandered in.

"You okay, Sun?" He gave me a pat on the back.

"I don't know, Ricky. I don't know."

Drocco looked at me kindly and gave me a sharp nod. "You oughta know that three or four inmates came rushing up to the gate yelling bloody murder, telling me to call the code three. They had your back."

I guess I was glad to hear it. There were two other deputies standing out in the hall. I could hear them laughing.

"Did you see the look on that guy's face?" one said. "He practically wet himself when we tackled him."

"Yeah, that asshole had it coming."

"And Dawn . . . that dyke can really dole out a beating! Imagine what she'd do to you in bed."

"That's sick, man, that's so sick."

There were reports to be filed but I got the hell out of there as soon as I could. I told people I was fine as I headed for the door, but the ground swam a little beneath my feet. My hands shook on the steering wheel. I was awash in adrenaline. It was a miracle I didn't get into an accident driving home. What would have happened if the man had reached me? Would I have reacted? Dawn hadn't hesitated. She turned her body into a weapon and rushed in. My car slid north from San Bruno back into San Francisco. The sun was setting and San Francisco Bay off to my right turned golden in the changing light.

I replayed the scene in my head. I gave myself another chance to react, picturing different ways for it to play out. In one scenario, I leaped from the table and ran around him, a base runner avoiding the tag. In another, I found my voice, and recruited the inmates around me to help. But in some, I took my fist and slammed it again and again into the man's face until my knuckles came away bloody just like Dawn's.

I went back to work the next day. My supervisor, Randy, told me not to come back for at least a week, but I wasn't going to let a lunatic with a mop wringer change my schedule. I went back to the Queens' Tank. Deputy Drocco gave me a smile as he let me in, and a warning. "They decided not to segregate Dawn. He's still in there."

Dawn and Barbara came to see me the minute I started my rounds.

"Hey darling," Barbara said, her eyes gentle and warm. "You doing okay today?" Dawn just nodded at me.

I smiled back and thought, Not yet, but I will be. I will be. I'm tougher than you think.

The guy who came after me was returned to the Queens' Tank later that afternoon. After a trip to the infirmary, he was sent back to his cell with two black eyes and a swollen lip. There wasn't anywhere else to send him. For a week he was in lockdown, which meant twenty-three hours a day in his cell, one hour out for supervised exercise.

I was still working the tier when his lockdown ended. One afternoon, he sidled up to the table where I was working, his face an unsightly mix of black and blue and green bruises. I jumped when I realized it was him. I looked around and saw that a table away, Dawn and Barbara were keeping a vigilant eye on me. The man looked sheepish.

"Sunny, Barbara said I should come talk to you," said the inmate. "I'm sorry about what happened last week. I guess I drank too much pruno, you know." Pruno was an illegal liquor the men brewed out of orange juice, sugar and bread in their toilets. I'd been told it was like drinking fermented gasoline.

"I drank too much, you know what I'm saying, and I lost it. I didn't mean it. If my head was straight, you know, I wouldn't have done it."

I looked at him. I was both touched that Barbara would have thought of this, and angry with what the man was saying.

"All right . . . what's your name?"

"Derek."

"Derek . . ." I hesitated, trying to find the words. "I accept your apology but you know what? I'm also disgusted. What kind of excuse is that?"

Derek's eyes widened. He blinked twice. "Excuse me?"

"'The booze made me do it'?" I answered him. "It's always someone else's fault. It's 'the drugs,' 'my old lady,' 'my abusive dad,' always someone else. When is it your responsibility?"

He seemed stunned. But he played his part, did what I expected him to do. He stayed hard, unreachable.

"Damn, I was just trying to apologize." He turned on his heel and stalked off.

At the end of the tier the TV blared. A table away, a man eyed me warily. An argument was echoing from the far end of the tier. A crowd of preops, looking a little like a football team in drag, were milling around waiting to meet with me, each with her own story to tell.

CHAPTER 5

1983

The phone rang in the law interns' office. It was Friday. I was the last one there for the day and should have known better than to pick it up. A mother was on the other end and she started pleading with me.

"Please," she said. "Please. My son is getting out on Monday, and he won't call. He returns my letters." The woman was desperate, which was unusual. Many of the family members I dealt with had checked out, had given up on their convict child or brother or father or mother. But she was begging. "I just want to help him but he's not right in the head. He's sick, you know, he's got mental problems. They've got him up on Three North." My heart sank.

The 3 North tier, otherwise known as the psych tier, was the only place in the jail system that creeped me out. I could get in a deputy sheriff's face and tell him I thought he was a grade-A asshole, or walk up to a group of thugs on 6 North or South, the hard-core felons, and confront them about being bullies, or walk through the Queens' Tank and pull down the sheets the men had slung up so they could have sex in private while the deputies looked the other way. I confronted the monsters every day. I didn't run from them. But the psych tier was the one place I could not face. The men on the tier were a random combination of paranoid schizophrenics, manic-depressives, addicts suffering drug-induced psychosis and Vietnam vets with posttraumatic stress. They were cutters, biters, spitters, men who pulled their own hair out and roof jobs. I hated it. The men shouted for no reason. They were calm one second, and the next they were screaming. Psych services was little more than a MASH unit doing crisis management.

The population was heavily dosed on antipsychotics. The men had what we called the "Prolixin and Thorazine shuffle" and every time I was there I thought of Stevie.

I think the woman who called me that Friday afternoon heard me hesitate, because her voice cracked as she pleaded with me. "If you could just please get a note to him. Don't tell him who it's from because he'll throw it away. Please just let him know that we'll be there to pick him up when he gets out. Please tell him we'll be waiting at the gates. Please."

I felt like I was talking to my mother. If I closed my eyes, I could picture Frieda, with the quivering lip she had whenever she talked about Stevie, her uncertainty over what to do about a son who was not her son anymore, not in any way she knew. My stomach was churning but I agreed to help.

I wrote the note and went to 3 North. I didn't go in. I couldn't. I asked the deputy, who was a friend of mine, if he could pull out the guy for me. "Really?" He looked at me skeptically. "That guy's kinda out of it." The inmate wandered out looking like the bottom of my shoe. His hair was a mop, a tangled dirty mess on top of a scraggly beard. His eyes were dead. He was one of the medicated zombies.

I handed him the note. "Please look at this right now," I said. "This is a very important message. I'm gonna stand here while you read it."

He opened it and stood there swaying. His eyes widened ever so slightly as he read it. Then he closed the note and popped it into his mouth. He chewed it with a quiet, angry intensity. His head bobbed forward, pigeonlike, as he swallowed. He glanced at me and then, without saying a word, shuffled back onto the tier.

Stevie had been living with my parents, on and off, for the past four years. He'd been unable to hold a job, and unable to find a doctor that could help him. When he was doing well, he was usually paralyzed on Prolixin. At one point, my dad called me up, sounding exhausted, to tell me Stevie had torn up all of his family photos. These photos were irreplaceable, and especially precious to my orphan dad. I'd visited Stevie and my parents a few times and came away worried. It seemed entirely possible that Stevie could take the next step and turn his anger not just on my dad's things, but on my dad. My parents were running out of money and ideas about what to do. The only time Stevie hadn't lived at home since his diagnosis was when he went to Los Angeles for a few months to try to become a boxer. No one had thought that was a good idea. He'd been beaten badly in the ring and came back to Chicago ranting about the *shvartzes* and goyim who had beaten him up.

I watched as the hairy roof job who'd just eaten the note disappeared back into the tier and I shivered. It might as well have been Stevie going back onto the tier. I did not know how to help my brother. I didn't know how to help this man.

I caught the Queens' Tank assignment more than my colleagues. It was tit for tat. They picked up slack for me on the psych tier; I took the Queens' Tank. It suited me. On good days, I felt like I could help the messy lives of the she-males.

That didn't mean I didn't feel like Sisyphus every time I walked in there, eternally pushing a rock up a hill. A four-hour rotation always left me with a headache and deep desire for a tequila shot, a cigarette and an empty-headed conversation with a lovely stranger at my neighborhood bar.

It was another Friday afternoon and I'd nearly hit the gate when a prisoner rushed up to me, sweating and anxious. I'd never met him but I'd seen him before. He was white, middle-aged, pudgy and wore horn-rimmed glasses, like a suburban dad or somebody's accountant. "Hey, hey, hey." He stepped into my path. "You need to help me. No one's paying any attention to me."

"Listen, buddy, my day is over. It's going to have to wait till Monday."

His eyes were darting around as if someone were chasing him. "I'm here on a child molestation conviction and was sentenced to a year in this hellhole. I've sent letters, letters to everyone, and nobody has answered."

I was on alert now. His desperation, his fidgetiness, his overall energy, was a warning sign. He took a deep breath and was practically spitting at me by the time he unloaded his full confession. "I'm getting out of jail in two weeks and I have been asking for help for a year and nobody has responded. I'm promising you I will do it again! There's a little girl whose mom is renting a room in the apartment where I live, and she will be my next victim."

I didn't want to be standing there, didn't want to be anywhere near him. But I swallowed, and tried to do my job.

"Okay, hold on, what are you saying?"

"What, you can't hear me? I promise you that the little girl living in my house will be my next victim."

My brain finally caught up with what he was saying. I didn't want him to clam up so I asked follow-up questions.

"Who is this girl? What is her mother's name?" He slowed down while I wrote down his answers. I looked back at him. "You need help. If I found a program that would help you, would you do it?"

He nodded yes.

I was trying to do the normal things I do in my job: write down the details, spend time with the client and set up a game plan. But I felt itchy, almost sick. I finally wrote down his name, Fred Johnson, and his inmate number and took off.

I went straight out the front door of the jail. I felt like I was drowning. I lit a cigarette and tried to clear my head. My job was to be that monster's advocate, to fight for him, almost like a defense attorney. But this was something different. He asked me for help but all I could think of was the girl living in his house. Who was her advocate? He wanted help; she needed it.

He was getting out in two weeks.

I jammed another cigarette into my mouth. Back in the front office, I pulled Fred Johnson's custody card. Johnson had been sentenced to a year in the county jail on child molestation charge 288 of the California penal code. His attorney must have struck a deal with the DA because he faced up to eight years. A defendant would get only a year under specific circumstances, such as if the victim couldn't or wouldn't testify because she was too young. It was as bad as I had imagined it.

I stewed over it all weekend, driving my girlfriend nuts. I had a mountain of homework to do for law school, including a presentation I was scheduled to give in my constitutional law class, but every time I tried to get started, all I could think of was Fred Johnson.

First thing Monday morning, I went to see my boss, San Francisco Sheriff Michael Hennessey, at City Hall, a beaux arts confection that is both majestic and imposing. It doesn't really fit Hennessey's style. He's an even-tempered, smart Irishman from Iowa, with an impish sparkle in his eye. I liked him. I was pretty low on the totem pole in the grand scheme of things. Legal interns were at about the same clout level as a cadet in the department, which was, if not at the bottom, very near it, but Hennessey didn't treat me that way. Hennessey created the office where I worked, and had a special place in his heart for the interns. He was a lawyer himself and liked talking through problems with us.

I gave him a quick nod as I walked in. But I was too anxious to chat and quickly spelled out the story.

"Sheriff, I'm at a loss," I told him as I finished. "We've gotta do something, right?" His lips pursed and settled into a scowl. Hennessey started twiddling his pen between his fingers, a nervous habit of his. He wasn't much for confrontation, and he did not speak hastily. So I kept going.

"Listen, I know my job is to advocate on his behalf. But I don't know what that means here. Am I supposed to try to have him brought up on charges for making a threat? His sentence is about to run out. How are we supposed to hold him longer?"

"Is that what you want to do? Hold him?"

"Hell yeah! I want to lock him up and never have to think about him again. But since that's not an option, I want to hold him at least until we can maybe get him some help, maybe get him into a program."

"Well, listen, Sunny, I agree that you're supposed to be helping these men, no matter what kind of crimes they've committed. But he asked you for help, so you've got a responsibility to pursue that." The pen twirled a few times in his fingers. "That being said, you have no *legal* obligation to report it. It's only a threat, and not exactly actionable. You know making a case on something like that would be a tough sell. But morally, that's another story, and that answer is easy: we've got to do something." The pen finally came to rest in his hand. He leaned back in his chair. Finally, he cleared his throat.

"Why don't you start with the sentencing judge? See what he has to say. Johnson's statement to you may represent a violation of the terms of his probation. Other than that, the law isn't really on your side. Trying to prove that what he told you is a criminal act is not easy. Intentions are not actions."

I got moving, heartened by what he said, but anxious. This was new territory for me. My colleagues and I in the Prisoner Legal Interns office had a specific identity. We were supposed to fight for the inmates' often overlooked rights. But here I was trying to bring the full weight of the system down on one of my clients, and that made me feel like a turncoat.

My next stop was San Francisco's Hall of Justice, the building that housed Mainline and most of the infrastructure of criminal justice in San Francisco County. It was built in 1958, a gigantic blank of a building, sheathed in marble, and utterly characterless. The top two floors were jail facilities, which included Mainline. The bottom floors housed the office of the district attorney and the adult probation offices, as well as various divisions of the San Francisco Police Department. Traffic court, some of the municipal courts, and the superior court rooms were there as well. Despite its having the charm of a big-box department store, I always liked going to the Hall of Justice because you saw more civilians. At County Jail 3, where our offices were, it was all deputy sheriffs and inmates. Orange and green made you depressed if that's all you saw. I was headed to the office of the honorable Judge Randall Scott, who had been Fred Johnson's trial judge. The judge's secretary, Mrs. Hendricks, knew me. I'd called her half a dozen times about inmates I was representing.

"Now who are you trying to set free this time?" She sighed.

I said it was an emergency, and she ushered me promptly into the judge's chambers. A veteran jurist, Scott looked like a Jewish Santa Claus, and had a reputation for combining compassion with toughness. He was respected by both prosecutors and defense attorneys, no easy feat. Hanging behind his desk was a large portrait of Martin Luther King Jr., and next to it, a hand-painted, framed replica of the Bill of Rights. I launched into my story about Fred Johnson, and he blanched as if I'd kicked him when I reached the heart of the story and Johnson's threat. There was a pause as he removed his glasses to massage the stress out of his brow.

"Ms. Schwartz, I appreciate you trying to do something here, but what can I do? His sentence was his sentence. Once it runs, he's served his debt. I'm not the jury. I've got no legal way to hold him."

"Judge, somebody has to do something. We are talking about a child. I can guarantee you he will hurt that little girl if he's released."

"I'm not arguing that point. I wish I could. I really do. But it's outside my authority."

"What do I do?"

He gave me a rueful smile. "You're doing what you can. You're trying. Try talking to the defense attorney. His advocate might know a way to work the system to protect everyone involved."

As I left, he looked as depressed as I felt. I wanted to argue with him but I knew it was pointless. A day later, I was back at the Hall of Justice, this time in the public defenders' corner of the building. This was the land of no empty surfaces. I don't know if I'd ever met a public defender with a tidy desk, and Fred Johnson's attorney, Susan, was no exception. Files teetered around as if she were a character in a Dr. Seuss book. I wondered if this was the life waiting for me when I finished law school. Susan gave me a haggard glance when I walked in, and I had to remind her who I was talking about. It didn't take long before her face scrunched together. "Augh, that pedophile. That guy was a creep."

"Right. Unfortunately, Susan, I hate to tell you but he is still a creep." I then told her my story, as I'd told the sheriff and the judge already.

"That guy really is a piece of work, huh?" she said.

"Yeah, so what do we do about him?"

Susan didn't skip a beat. "Listen, Sunny, if you try to raise any of this, or try to do anything to revoke his release date, I'll kick and scream about it in court."

I was afraid of this. "Why?" I asked.

"That's my job. It's not always pleasant, and I can tell you, this is about the least pleasant part of it. But if you want to hold him any longer, you have to convict him of something. No crime has been committed. He can't be held because of something he might do in the future."

I liked Susan. She was tough, juggling fifteen million things, and clearly a principled advocate. I'd been getting the same lessons in law school the last four years—every client deserves a vigorous defense, be a fighter, your job is not to sympathize, it's to strategize and win. I knew that even with a threat as specific as Fred Johnson's, any defense attorney worth their salt could have it bounced. There was no proof he had any intent to carry it out. In court, Johnson's attorney had only to claim it was idle chatter, something he said out of fear or anger, or better yet, just deny he said it, and the case would evaporate.

"There has to be something we can do, Susan," I said. "I think a true defense is to try to get your client the help he needs so he doesn't reoffend and end up doing harder time. Come on now, please, let's do something about this." At this point I sounded pathetic. Susan's eyes softened, but she didn't give me any rope.

"Sunny, listen, we're not social workers. I'm his lawyer. I can't go after him. It would be unethical. You know that." There was exhaustion in her voice but I knew this was the oath she took as a defense attorney and I didn't push it. The men and women we would be called on to defend would be despicable, most would be guilty, but the thing we were defending was the right to counsel. In my law school, and in law schools across the country, this idea was sacrosanct. I, too, held it dear to my heart. I looked at Susan, and she looked like a very weary crusader, but not one who was ready to lay down her sword.

By Friday, I felt beat up. All week I'd been told by the lawyers I consulted to drop it. Judge Scott had recused himself from Johnson's case, which I presumed was because my visit had biased him and he was no longer impartial. The case hadn't been reassigned yet but it was tough to lose a good judge. I was anxious about how much time this was taking away from my job and my schoolwork. My other colleagues were taking notice. I'd had to ask one to cover part of my shift the day I went to see the defense attorney and he'd agreed to do it begrudgingly. I felt like he was judging me. I knew I was judging me. The right thing, by the definition of my job as this monster's advocate, was to drop it.

Monday morning I sought out the last person I could think of—Fred Johnson's probation officer, or PO. I found the PO, Allen, in his office, a nondescript cubbyhole on the third floor of the Hall of Justice. I liked Allen from the moment I met him. His eyes were generous and warm, and he asked me questions. Many people who had a number of years under their belt in criminal justice were cynical, pushing their papers through the system, doing just enough to keep up with the workload. Allen had none of that attitude. He let me tell my story, and he didn't find a way to say no, or to complain that I was adding to his workload. Instead, he came up with solutions.

"Well, it's interesting, Johnson's release isn't a done deal, you know," Allen told me. "Johnson has to agree to two conditions. First, he has to register as a sex offender, and second, he has to enroll in a group to deal with his pedophilia. If he doesn't do both things, he would technically be in violation of his probation and I could send him back for that."

"Sounds pretty flimsy."

"Yeah, well, I bet he won't sign anything I give him. And I can guarantee he'll be a pain in the ass in court. It'd be flimsy, but it might be enough to do the trick."

I sat up in my chair and clapped my hands together. I wanted to hug the guy. This was the first sign of hope I'd had since this ordeal began. I told Allen that I'd found a locked facility in Los Angeles that worked primarily with sex offenders. It'd be the right place to send Johnson. Allen assured me that he would make sure that Johnson's confession to me was part of the record and that this thing would go to a hearing. Out on the steps of the Hall of Justice, I started a new pack of Tareytons and felt almost giddy.

Five days later, I was summoned back to the Hall of Justice, this time to the courtroom of Superior Court Judge Richard Daniels, who had taken over the case. As Allen had predicted, Johnson had refused to register as a sex offender and this was the probation revocation hearing. Judge Daniels was a law-and-order Republican who subscribed to the old saying "Justice moves with a leaden heel, but strikes with an iron fist." Normally, I would have been annoyed to be in his courtroom. But for this hearing, he seemed like the right SOB for the job.

It was just after 9 A.M. when I arrived. I went in through the back where the judges, defendants and bailiffs enter the building. I passed by the holding cells for the defendants who had a court date that morning. In the corridor, I passed a line of prisoners being transferred over. They were shackled together, ankle to ankle, waist to waist. Many knew me and called out, "Hey, Sunny, are you here to get me out?" "Hey, Sunny, whatchoo doin' for me today?" "I gotta talk to you, Sunny. I gotta get out of here . . . my woman's about to give birth."

I smiled weakly and hurried down the hall, feeling confused. Fred Johnson had asked me for help, but he hadn't asked me for more prison time, and that's what I was trying to give him.

When I got inside, I learned that, like the original judge, Johnson's attorney, Susan, was gone. A colleague was covering the case. I didn't know if it was the press of work or that she wanted out, but chose to believe it was the latter. That brightened my mood. There weren't many circumstances where a defense attorney, especially a public defender, would drop a client. It's hard to do; judges often won't allow it. A guy has to be pretty despicable for that to happen. I sat down in the gallery as the bailiff called out the introductions and Judge Daniels took his seat. Fred Johnson sat hunched over at the defense table with his new attorney, a man I didn't recognize.

After a few preliminaries, the new defense attorney said that contrary to what his client had told Allen, the probation officer, Fred Johnson would indeed register as a sex offender and was prepared to live up to the conditions of his release. The lawyer had the signed paperwork with him and Johnson told the court that this was all a big mistake.

It could have ended there, and Fred Johnson would have been released except, as the DA pointed out, there was my story to tell. I was sworn in by the bailiff. Johnson looked at me warily as I sat down in the witness box. I took a moment to give him the once-over. He seemed calm. I saw none of the panic that he had when I first met him. I caught his eye and he quickly looked down and wrote something on a legal pad. The DA walked me through the story leading up to Johnson's revelation to me two weeks earlier. When I explained how Johnson had begged for help and promised to molest a girl in his home, he jumped out of his chair.

"You're a liar!" he bellowed. "Why would you do this to me?" The judge started rapping his gavel. Johnson's new attorney was also on his feet yelling objections.

"Your Honor," he bellowed. "This testimony is outrageous hearsay and shouldn't be allowed."

The judge finally gained control of the courtroom and told the defense attorney to sit down. "Counsel, I'm going to overrule the objection for now." The judge then turned to me with an arched eyebrow. "All right, Ms. Schwartz. You're creating quite a stir. What are you suggesting we do?"

I knew this was probably going to be the one chance I had, so I took a deep breath, and dove in. "Fred Johnson asked me for help, Your Honor. He said he was going to get out and molest a young girl. I think he should be in a locked facility to deal with his problem and I've found one in Los Angeles that would do the job." As I said it, it didn't seem like such a long shot anymore; it seemed like common sense. Here, a child molester was saying he was going to molest again. I'd put a solution together. No one had to think about it. The judge just had to rubber-stamp it and you could almost call it justice. It was patched together, but at least the girl living in Johnson's house would be safe. But the defense attorney was having none of it and as I finished he started objecting like mad, almost screaming. Veins were bulging in his neck.

"Objection, Your Honor, this is irrelevant and so prejudicial that it outweighs any probative value. This testimony is also clearly outside the scope of this witness's expertise. Who is this person, Your Honor? She's only a law student. She's supposed to be his advocate?"

Now I got mad. "Wait a minute. I've spent more time with this man than anyone in this courtroom. And your client wasn't asking for help, he was screaming for help! If you want to do true defense, you'd make sure your client got the help he needed. You wouldn't be lecturing me about credentials. Everyone in this room is responsible, and if we don't do something now, we'll all have blood on our hands!" The judged rapped his gavel to shut us up.

He said he'd take it all under advisement and I stepped down. I'd barely gotten myself settled in the gallery when the prosecutor and defense attorney finished their summations. The judge paused for a moment, and then, without taking a break, announced his decision. I was stunned. What was I expecting? I thought he'd at least take a minute to think about it.

"On the issue of Fred Johnson's probation," the judge said, "I find that there is not enough evidence here to warrant a revocation of his probation. But I do want to put some safeguards in place." He did *not* send Fred Johnson to a locked facility. The safeguards he mentioned, from where I sat, sounded like a Band-Aid. The judge extended Johnson's probation from three to five years and imposed more court appearances and progress reports. Fred Johnson was released immediately.

I walked out of that courtroom boiling with rage and heartbroken, knowing for a fact that Fred Johnson was going to molest again, and I was pretty sure everyone else knew it, too. I stepped out onto the top stairs of the courthouse, which looked out at six bail bondsman storefronts and a mechanic's garage, a view as bleak as my mood. I lit up a cigarette.

On the side of the Hall of Justice is a plaque. It reads: TO THE FAITHFUL AND IMPARTIAL ENFORCEMENT OF THE LAWS WITH EQUAL AND EXACT JUSTICE TO ALL OF WHATEVER STATE OR PERSUASION. I ground out the cigarette under my heel. We'd followed the law "with equal and exact justice" that day but no wrongs were righted, no debts were repaid to society, everyone lost.

I kept thinking of something Susan had said when I met with her: "We're not social workers, Sunny." It was a line I'd heard from lawyers, judges, deputy sheriffs, almost everyone who worked with prisoners. In other words, it's not my job. In a fundamental way, Susan was right. Her job was not to help Johnson, but to protect his constitutional right to a defense. But I had to wonder whose job it was to fight for justice, to try to do what was best for everyone. It was no one's job.

I checked in with Allen over the next few months. He contacted the woman living with her daughter in Fred Johnson's house to warn her of the threat, and he did his best to try to keep track of Johnson. But he wasn't a babysitter, he had other clients he had to follow, and he couldn't watch the guy day and night. Three months later, he reported to me that Fred Johnson had been arrested for molesting a different girl, a six-year-old immigrant from Nicaragua.

CHAPTER 6

1985

The paint was bulging along a seam on the wall. There must have been a leak. County Jail 3 was old enough that there were leaks behind most walls. I was in one of the hearing rooms. Inmates did not get to testify in stately courtrooms with stained wood and moldings. They got dirty linoleum, fluorescent lights, uncomfortable chairs that were nailed down and no windows. Of course, that meant that's what we got, too—the law interns, deputy sheriffs and administrators who worked with them. I was desperate to get out of the jails.

A year earlier, after I finished my law school course work, Sheriff Hennessey put me on his legal counsel team. In one sense, it was a step up. I was paid a little more. But it was an unforgiving set of responsibilities. My job was to go after rogue deputy sheriffs and to act as something of a prosecutor in their administrative hearings. The deputies were accused of anything from sexual harassment to use of excessive force. When I was a legal intern, deputy sheriffs tended to eye me with suspicion. We were the liberal pinkos always taking the side of the prisoners. Now that my sole job was to go after deputies who broke the rules, I barely had any friends left among the deputized staff. I looked over at the deputy who was my target for the hearing. He was charged with an assault that left a prisoner with a permanent limp. I knew the deputy was a first-class bully who was just as likely to tell me to "move my fat ass" as he was to jack up an inmate for looking at him funny. The deputy stared back at me and smirked.

The bar exam results were coming that day. Some of my friends had received them that morning. A former classmate of mine had already reached me to say she'd passed and another friend had failed. Just the word *fail* made my stomach do flips. The California bar was one of the hardest in the country. I'd already failed it once along with two-thirds of all the other test takers in the state. I failed even though I studied ten hours a day and, near the end, barely slept. I promised myself I'd be healthier the second time around, and I gave myself a little more room to live. I went out, saw friends, studied six hours a day, slept a reasonable amount at night. Still, I walked out of the second test certain I'd failed again. I would have put money on it. My closest friends were helping me through it. I had three Hallmark cards by my bed, which were really condolence cards. "Whatever happens, we love you," one said. It might as well have said, "When you fail, we will still love you." If I thought about the test for more than a minute my monologue started up in the back of my head, an insistent jab, Who the fuck are you? Of course you're going to fail again, you always do.

I looked at the clock. Even if we won, the most the deputy would get was a suspension. It was highly unlikely he'd be fired, and even if he were, the cure might be worse than the disease. The fired deputy would become a martyr, the deputies would hold fund-raisers for his legal defense and the divisions would widen between the civilians like me who worked in the jails and the deputies.

I was fighting as hard as I could but it felt like I was accomplishing nothing. I thought often of the famous Stanford Prison Experiment, which I'd recently read about. In 1971, Stanford professor Philip Zimbardo had recruited male undergraduate students to populate a fake prison. Most were given the role of prisoner; a few were given the role of guard. On day two of the experiment, the prisoners revolted and the guards took extraordinary means to put down the rebellion. Over the next couple of days, "guards" withheld food, punished inmates with nudity or sexual humiliation, withheld bathroom privileges and took mattresses away from "bad" prisoners. Some prisoners started exhibiting such high levels of anxiety they had to be sent home. The experiment was supposed to run for two weeks. Zimbardo was forced to shut it down after six days. The methodology of the experiment has been questioned but one of the simplest conclusions was inescapable: captivity can create its own moral universe, and it doesn't take much to push even law-abiding citizens into despicable behavior.

I'd been an eyewitness to some of the worst behavior that captivity could provoke—the simple lack of respect some deputies showed toward inmates, and the disgusting behavior many inmates displayed toward the deputies. In the case I was working on, the inmate the deputy maimed was a world-class asshole himself whom I'd had to defend a few times for rule violations. Though no one deserved a beating, I was sure he'd done something to provoke it.

I'd listened to stories of men who'd been gang-raped while deputies looked the other way. I'd heard stories of men getting shanked in the yard because they'd disrespected an opposing gang member. I'd listened to stories of men who complained and complained and complained about being in jail but never once stopped to say anything about the people they'd hurt. I couldn't do anything about this culture in my job. It just was what it was. I needed out.

My roommate, Judith, was on the phone when I got home that night. I dropped my things, popped open a beer and made my way to the bedroom. My mail was on my bed. I wanted to sit down with the remote control, watch *The Cosby Show* and zone out for the night. But there it was, a letter from the State Bar of California.

I reached over and shut the door. I sat on the edge of my bed, stopping myself from throwing things around the room. I dug my fingernails into my hand, released them, took a breath and slit open the envelope.

I went running out into the living room, tears streaming down my cheeks. I gave Judith one of those ridiculous crazy-person looks.

"Sunny, what is it? What is it?"

I shoved the card at her. "Read it, Judith. Does it say what I think it says? Please read it out loud in case I'm hallucinating."

She gave me a queer look. "Okay, this one is from the California State Bar Test Committee. And, oh my God, Sunny, oh my God! *The committee of the State Bar of the State of California is pleased to inform you that you passed the bar of California!*"

She let out a squeal of delight for me. I almost fainted.

"They made a mistake," I finally managed to say.

"No, they didn't, Sunny. But even if they did"—she winked at me— "looks like you're a lawyer now!"

I sat down on the couch and let out an enormous, chest-heaving sob.

As soon as I collected myself I picked up the phone and called my dearest friends in the city and told them to come over.

I called my sister, Cindy. I called my mom and dad. Frieda laughed and without embellishment said, "Dolly, we are so proud of you." I called my friends in Tucson, my friends everywhere, anyone who knew where I'd been, how I'd tried to change the grades on my elementary school report cards with a pencil before bringing them home to my parents, how I'd gotten onto a first-name basis with my truant officer in high school, how every paper I turned in came back with so much red on it, it looked like someone had died. I called them to tell them how I'd finally pushed away all of the shame and fear and brutal self-doubt. I told them a miracle had happened.

And soon my friends were at my door, bewildered because I didn't tell them why they had to come, just that they did, and before you knew it we were pulling out champagne, hugging and crying and laughing, whooping it up. The music went on and we were dancing to James Brown and Prince, and life, for once, was fine. I had a way out of the jails. I had a way, I thought, to really help people.

After everyone went home, after I collected the empty bottles and cleared out the ashtrays, and the apartment was quiet and peaceful, I called Stevie.

It was late in Chicago, past one in the morning. He was still living with my parents. (I'd asked them not to tell.) I was half hoping my mother would pick up and that Stevie had already gone to bed. The phone rang a few times before the line clicked.

"Who's there?" It was Stevie. He sounded timid.

"Stevie, it's Sunny. It's your sister."

"Hey, Sun, what's happening?" I could hear sleep in his voice.

"Stevie, you're not gonna believe it. I got some great news today."

"Well then, go on and tell me, Sun. You got me up out here, it's like the middle of the night." He said it with vinegar in his voice, a hint of the old Stevie. I smiled and got to it.

"Stevie, I passed the California bar exam."

"Wow, Sunny, wow! But help me out here. What's that mean?"

"It means I'm a lawyer, Stevie. I'm a professional."

My brother laughed. I hadn't heard him laugh in a long time. "That's great, Sunny. Really . . ." He paused for a second. There was a catch in his voice. "You really stuck it to them, didn't ya? You showed 'em what's what."

I could feel time tick by and wanted to bottle it, save it for when I lost Stevie again. He felt present, the old Stevie. My brother. I was grinning, and calm, and giddy.

"Stevie, if I can do this, you can get better," I told him. I really believed it, too. I was supposed to fail, to reach and reach but be disappointed. But there I was, in a new world, a brand-new, unexpected world where my old identity didn't matter.

"You really think so, Sun? I'd like that. I would."

"Yeah, Stevie. If I can do this, I am telling you, why not you? We can take care of each other, do this together."

I closed my eyes and in that moment, I believed it, too. It was easier for me to remember my brother the way he was when he was healthy. He'd already been in and out of most of the psychiatric facilities in Chicago. Most wouldn't take him back because of his "violent tendencies." My mother said it was the boxing that changed him, "made him goofy," and that he must have been injured in the ring. I didn't have the heart to argue with her that he was sick long before that. I'd stopped believing I'd get Stevie back. But that night, I had hope.

A few months later, Stevie called me in a panic. I picked up and he was on the other end, out of breath. "Don't tell anyone, you have to promise not to tell!" he whispered.

"Stevie, is that you? What is it?"

"Sunny, Jesus, Sunny, you have to help me. I can't live here anymore. It's Dad. I can't live with him anymore!" His voice sounded almost like he was in a nightmare. I tried, gently, to wake him up.

"Hey, Stevie, it's all right, it's all right. Just take a deep breath."

"*No*, Sunny, you don't understand." His voice dipped and shook. "You have to listen to me."

"Okay, okay, just talk to me." Some of the panic left his voice and he started explaining to me how it was Dad who was the sick one. It was Dad who needed help and how he didn't feel safe living with him.

"You know him, Sunny. You know how he gets, how he stomps around the house, and is always so selfish. Well, it's a hundred times worse than it was. I'm afraid he might hurt me." Stevie almost sounded reasonable. I always thought Dad was a lunatic anyway, so why couldn't Stevie be right about this one? I desperately wanted it to be true, for Stevie's sake. I wanted to believe him.

"He's trying to hurt me, Sunny. You've got to get me out of here. I think it's in the food."

"What's that, Stevie?"

"I think it's in the food. I think Dad is trying to poison me." I came back down to earth. This was another one of Stevie's delusions.

"Stevie, you have to try to believe me. I know Dad is tough to be with, he can be a real creep. But I know he's not trying to poison you."

Stevie wigged out. I'd challenged him, and he couldn't stand being challenged.

"Sunny, God damn it, you are nothing. You are queer and abnormal and a loser and sick. Who the hell do you think you are, telling me anything?"

"Hey, Stevie, come on."

"You think God's gonna have mercy on your sick, queer-ass ways? He's gonna punish you, torture your arrogant stupid ass! Fuck you, you stupid queer fuck."

I knew he was sick. I knew it. I knew he wasn't responsible for what he was saying. His illness was talking.

I hung up.

Later that night, I went to my desk and opened my stationery drawer. I had a stack of Ansel Adams cards with Arizona landscapes, pictures that always calmed me down. Hopefully, they would do the same for Stevie. I picked one out and wrote: *I believe in you, Stevie. I believe you can get better. I want you to believe it, too. I will try to do better myself, keep calm, not push you. I just want you to know how much I care about you. Love, Sunny.*

I never knew whether he read the card.

*　*　*

On January 12, 1987, right before I went to sleep, I wrote this in my journal:

> *I feel so sad.*
> *I feel such guilt.*
> *I feel scared.*
> *I want so much to be normal—consistent—normal, God damn it.*
> *I want so much to rid myself of my past, my crazy family.*
> *I've felt too many times this year about wanting to end my life, something I never could relate to in the past. Such self-hatred.*

I'd been fighting with my girlfriend again. I fought with all my girlfriends. I fought and raged, and threw things until I hated myself and them. Even as it was happening, I knew I was imitating my father. I could stand back from the argument, and feel his shadow. "You don't love me," I'd yell, and I might as well have been saying it to him. I could feel the power of my anger as I let myself catch fire, that animal ferocity, and I felt addicted to it, and ashamed by it. The exuberance of the bar exam had not erased everything else going on in my life. It turned out I was still myself, an angry fighter who wasn't quite sure who or what I was fighting.

The next morning, I had to be up and in the office early. I had joined a small civil litigation firm that was a world away from the jails and the inmates. We did sexual harassment cases, job discrimination and civil rights claims. It was a good firm, tight-knit, and the partners' hearts were in the right place.

I couldn't have been more miserable.

One client we had was suing her former employer for discrimination. She worked at a bank for ten years and made forty percent less than her male counterparts who had the same responsibilities and less seniority. If I'd seen it in a law school case study, I would have been fired up. But trying the case had made me question everything I ever believed about the law. My senior partners were fed up with the client because she complained all the time, and the posturing on both sides made me want to gag. We sat in these meetings with opposing counsel and no one could look another person in the eye and say, Let's just make this right. I knew there was a game to be played. I knew this was what I had signed up for but it felt counterproductive. Truly resolving the situation, trying to make this woman whole, was not going to be accomplished with lawyers. I'd been sitting in our conference room the other day, one I'd been in countless times before, when I started staring at the painting on the wall. It was an abstract, squiggly lines in browns and blacks. I saw the title for the first time: *In the Company of Wolves.* Someone's idea of a joke, I guess. I didn't think it was funny.

I fell asleep that night with my mind racing. I wanted to escape into my dreams and wake up somewhere else, where Stevie was well, where my parents knew how to respect me, and where I knew how to love and be patient and went to work in a place where people's lives actually got better.

I woke up in a foul mood, banging things in my apartment as I made coffee and took a shower. The ringing phone broke through the blast of my hair dryer. It was seven-thirty in the morning. No one called me at seven-thirty. I let it ring an extra time before I moved to pick it up.

"Sunny?" It was my father but somehow not my father. His voice sounded strange.

"Yeah? Dad, what is it?"

"Sunny, Stevie's gone."

"What?"

"Stevie's gone. He took his own life."

Stevie's gone; he took his own life. I fell to my knees. The room turned gray and the floor came rushing at me. I was a puddle, a damp mess, a ruin, and then I was flying to Chicago.

CHAPTER 7

1987

Stevie had gone to live in Baltimore with Jerry, who was a resident at Johns Hopkins medical school. Jerry's wife had just had their first child, they'd moved to a bigger place, and Stevie took their old apartment. My parents were worried, but they'd exhausted every resource in Chicago, and in Baltimore they were able to set him up with a nurse for twelve hours a day through a Jewish charity. One morning, the caretaker for the morning shift hadn't been able to get into the bedroom. My brother's body was blocking the door. He'd hung himself in his room.

Going home hadn't been easy for me since I'd left for Tucson. Cindy was the only one in my family who had come to terms with my sexuality. My father always circled around to the same subject when I talked to him. "Sunny," he'd say, "it's a waste. You're too good for this. You'll make a man very happy and you'd be a great mother." After he finished that speech he'd almost always move on to the questions. "Did anything ever happen to you?" he'd ask.

"What do you mean?"

"Did anyone ever hurt you? Is this my fault?"

"Dad, if it was your doing then I thank you for it!" I'd shout back while he scowled. My mom never brought it up, and she never asked me about girlfriends, either. Jerry stopped talking to me, and barely acknowledged me when I did see him. He was living in an Orthodox community in Baltimore. His wife, when she left the house, wore a wig or *sheitl*. They didn't use electricity on Saturdays. He believed God had abandoned me. He didn't let me meet his child.

I stood in front of my parents' door for a minute before I worked up the courage to go inside. The mirror in the front room was covered, the custom during Shiva. There was an instant where it felt like if I turned and ran, I could escape the grief, leave the mirror and its horrible meaning behind. Tears started in my eyes. Then my mother found me and threw herself on me. She was wailing, "My baby, my baby." I gripped tight and tried to ride out her grief for her lost child, her favorite child. My father was a wreck. He sat on the floor in the corner, his mouth slack. My mother hung on to me until I could deposit her on a couch and she fell asleep. Jerry and his wife came. They were polite to me. They'd brought their second child, a newborn girl, because she was still nursing. It was the first time I'd met one of his children. The baby looked like my mother.

I slept in Stevie's old room. In the drawer of his desk I found his grammar school autograph book with its fading pages and ribbons. All the girls had signed it. Felicia from two blocks away wrote, "Don't forget me, ever!" I fell asleep sobbing.

The next day we buried Stevie in a pine box at the Jewish cemetery. Chicago's January sky was slate gray, the wind a jagged saw. I hung on to my mother, and she to me, and kept my face shielded from the wind. Stevie had left a note. Most of it was illegible, no matter how hard we tried to decipher it. The only line we could make out only served to remind us that his mind was broken. *The maharishi told me to kill myself.* Stevie used to tell my mom not to worry. "I will take care of you," he'd say. "I'll make money and get you out of this neighborhood and buy you a white Cadillac with red patent leather seats." He said it all the time. I will take care of you. I'd told him the same thing a year ago.

There are so many ways for life to fall apart. When I'd moved to San Francisco, I was full of hope. I was full of fear, too, but mostly I was full of this sense that I could fight through it all, conquer my demons and slough off the uncertain legacy of my family—my father's fiery anger, my mother's embarrassment, the insensitivity of my brother Jerry, and Stevie's madness. I still carried a needy rage that I used to attack every woman I'd ever let get close to me but I'd also managed to cultivate another lesson from my parents. For all of their faults, they had always sent my brothers and me out the door with a simple instruction: "Be a mensch." Be a good person. Do the right thing. That was the legacy

I'd carried into the jails and into law school, and that I'd used to pass the bar. I'd conquered the worst parts of my shame, I'd become a lawyer. I'd fulfilled my dreams. And I still felt awful.

Back when I worked in the jails, I'd had to stand by and watch the horror show—the men stewing in their sick crimes, left idle to learn nothing and do nothing but wait for their release. I'd watched deputy sheriffs, a few who were sick bastards, taking out their frustrations on inmates by jacking them up, squeezing them with rule violations, taking away privileges. I'd watched some try, just as I was trying, to help someone here, another one there. But I watched many punch the clock, believing there wasn't anything to do except ride it out until retirement. I'd felt like a collaborator, that all of us—civilians, prisoners and deputy sheriffs—were collaborators in a system that accepted and invested in failure. When I became a lawyer, that feeling, much to my frustration, remained the same. I felt like I was trying to win battles that shouldn't be won.

Standing there, burying my brother on that terrible winter day in Chicago, I could feel the last of my dreams collapsing like leaky balloons.

Before they gave me the cocktail of Valium and Demerol they asked me what I wanted to listen to. When my eyes wedged open, Bach's "Brandenburg Concerto" was playing in the background. My head hurt as if someone had whacked it with a two-by-four. I opened my mouth. A shard of pain greeted me. Could I still talk? Dr. Hiashima had said anything could happen. This was brain surgery after all.

I'd had a cold. That's how it started. One of those wet, damp colds where everything was running. I'd finished a deposition, and was collecting my papers and found myself staring at the painting again. *In the Company of Wolves.*

Am I the wolf, or am I the prey? I asked myself.

I blew my nose. A mild thumping started in the back of my head. The pounding started behind my right ear, and it beat in time to my heart.

The sound was still there when I woke up in the morning. It was there when I went to work, as I sat through endless meetings, and went home in the evening. I had a washing machine in my ear, spinning and swirling without pause. At first I was annoyed, but after two days, I began to feel nervous.

I received eardrops from an ear, nose and throat doctor but the Laundromat was in my head so I booked an appointment with a neurologist. I got MRIs. I got CT scans. I got almost every picture they could take of my brain and I was soon sitting with a radiologist, Dr. Hiashima. Pictures of my brain were spread around the examination room and the doctor had a grave expression on his face. I'd brought my girlfriend, Jan, along for moral support. We'd been dating for about a year and we fought like cats and dogs. But she was there when Stevie died. She'd helped me push my life back into shape and so she came with me to the hospital.

The doctor was straightforward. He told me I'd developed a leak in my vertebral artery at the base of my brain. It probably happened when I'd sneezed. The blood vessels were weak, he said, and could burst.

"Okay, fine, doctor, I'm with you. Let's fix it," I told him.

I looked at Jan. She was crying. I realized that maybe I might be missing something.

"Wait a minute. Am I hearing what you're hearing?" Jan whimpered a little.

"The problem you've got is very serious," Dr. Hiashima told me solemnly. "It can be attacked using a procedure that snakes a small latex balloon the size of a grain of rice up to your brain. It's experimental, but far better than the alternative: open brain surgery."

That was the good news. Then came the bad. It was still brain surgery. It was experimental. I had to sign a waiver saying I understood that as a result, I could become deaf, blind and paralyzed. In other words, if something went wrong, death might be a blessing.

I had two weeks until the surgery. It had to happen immediately. I was supposed to leave in a few days to go to Hawaii for a vacation with Jan. The doctor said I should go.

"Just don't do anything overly strenuous or stressful," he said.

I looked at Jan. She'd come with me for all of these doctor visits. She was also the focus of a good deal of the stress in my life. How was this going to work?

I'd told myself we fought so much because of Stevie, because I didn't know how to deal with his suicide. But she'd finally gotten the guts to point out to me that I was angry before he killed himself.

We went to Hawaii. I stumbled off the plane into the salty island air and learned to float. I'd been afraid of the water most of my life. I was a poor swimmer, and got nervous in the deep end of pools. But in the ocean, the fear inexplicably disappeared and I swam out past the break without hesitating. I snorkeled over reefs and got lost in the teeming world beneath me. I kicked gently, finding my way into protected coves, watching the flashing kaleidoscope of life scatter at my approach. I saw the same magical displays out in the open air, too. Even waiting in line at the supermarket was beautiful to me. It was then that I started bargaining with God.

For years, I had been too angry to pray, angry about Stevie, about my family, about how alone I felt. But standing there while three perfectly ripe mangoes were lifted into a paper sack, the misery I carried through so much of my life seemed, at least for a moment, very far away, brain leak or no brain leak. I gave thanks for the beauty right in front of me, and prayed that God might let me hang on to life for a little while longer.

When they snaked the tube up into my brain a week later, I was daydreaming about Stevie. Questions a ten-year-old might ask invaded my thoughts. Both our brains had malfunctioned. Why was he shifted from hospital to hospital, a burden to my parents and a lost cause? Why couldn't they have just gone up into his brain, and replaced a pipe, tightened some screws, and shut some doors that had been left open?

That afternoon, after I was out of surgery, my doctor dropped by my hospital room to check on me. Jan was there, and a bunch of other friends. Dr. Hiashima smiled and sat down.

"I have just three don'ts you've got to avoid to make sure this operation holds and you remain healthy. You with me?"

"Sure, doc."

"Number one: quit smoking. Number two: don't get angry because when you get angry your blood vessels expand and contract and that will be bad for the balloon I just put in your head. Number three: reduce stress in your life. That's all I ask," Then the doctor gave me a wink. "Simple, right?"

Some of my friends cracked up. A few wiseasses clapped.

"Doc, everything you just said I shouldn't do are the most habitual things I do as a human being. Anger and smoking and stress . . . those are my three middle names!" Dr. Hiashima looked me right in the eyes, he was good at that, to respond.

"Sunny, if you want to live, you need to figure out a way to stop."

After my first follow-up appointment I quit the law firm. The cigarettes went into the garbage. I'd already left the San Francisco Sheriff's Department and the jails and the criminals far behind. I made a promise to myself not to go back to a system that invested in people's failure. I wanted to work to heal divisions the way I was working to heal myself, not drive them apart.

I needed new dreams.

CHAPTER 8

1988–1990

I was smoking on the front steps of a brand-new jail, San Francisco County Jail 7, and a refrain from a Talking Heads song was running through my head: *How did I get here?* Life can take some funny turns if you let it.

One year earlier, I'd been on a bus in Thailand. I was terrified and alone and in a foreign country for the first time in my life. I was headed to the beach to float some more in solitude. Jan and I had broken up months before, just one of the many things that had come to an end after my surgery.

The bus was rumbling over a deeply rutted mountain road. Chickens were running up the aisle, having leapt from the arms of their dozing owners. Sinewy Thai men jumped off and on the bus at each stop, clinging to the side even after it started up. The people were patient in a way I wasn't used to. The bus stopped sometimes and did not move for half an hour. No explanation was given, and no one asked for one. Time was a meandering stream.

We were moving again when the bus lurched and I bounced against the window. While I swore under my breath, howls of surprise started up from the front. We ground to a halt. Another bus, coming from the other direction, had run off the road and rolled into a ditch. It lay in the tall grass, twenty feet down the hillside, twisted and broken like a bird that had slammed into a plate-glass window. Everyone around me started praying. Their hands went up, their heads lowered, their combined murmuring created an oddly musical chant, a gentle surface of sound. Then the bus doors flew open and everyone in a single motion stood up and filed out of the bus, and clambered down the hillside to help. No one talked about it. No one complained. Knowledge became action.

I went from Thailand to Seattle, where I worked for a hospice program as a part-time caretaker for the sick and dying, making macaroni and cheese and giving foot massages to old folks. But I'd missed San Francisco and had returned to take a part-time job at ALRP, the AIDS Legal Referral Project. It provided end-of-life legal assistance to people dying of AIDS.

It made sense to me that in my last two jobs I'd been working with terminal patients. The way I figured it, I didn't get to say good-bye to Stevie and this was my way to try to make it up to someone. Stevie had performed this long exit, as if he were bowing and backing out of a room, and I felt as if I'd just sat there and watched him go. He'd taught me how to throw a curveball, he made jokes just for me, he was the best ally I'd had. But he didn't let me say good-bye, so I was left trying to help his replacements die.

I came back to the jails during a bomb scare. It was just after lunch and someone had called in a threat to our office. This happened periodically. Even in San Francisco, there were plenty of folks who didn't like homosexuals, even ones who were dying. I'd grabbed my smokes and the messages from my mailbox. There on the top was one from Ray Towbis, Sheriff Hennessey's right-hand man at the Sheriff's Department. It was marked urgent and underlined three times. Ray was a piece of work. I don't know how the guy managed to yell at me through a "missed call" note but he did. I called him from the pay phone out front.

"Ray, what's happening? Where's the fire?"

"Schwartzy. Whatcha doing right this minute?" Ray barked at me. Ray Towbis was one of the most unusual-looking human beings I'd ever met. He stood about five feet three, had huge Coke-bottle tinted glasses, a flyaway comb-over and a potbelly that was almost perfectly spherical. But his energy was infectious. I got to know Ray when I had joined Hennessey's legal counsel, and he and I became fast friends. After I passed the bar, he had even hired me and my law firm to help him with some personal legal matters. I knew he had my back, and I had his.

"I'm in a phone booth waiting out a bomb scare I'm sure you called in," I told him, teasing him. "Why are you trying to scare me? What're *you* doing?"

"Sandra." He called me Sandra when he wanted to get my attention. "Get here now, we want to talk to you."

"Who's 'we'?" I replied, but I'd already asked too many questions.

"Sandra! Don't ask questions. Just get here. You're going to like this!"

I looked around. The fire fighters were just pulling up, and no one seemed to be in a hurry. I figured, why not?

"Schwartzy!" Ray yelled out as I stepped through the door, and he lumbered to his feet. He gave me a slap on the back. "Sandra, Sandra. This is perfect. We need you. We need someone with moxie. We've got a job that was made for you!" Ray was up for the sale that day. His tactics were pure. He'd happily sell you something you didn't want, but only if he thought it was for the greater good.

"Ray, what are you talking about? I'm a big-shot lawyer, you sure you can afford me?" I winked at him.

"C'mon, Schwartzy, we need someone with real vision about what to do for the prisoners." Ray was leading me into the sheriff's office. I gave Hennessey a wide-eyed stare when I saw him but didn't say anything. Both he and I knew not to interrupt Ray when he was on a tear. "The sheriff and I are throwing out the old rules. We need someone with your courage to do this. Get the deputy sheriffs working with you, and get the inmates ready to work and join society when they get out."

Ray went on like this for five minutes and I still had no idea why I was there. Then Hennessey piped in. "Sunny, we want you to take over all the programs in the jails. We've decided to overhaul how we're doing it, and we're putting all the programs into the new jail that just opened. We're taking a big risk on this jail, and we don't want to blow it. That's why we want you."

They made a good pitch, these two. I'd listened, and despite every voice in my head telling me to walk away, I agreed to go visit the jail. And that's how I found myself stubbing out a cigarette on the steps of County Jail 7, which had just been opened in San Bruno, and which happened to be a few hundred feet down the hill from County Jail 3, my old stomping grounds.

I felt a familiarity that was bloodcurdling. I'd spent four years tramping up and down the tiers of the San Francisco system. I'd inhaled enough smoke on steps like these to kill a horse. I'd tried quitting but the dirty habit crept back into my life. Did I want to add the stress and heartbreak and devastation of the prisoners and deputy sheriffs and this whole twisted industry, too? I looked around. No one thought of landscaping when they built a jail. They just dug a pit and dumped in the concrete. Of course, I got it. Why make it pretty for the criminals? But that was the question, wasn't it? Why not make it pretty? Why withhold easy grace? The view was here, the glory of God spread in the valley around us, but it was not intended for the men and women inside.

I was going to meet with the most unexpected director of a jail facility ever appointed, a guy named Michael Marcum, whom I'd known only slightly in my days as a legal intern. Marcum had been part of Ray and the sheriff's sell. He was a civilian in an industry where jail directors *always* came up through the ranks of the deputy sheriffs. They'd paid their dues, and if they'd shown a talent for administration, they'd been given a jail to run. Marcum was the first civilian ever appointed to run a jail in San Francisco County, and he wasn't just any civilian. Marcum was also a former inmate who had served time for a murder he committed when he was nineteen. He had shot and killed his father, an abusive drunk who'd abused Marcum and his mother for years. He'd worked in the jails ever since his release.

I'd had only one memorable interaction with Marcum when I was a law intern. He was the director of prisoner services, which meant he managed the staff members who taught classes in the jails, and the social workers who did postrelease programs. One of his employees was a jackass, a social worker named Hank. Every time I passed him, and I wasn't the only woman to have this happen, Hank said something vile. One day, I'd had it and barged into Marcum's office.

"Hey, Marcum, I got a complaint about Hank. You have to tell him to knock it off because I'm about to kick his ass." Marcum was as even-keeled as they came, and all business.

"Uh, first of all, hi, Sunny. What happened?"

It was a quick story. I'd walked by Hank's desk and he'd smacked his lips at me, and told me he was ready to "treat me like a real woman." Marcum listened patiently and, to my surprise, asked follow-up questions. I'd run into plenty of men in his position who considered my complaints a hassle.

"Did you tell him anything?" he asked.

"I told him if he ever did that again, I would break his feet." Marcum stifled a laugh. I think he was impressed. Hank had the build of a bar bouncer. A few months later, Hank was gone. Marcum was good people.

I found his office in the administration section. He wasn't there so I took a seat to wait. On his walls, there was a giant poster of Angela Davis alongside pictures of Jean-Paul Sartre, Roland Barthes and Michel Foucault. I smirked. This guy was running a jail? Another poster hung on his door—a picture of Woody Guthrie's guitar with the famous words written on the side: "This machine kills fascists."

Marcum rushed in looking exactly as I remembered him. He was a skinny, fastidious man with flipped-back, impeccably groomed hair. He always sat up straight, making no inefficient moves. He graced me with a big smile.

"Sunny, sorry to keep you waiting. It's great to see you."

I grinned back at him. "This is crazy, Marcum. Talk about putting the lunatics in charge of the asylum!" Marcum reached out to give me a hug. He was all right angles, like hugging a two-by-four.

"I'm glad you're here. So tell me the truth, are you really thinking of coming back?" Marcum didn't want to waste time with me if I wasn't serious and he had no reason to believe I was. When I'd left the Sheriff's Department four years ago, it was the no-looking-back kind of exit.

"You know, before I talked to Ray and the sheriff, I would have told you no, flat out. But they sold me pretty well. Now you gotta level with me. Are the deputy sheriffs going to play ball? Are they really gonna let you do anything?" Deputy sheriffs had always held the power in the jails. They controlled the culture of the place. If they didn't like you or what you were doing in programs, then you weren't going to succeed. It didn't matter if you had developed a pill that would solve all the prisoners' problems in one swallow. If they thought prisoners were animals who deserved to be treated like garbage, then that's how they were treated.

Marcum gave me a piercing look. "I know what I want to do, Sunny," Marcum replied. "I want to pull the jail culture down, down to the studs, and rebuild so it might actually help prisoners and make it a better place to work. And if the deputy sheriffs who are here won't play ball, I'll get some who will. What do you think?"

I shook my head in disbelief. There weren't many people who could leave me speechless. Marcum beckoned me and I followed him out the door and down the hall. He pressed a button on the wall leading into the prisoner section, and a speaker squawked at us from the wall. This jail was much more high-tech than County Jail 3. Here there was an interconnected camera and speaker system. Many doors were unlocked remotely by a deputy in a security room. But the smell of fresh paint didn't obscure the institutional assault of this place. This was still a building of gray cinder-block walls, glaring fluorescent lights and hard edges. It was the kind of place where dreams went to die. We went through a set of doors into a wide hallway with a couple of doors scattered at wide intervals down the right side. Marcum motioned me to one of the doors.

Inside was a giant dormitory, almost like an airplane hangar with gray walls and open bunks spread throughout. Prisoners filled the space. In the middle of the room, up on a slightly raised square pedestal, was a large console where a deputy sheriff was sitting.

Marcum explained, "You know the long tiers from County Jail 3 where you have the deputies at one end, and who knows what's happening at the other end? There's none of that in here. This is the new direct supervision model. The dorms are designed so that the deputy can see what is going on throughout the dorm. It's helping us."

It actually looked like a huge step up from County Jail 3. In the old system, the deputy posted outside the tier couldn't see into any of the cells. The men were on their own except for certain times of day—counts, bed checks and the like. The only other time they had contact was when a fight broke out. Then, the riot unit of eight to ten deputies was sent in to control the situation. It always seemed to me like having a high school detention hall filled with the worst bullies you could imagine, and putting the teacher out in the hall to wait for something to go wrong. Or as one deputy described it to me, it was the "warm water, fish-head soup, lock the door, forget about them" approach to corrections. This new design handed control of living areas, which had been in the hands of the biggest thugs in the dorm, to the deputies.

"Come on," Marcum said, keeping to his schedule. "Let me show you what we're trying to do. This is a top-down overhaul. We're assessing every deputy and we're assessing every prisoner, and making sure everyone is accountable for what goes on in here."

That got my attention. "Accountability, huh, Marcum?"

"Yeah," he said. "Absolutely. I want prisoners to feel like they are living in a humane society here, same as deputies. So we're watching everyone's behavior. This doesn't mean we're going to be nice to the prisoners, you know that. But I sure would love it if the punishment was productive, that these men could come away from this experience having learned something." Marcum then started ticking off his ideas. He wanted domestic violence prevention programs, new high school and college classes, as well as an array of counseling resources.

I was listening and thinking, this man has been smoking something. Either that, or Allen Funt was about to jump out from a secret hole in the wall and announce I was on *Candid Camera*. Back when I was a legal intern we'd talked about what we would do if we controlled the jails. But we never got much further than the light-a-match-and-burn-it-all-down approach. We all had dreams, ways we wanted to make a difference in the lives of everybody who lived and worked here. But they seemed like such an impossibility, why waste your breath talking about it? But here I was, hell was freezing over. Was it possible to do something good here?

"Come on," Marcum said. "I've got something good to show you." He looked at me with a mischievous glint in his eyes.

We wound our way through the halls until we arrived outside Pod A. It looked like the other dorm I had seen—an industrial gray airplane hangar. This was the workers' dorm. The workers had better discipline records than the general population and received special privileges to work in the mailroom or cafeteria.

"All right, Marcum, what are we up to?"

"Last night, we had an incident here, and this is the dorm meeting to deal with it." Dorm meeting? I'd never heard of such a thing. No one held meetings with prisoners. I'd seen deputies yell at them, or avoid them, and civilians meet with them individually, but never anything like a group meeting.

Marcum told me that they had a meeting every week to handle routine business, but this one had been scheduled specifically to deal with the incident. He told me about it as we stepped inside. The night before, a female rookie deputy named Teena Franklin had been harassed after lights-out. She'd been walking up and down the rows of bunks doing night rounds. This was a routine check to make sure everyone was still breathing and no one was escaping. In the middle of her rounds, a few men started yelling from the other side of the dorm.

"Hey, dyke bitch, you wanna come tuck me in?"

"Yeah, lady, why don't you try men for a change?"

There'd been more catcalls and homophobic jeers. This was the run-of-the-mill bullshit that was common in the old jails. We called guys who did that "cell soldiers" because they only got tough when their cell door was locked, or in this case, when the lights were out and they were anonymous in the dark. In my day, if the deputies figured out who did it, they might restrict some privileges, maybe even bump the prisoners from the dorm. But more likely the whole incident would pass unnoticed. Living with that kind of verbal abuse was considered standard operating procedure, something you had to get used to when you worked on the tiers. But Marcum was telling me that this was precisely the kind of thing that he wanted to change.

"We're going to confront it. These guys are the workers; they can't be behaving like this."

"But, I don't get it." I was feeling dumb. "How's it going to work?"

"You'll see." And he left me to go say hello to the deputy sheriff. The men were gathering at the bolted-down metal picnic tables in their common area and I decided to sit down with them. I parked myself at a table full of Latino men, who looked up at me a bit stunned. I stared them down, and then said, "*Hola.*" They smirked.

The staff assembled. Lieutenant Becky Benoit stalked into the room. When Marcum had mentioned that she was the watch commander, I'd raised my eyebrows. I'd barely known her before but what I did remember was that she was a hard-ass who rarely smiled and was not very approachable. She was also about five feet two and petite. I wondered how she survived. Marcum had sung her praises but I wasn't so sure.

The men were assembling. I could see they'd done this before. To my amazement, with almost no prompting, they quieted down when Benoit walked out to start the meeting. She was carrying a book with her and she opened it and started to read. Her voice was quiet, a bit gruff, but it carried.

"After climbing a great hill, one only finds that there are many more hills to climb. I have taken a moment here to rest . . . But I can rest only for a moment, for with freedom comes responsibilities, and I dare not linger, for my long walk is not yet ended." She closed the book. "Nelson Mandela said that. Who knows who Nelson Mandela is?" A scattering of hands went up.

"Well," Becky continued, "Nelson Mandela is a great leader in South Africa. He was once imprisoned for many, many years because he was black. He hadn't done anything, hadn't committed any crime. But he kept his dignity, and after he was released, he went on to become president of his country. He is coming to visit San Francisco next week and I think you ought to know about him. He is a man who understands and talks constantly about how hate corrodes the spirit. It's like a poison. Mandela knew that he could hate the men who imprisoned him, but if he lost himself in that hate he would lose his soul.

"Now I want to talk about what happened in here last night. Some of you took it upon yourselves to yell homophobic language at Deputy Franklin. Those words were designed to do nothing but humiliate. We do not tolerate that kind of behavior here. We don't tolerate racism, we don't tolerate homophobia. We do not tolerate it in ourselves; we do not tolerate it in you. Our covenant with you is that we will treat you with respect and dignity. But we expect the same treatment in return. I want you to think of Nelson Mandela, a role model for all of us, and how he would have responded to this kind of behavior, and what he would have said to the men who said it."

The men had sat quietly through Becky's speech. Some looked bored, some were rocking back in their chairs, a few were falling asleep, but most were paying attention. My jaw was on the floor. Marcum joined in when Becky finished.

"This is our community," Marcum said. "It is everyone's problem if hate is tolerated." Marcum asked if anybody had anything to say. I was stunned to see a few hands go up. Raising their hands? In a jail? I looked at Marcum. He was looking at me as if to say, "See? I told you." He called on three of the men. They stood and apologized for not stepping up to stop the foul language. Finally, two more hands went up in the back of the crowd. They stood up together.

"Hey, we just want to apologize, and apologize to Deputy Franklin. We were the ones who did it."

"Yeah, we're sorry."

Both men looked like they were in their late twenties. They were scraggly, unremarkable. Both would have looked at home in a dive bar or a methadone clinic. I'd never seen anyone stand up and take responsibility in any corner of the criminal justice system where they weren't being offered a deal. I'd never seen such simple, healthy communication in a jail setting. Marcum was now talking to the two who had confessed.

"Thanks for your honesty, gentlemen. Thanks for standing up like real men."

There was scattered clapping in the dorm, which Marcum stopped. "This is not a show. This is not an exercise. This is serious, painful stuff. Your words have an impact, the pain you put out into the world is on you. And it's up to you to stop it."

Now he looked at everyone in the room, taking in the civilian staff and the deputy sheriffs in the room. "And that's on everyone. We all are making an agreement to stop hateful speech, to stop abuse of any kind. If we have to play cops and robbers, we will. If you act like criminals, you'll be treated like criminals, but if you act like men, you will be treated like men." Marcum then turned to other announcements, and even that incredibly pedestrian activity felt revolutionary. In the world, this was ordinary, ho-hum stuff. It was just a meeting. But here, a meeting meant something. It meant there were standards, a schedule, a community, and not just a roomful of lost souls waiting for their lives to resume.

Marcum made sure there were consequences for the two men who'd come forward. He gave them extra work shifts and a writing assignment. I was laughing when he finally circled back to me.

"Did you set this whole thing up for me or what?"

He smiled and then turned serious. "Listen, Sunny, I'm about as surprised as you are that we're getting this chance. But we need you to make it work. This was a good meeting today. They all aren't quite so dramatic, I promise you that. But these are the first steps. We want to build a respectful, dignified community so people are more prepared to go back to society. We need programs, we need you here, and . . ."

Marcum was no longer looking at me. He was giving a stump speech, the kind of speech I'd always wanted to hear from a boss or supervisor. They say you don't get too many fat pitches up over the plate. You have to swing when they come your way. I knew this was my pitch. I just needed to pick the bat off my shoulder and swing.

"Marcum, shut up for a second, would ya, and *count me in!*"

CHAPTER 9

1990

I had my own office. There were windows. Okay, so they were narrow slats of glass but I still had a view better than any I had when I was a lawyer. From my office chair, I could see a pristine patch of the San Bruno Mountains. I felt lucky when I wasn't feeling scared.

It was my second day on the job and my phone wasn't ringing. I'd looked at it at least fifteen times, wondering when someone would call. I had a scribbled list of priorities that Marcum had rattled off to me this morning, and I was hoping someone would tell me how to start. I'd checked in with Becky (Lieutenant Benoit to everyone else) to say hello but I hadn't seen either of them since. There had been a fight in the dorms this morning. We'd had a lot of fights since the place opened, and there were deputy sheriffs to debrief, a dorm meeting to hold, paperwork to fill out. This place was new to everyone, and until the inmates and staff got used to it, there would be fights.

No one knew yet what to call me. No one had ever had my position. I was in charge of programs for County Jail 7, and I was starting with Marcum's short unfinished to-do list:

1. Get a school back in the jails.
2. Start a parenting class.
3. Get a Domestic Violence (DV) group going.

The list wasn't supposed to be exhaustive, just a place to start. And we were starting from almost zero. The jail had a GED program that could accommodate twenty inmates at a time. There was an auto shop and a print shop that taught vocational skills. There were a few inmate worker positions in the kitchen, laundry room and library. The best program we had was the horticulture project, run by a woman named Cathrine Sneed. Sneed took out forty inmates at a time to work in an organic garden we had on the south end of the property. Planting seeds, weeding, fertilizing and tending a garden was a pretty good metaphor for what men had to do in their own lives. That was a heroic project, but all in all, we didn't have much more to offer. The city colleges had been teaching a few courses but Marcum had fired them recently. They'd been sending their worst teachers. We'd caught some sleeping on their desks during class, and one sold drugs to his inmate students. The vast majority of the 362 men and women in County Jail 7 did nothing all day, which was no different than any other jail or prison in the country. I glanced at my phone again, still nothing.

Deputy Richard Drocco stuck his head into my office at around eleven.

"Hey, babe. Good to have ya back in the fold." We caught up a little, then Ricky told me he needed to let me in on what people were thinking.

"Those knucklehead deputies," he said. "They think you're a prisoner lover and a cop hater. That's the rumor, at least." He was talking about the chatter in the deputy locker room. Drocco was smiling, making dramatic gestures with his hands, giving me an insistent finger waggle. "Don't pay any attention to them! I told them you're for real. But listen, babe," Drocco crossed his arms, turning conspiratorial. "We hear you're planning on doing all this stuff for the prisoners, planning to bring in a lot of programs. Don't be planning all these bullshit-type programs. Make sure these guys get some straight talking to. There are some real assholes downstairs." I knew what he meant by bullshit programs. There were a lot of flaky people in the prisoner services world, as well as plenty of con artists and good-for-nothings, trying to suck some easy money out of the correctional bureaucracy. They peddled self-esteem classes, addiction programs and anger management classes that were as effective as a Band-Aid on a broken leg.

"I hear ya, Ricky. Got any ideas?"

"Get these guys jobs. They need to make a living and start paying taxes instead of mooching off all of us." He was punching his palm with his fist. "And maybe you can get some classes for us, too?" He said it as a joke, but I loved the idea. To change the culture, everyone would need new training, including the deputies.

Drocco high-fived me on the way out. Seeing him was a good reminder. When I first started in the jails in 1980, my view on deputy sheriffs wasn't that much different from the inmates'. I saw them as the enemy. I knew one of the things I would have to do in my job was to break down the wall between civilians and deputy sheriffs, and get us all to work like we were on the same team. Luckily, Marcum had been able to pick and choose staff over here. But earlier this morning I'd seen Lieutenant Bill Hunsucker stalking the halls. I remembered Hunsucker as a mean, snarling bulldog of a deputy whose temper had reminded me of that of my father. I had asked Marcum about him and he just rolled his eyes.

"Yeah, I know, Sunny. Hennessey sent him over, told me I needed to give him a second look." I'd have to watch him. And then there was Lieutenant Becky Benoit, the watch commander. In every other jail, her position would have meant she was running the place, but here she was reporting to Marcum, as was I. I'd met her only a few times and hadn't figured her out. She was a quiet Cajun (an oxymoron if I'd ever heard one) from the bayous of Louisiana who managed the impressive feat of being feared and respected by both the other deputy sheriffs and the prisoners. I was her opposite—hugging and snarling and living as large as I could. Yesterday, we had already had our first confrontation. I had lit up a cigarette in the staff dining room. She told me to put it out. I told her that wasn't going to happen. The deputy sheriffs at the next table looked up alarmed, but Becky let it go and walked off. Deputy Hunsucker had motioned me over. "Never seen anyone stand up to Benoit like that. She freaks a lot of people out. Nice going." I was willing to give Becky the benefit of the doubt after the presentation she'd made in the dorm meeting, but I was wary. I'll admit it. I didn't trust the deputy sheriffs and I was dreading the fights we would have.

But they weren't the only ones I was working with. I had ten inherited staff members who reported to me and were waiting for me to set an agenda. I knew a few of them. They were long-serving prisoner service counselors, a job that bore some resemblance to what I used to do as a legal intern. Prisoner service counselors were liaisons to the outside world, but didn't handle any of the legal stuff that I used to. They were a mixed lot, just like the deputy sheriffs. Some were amazingly dedicated and hardworking. Others were collecting a paycheck—clock-punchers and do-nothings.

But I was grateful not to be surrounded by a bunch of bullshit lawyers. I felt recharged by Thailand and Seattle, and was profoundly thankful to be alive and not a vegetable in a wheelchair. I thought of the balloon in my brain every day, a finger in the dam holding back the flood. I wanted a second chance with this strange community of people. I wanted to be in this fight.

At the same time I had to swallow the fear creeping up in my chest. Beyond the three action items Marcum had given me, I didn't have a game plan. I had ideas, certainly, but I didn't have a list of programs I wanted to see in the jail by year's end. What I knew for certain was that no one else was going to show me what to do because we were making it up as we went along.

I began by cracking a book. Marcum had handed me *Jails, Reform, and the New Generation Philosophy,* by Linda Zupan, the day before. It wasn't going to be on the bestseller list anytime soon. It was by corrections people for corrections people. But it described the jail I was sitting in, which was new to the staff and me and relatively new in the world of corrections. Reading it made me hopeful. Compared to the normal "control and coerce" vibe you get in a lot of prison literature, there were good intentions in Zupan's words. She wrote that in direct supervision, contrary to older models,

> The rules are similar to the standards and practices of a civilized society. When rules are violated, management must promptly respond in an intelligent and equitable way. The housing unit should always be viewed as the "deputy's space" with the inmates in the role of the visitor; not vice versa, as is so often the case. The housing areas are divided into manageable units with the cells arranged around a common multi-purpose area.

It sounded good to me, I thought, and shut the book. I needed to force myself back into the monster factory, take its measure after a few years away, and I'd been dawdling.

Another door, another wait. I looked through the window into Pod B. Inside, I could see men playing Ping-Pong. Some were sleeping in their bunks. Others were playing cards. It was eleven-thirty in the morning. The men looked the same as I remembered them: an unsettling combination of innocence and experience swaddled in orange. It was always strange to see a crowd of grown men who all looked like they were wearing pajamas. They had the practiced stance I remembered. Emotion was missing from their faces. They held their arms away from their bodies, stuck their chests out, making themselves bigger. The door grumbled and slid open. A familiar soundscape rolled out to meet me. There was a radio playing too loudly, to compete with the television. Not everything had changed. I sighed.

The pod I was in was designed like the workers' dorm I'd visited when I first met with Marcum. Greeting me on the way in were four showers, four phones and eight open toilets. Men were sitting there doing their business and I made a mental note never to look there again. In the far corner of the room was a weight set. Clanging metal punctuated the constant chatter. The deputy sheriff was sitting at his desk at the foot of the door. I didn't know him. He was about 240 pounds with a buzz cut. Like the men in orange around him, he sat with his chest out, a face of stone, and his arms held out ever so slightly from his body. I introduced myself.

"Deputy Powers," he said. "Yeah, I know who you are. I heard you were starting this week." I told him I was doing rounds to talk to the men about programs.

"Be my guest." There was a touch of exhaustion in his voice. I picked out the nearest table, where a card game was going on. As I approached, the four men looked up. There was a loosely veiled menace in their eyes. I sat down and asked them what they were playing.

"Spades." It was little more than a grunt. They were near the end of a hand, so I waited them out. They'd been talking and laughing before I sat down, but now they were mostly quiet. The guy to my left, an older black man with glasses and deep creases at the corners of his eyes, seemed the most at ease. He was still whooping it up as the tricks turned his way and he made his bid. Once all the cards were out and the dealer was shuffling I started asking questions.

"So what do you do here all day?"

"You're looking at it," the older man said. The other three men snickered.

"What would you rather be doing?"

At this point, the guy to my right chimed in. He was a skinny inmate with baggy clothes.

"Getting out, man. What do you think? Can you get me outta here?" He gave me a poor-puppy stare. There were more scattered chuckles.

"What would you be doing out there?"

"Getting high," Skinny said, and the whole table roared. But the laughter died quickly, because I wasn't going along with it.

"Why?" I asked, as serious as I could. No one answered.

"Hey, why do you want to know? Who are you?" This came from the older guy.

"I'm Sunny Schwartz. I just started working here. I'm in charge of getting programs into the jail."

A third guy piped in. "Hey, are you Indian?"

"No, I'm Jewish."

"Oh." He looked bewildered. I don't think he knew what to make of that. The fourth guy wasn't looking at me. He was shuffling the cards.

"So, who has kids here?"

It turned out they all did. Cedric, the older guy, was fifty, and a grandfather. I couldn't believe Skinny. He barely looked fifteen. But he said he had two boys, ages four and seven.

"What was your last job?" I asked.

At this point, Cedric became exasperated.

"Lady, you ask too many questions. All I want is to do my time and get outta here. It ain't more complicated than that."

I wasn't going to let him off the hook.

"I get it. I do. I'd want to get out of here, too. But my job is to help you guys for when you *do* get out. So what classes would you take if we started some?"

"I need a job," the third one said.

"That's what we all need," Cedric chimed in. "But ain't nobody gonna hire us."

"Bullshit," I said.

"Oh yeah?" Old guy fought back. "They'd hire you. They won't want to deal with convicts."

"Some don't, but you're assuming that all you can do is commit crimes. You're also assuming who I am right now, aren't you?"

"Fair enough, young lady, fair enough." Cedric wasn't fighting me anymore. The others look annoyed, but they were listening. The fourth guy had stopped shuffling.

"You need jobs, okay. Have you thought about what kind of jobs you want to have?"

"Damn, lady." Skinny replied. "You think a motherfucker like me can be choosy about a job?" Normally, I wouldn't have let that kind of language pass, but today I only wanted to provoke so much.

"Come on, now. I'm not saying you get to do exactly what you want when you're released, but it's good to have dreams. What are your dreams for the future once you get out?"

There was silence at the table. Skinny folded his arms. Cedric looked down. The fourth guy, the guy who'd been shuffling the cards, set them in front of him, and quietly, almost angrily, said, "Shit, what's a dream, man? I don't know what that is."

I went from dorm A to B to C. The men spent their time watching *Jerry Springer* and slasher movies. They were dealing cards, playing dominoes and pumping iron. I could count on one hand the number of men who were reading a book, or writing a letter. The women's dorms—E and F—weren't any better. Some of the women were drawing cartoon figures on envelopes, which they would trade for candy bars. Others were doing each other's hair in front of a row of mirrors that gave off weak, cloudy reflections. Everyone said they wanted a job. No one had dreams.

I sat down with Deputy Powers at the end of the day in the break room. He was just getting off his shift in Pod A. I asked him how long he'd been working here. He replied that he'd been "in theater for a little over three weeks," and gave a short grunt of a laugh. He was funny in a hard-boiled sort of way. He also said he was scared shitless of Lieutenant Benoit. This last response I'd found to be pretty universal. The woman was beginning to impress me. I asked him if he thought the place was working and he threw up his hands.

"I don't know. I still don't get it. We can't get a break to go to the bathroom, you know. We're stuck in the dorm, and the inmates have nothing to do. Why the hell do they call this the 'program facility'?" Prisoners were saying this, too, though not quite so directly.

"What's with all the fighting?" I asked. "Direct supervision" was supposed to discourage fighting but so far there had been just as many fights as we used to have on Mainline or in County Jail 3.

"Yeah, well, there are some things that are better over here. The fights are short-lived and more controllable. They happen right in front of us, so it never has time to spread and get out of control. It's not like Mainline, where someone could be getting his ass kicked and we wouldn't know. We get to step in quicker, and that's better, I guess."

"But?"

"But it all happens right in front of us. We don't have any barrier. And there's no place to put them."

"What do you mean?"

"There are only two holding cells in this whole place. Fights happen, and we can't lock those guys down in their cells, 'cause they don't have cells. They either go to the holding cells for a few hours, and that's if no one's in them, or they stay in their dorms, watching TV with the guy they just had a beef with."

Two holding cells. Two holding cells for 362 inmates. That was incredible. That didn't allow for many options.

"Whoa, what happens if you lose a dorm?"

"Exactly, what happens if we lose a dorm?" "Losing a dorm" was our euphemism for a riot. Riots were the worst thing that could happen in a jail. We all feared them. I'd never been in one and I hoped I never would. The horror stories were enough. The deputies were vulnerable here in County Jail 7 in a way I hadn't imagined. There weren't the fallback positions, the way to isolate everyone for a mandatory cooldown like we had in the old tiers. If a riot happened, if you lost a dorm, you had to hope you got out. If the dorm was at maximum occupancy—sixty-two inmates—that was enough to make any deputy sheriff think twice about running in there. There was a twisted genius to it. Deputies couldn't jack someone up just to teach them a lesson, because the inmates would be watching. Still, it seemed burnout was a real threat here and I asked Powers about it.

"I don't really feel better at the end of the day, if that's what you mean. This wasn't just an assignment over here. They asked for volunteers and I raised my hand. Ray Towbis and Marcum said this was going to be a better working environment. It was going to be better for us and for the inmates. I liked that. The inmate should have more to do. And I'm not gonna argue if someone thinks it should be better for us. But right now, these guys, they've got nothing going on, so they give us problems. So I go home, and you can ask my wife, I'm as big a son of a bitch as I always was."

"So far, it's not better?"

"The only thing that's really changed is that I get to watch these guys take a dump all day."

I told him that I was responsible for programs now. And then, having listened to suggestions and complaints all day, I said something crazy. I knew it was crazy when I opened my mouth, and yet, I believed it ought to be true, so I said it anyway.

"Mark my words—this place will have each and every prisoner in class every day for most of the day—all three hundred sixty-two of them will be in some program!"

He nodded at me as if I were nuts. Neither of us had ever seen anything like that in the jails. He had no reason to believe I could deliver on my promise. Neither did I. But it should've been true. These men and women needed things to do. They needed to learn something before going back out into the world, and it needed to be something different from the rage and frustration they normally came out with. They owed it to us to get to work, to make something of themselves. I was going to demand it of them.

CHAPTER 10

1990

We took control of the televisions. I'd come to that decision early on. One day, I was talking to a deputy sheriff in one of the pods when a prisoner started whistling at the far end.

"What's that for?" I asked. It was loud and, strangely, no one seemed pissed. It was the middle of the afternoon. Prisoners began to gather around the television.

"That's the Woody Woodpecker alarm," the deputy sheriff told me. "Someone does that every day at four."

"It's the what?"

"The Woody Woodpecker alarm." He looked at me for a few more beats and then explained. "For the cartoons. It's the one thing the 'bangers all agree on, actually. You know, Woody Woodpecker, Chilly Willy, those guys. It's about the only thing that gives me any peace in a day."

"Well Jesus, that's just sad." The men had spent all day doing nothing. Now, in the only organized activity of the day, they were going to spend another half hour watching cartoons. That pretty much made my decision. Changing a culture takes a thousand small steps, and this was one of the first. But this step provoked a pitched battle against an especially annoying adversary whom I came to know intimately, an inmate named Leroy Clinton.

Clinton's arrest record was extensive, depressing and entirely typical of the men we had in the program facility. Leroy was what we called a retread. He was caught in a vicious cycle of incarceration interrupted by brief moments of freedom. Leroy had begun committing crimes in his teens and followed a predictable path from minor to major offenses. In the three years before I met him, he did three stints in our jails on drug and car theft charges:

- 3/87: Vandalism/property damage. Fine and probation.
- 7/87: Malicious mischief to a vehicle. Dismissed.
- 8/87: Malicious mischief. Convicted. Ninety days in jail and three years probation.
- 3/88: Possession and sale of cocaine. Dropped for lack of probable cause.
- 8/88: Vehicle theft. Dismissed for lack of evidence.
- 11/88: Vehicle theft. Dismissed for lack of evidence.
- 12/88: Grand theft auto. Dismissed for lack of evidence.
- 4/89: Numerous counts of possession and sale of cocaine. Convicted and sentenced to ninety days in jail and three years probation.
- 12/89: Probation violation. Remanded to one year in County Jail 7.

Leroy entered the program facility when he was thirty-four and quickly became one of our most notorious inmates. It wasn't that he was stabbing people in the bathroom, or smuggling drugs, or setting fire to his mattress. But Leroy was consistently, infuriatingly defiant. If the staff said yes, he said no. He was five feet eight, balding in front, and he had dreadlocks down his back so thick they could be used to tie up a boat. Leroy must have been at least 350 pounds, and he was a giant pain in my ass.

We announced the new television policy at our weekly dorm meeting. All the details had yet to be decided but the bottom line was that the deputy sheriff in the pod would now supervise the remote, and prisoners would no longer choose what was playing. *Jerry Springer* was out. Educational programs were in, as well as some occasional entertainment, but none of the slasher-film screamfests the prisoners liked.

That afternoon, I was in Leroy's dorm talking with the deputy about a schedule change. I was in midsentence when Leroy's voice leapt above the din.

"They are a bunch of dictators. These people are trying to control everything we do. We have a right to watch *Jerry Springer*," he yelled. "Hell, these fascist fools won't even let us go outside!" (That last complaint was purely Leroy's issue. Marcum had denied his request to join the organic gardening program because, as Marcum said, he had "too much rabbit in him.") Other men were joining the cry.

"Yeah. What the hell is this?"

"Fuck this shit!"

Just then, by chance, Lieutenant Benoit came into the dorm. She and Deputy Drocco and I all exchanged angry looks. We decided, on the spot, to have another dorm meeting. We collected the men from around the television. Most peeled off from the protest easily. When he was nearly deserted, Leroy finally gave way and came over.

I introduced myself again. This time, unlike the morning, I heard people sighing, I saw some rolling their eyes. Disrespect. Respect is a currency in jail and if you give it up, it is not easy to win back. My voice took on an angry edge.

"I worked with some of you in the early eighties. Some of you younger kids, I actually worked with your parents. I was your law advocate, and I know I don't deserve the kind of reception I just got." Stillness settled over the room. "I have now been here for a month and I've been talking to everyone I can. Let me tell you, you are all saying the same thing! You want to get out of here. You want a job. You want to be with your family. I would have to be deaf not to hear it!" I was stalking up and down, my hand beating time to drive my points home.

"You're protesting the way the television is programmed? I can hear that, too. Let me make it very clear to you what I think. It is not my job to ensure that you enjoy your time here. My job is to make your time constructive." I told them that over the next few months, we'd be bringing education back to the program facility. I'd made good progress in my search for a school to come in with high school equivalency and college courses.

"You are going to have an opportunity to read. Learn how to talk to a potential employer. Learn how to raise your kids." I could hear more sighs and angry chatter. Most of it was coming from Leroy. The next thing I said I addressed directly to him.

"Who here thinks they are perfect parents? Anyone? Do you, Leroy? These classes are for your benefit." Now I pointed toward the television in the corner. "That box is not interested in whether you have a job, whether you have your dignity. It does not care about you or your kids. So before we start talking about your constitutional right to watch *Jerry Springer,* I want you to think about what it will really take for you to leave this place and not come back. I want you to figure out how you can show your loved ones, your community and yourself that you are in fact serious about getting the hell out of here!"

I opened the floor to comments. Leroy shot to his feet. He was steaming.

"Ms. Schwartz, we have a guarantee. Title Fifteen of the California code gives us the right to watch TV and if we want to watch *Jerry Springer—*"

I cut him off. "Look, Mr. Clinton. This is not a debate or a contest." The Title 15 regulations were California's minimum standards for jails in the state. It did not guarantee Leroy the right to watch whatever television program he wanted. But I wasn't going to get into that argument with him. "We are talking about matters of life and death. Your life. Your death. But one thing that is not yours is this jail . . . just as much as it's not my jail. And I will remind you what Mr. Marcum likes to say all the time." I liked to invoke Marcum. He had credibility with the men as an ex-con. "This is the taxpayers' jail. They pay for your room and board. They hired me to help decide how it is run. This is not your home, that's not your bed, and that is definitely not your TV. I would ask you to be the leader that you are so very capable of being. Recognize that this is a program facility. The programs we're putting together are for your benefit, and one thing that is definitely not benefiting you is *Jerry Springer.* So bury this idea about your right to watch his awful show."

I won a chorus of men singing "Ooooh, she got you, man," as if we were in the seventh grade. It was enough to put down Leroy's insurrection for today. In the end, we formed committees of deputized staff with inmates' input to select the TV and radio programming. This was how we managed most of the changes in the dorm. We sought buy-in, enforced discipline, and treated the men with respect until they did something to lose it.

After that second dorm meeting, Becky Benoit took Leroy aside to talk to him. She actually took him to the staff conference room. No prisoners were ever allowed in there but that's where she felt she could deliver the strongest message. She sat him down, and told him he was a pain in the ass, and that she wasn't happy she had to take time out of her day to deal with his petty complaints. But she also told him she respected him as a human being, and that she saw potential in him, and that, if he chose to, he could be a leader in the dorm.

She told me about the conversation at the end of the day. "Sunny, you should see the grievances I get from him. He's always going on and on about the food, or the deputies, the phones, the clothes. But you know what? It means the guy is alive. Leroy knows that this is no way for a man to live. That says something! I think he will be easier to deal with."

Leroy didn't stop fighting us, but Becky's intervention had changed him. He softened. The dorm deputies started asking me, "What did she do to him? Slip him a Quaalude?" I learned from Becky that day. I looked at the fire in her eyes, and thought about the other deputized staff I was working with, and I realized I might have to give up on some of my prejudices against deputy sheriffs.

Becky and Marcum both turned out to be remarkable colleagues. They were unstinting advocates for the jail, and for the essential dignity of everyone there—staff and inmates alike. Marcum became like my brother, or at least, the brother I always wished I had. He kept a tight lock on his emotions, was absolutely loyal and was a cunning administrator who played politics like a champ. He called me Sunshine; I called him Pencil Dick when I thought he was wimping out with the City Hall big shots. Becky scared everyone, she never backed down from a fight, and her attacks could be withering. She was fierce in her support for the dignity of prisoners, and did not compromise on their obligation to make amends for what they'd done. We shared these two desires, and it turned out, a lot more besides.

Many months after I started in County Jail, Becky and I found ourselves becoming intimate, drawn together by the passion we both shared for the work. She was the opposite of every woman I'd dated. I usually went for the mothering, nurturing types who took care of me, and overlooked or excused my temper. Becky was a cop, and a hard-ass, who had a temper and needs of her own. Plus I didn't want to mess up what we had at work. County Jail 7 was too important to screw it up with one of my patented dysfunctional romances. But Becky was persistent, and attractive, and so damn passionate about the work. That was a turn-on. We moved in together after seven months, though we fought like banshees. She was jealous. I was needy. I tried to bully her into submission, but she spit fire right back at me. We also fought equally hard for our programs in County Jail 7. Together with Marcum, the three of us kept taking each one of the thousand steps forward, trying to redefine what a jail could be.

One big step had happened before I even started. Marcum instituted a social contract for all new inmates. It was probably the single most important part of County Jail 7 in those early days, the thing that set it apart from other jails:

SAN FRANCISCO
SHERIFF'S DEPARTMENT
Prisoner Contract

As a participant in the San Francisco County Jail Programs, deputized and counseling staff will be available to assist you in your adjustment to dorm living, your participation in programs and assignments, and in understanding the basic philosophy of human decency and self-respect. The programs of this Facility are designed to help you take responsibility for your life and actions while you are in jail and when you are released.

- I _____ state and agree to the following:
- I have been informed of every Jail Rule and Regulation.
- I will obey the rules and regulations.
- I will participate in good faith in all assigned programs.
- I will attend all assignments on time.
- I will discuss problems with other prisoners and staff in a positive manner.

- I will work sincerely toward meeting the goals I establish to prepare for a positive reentry in the community.
- I will follow the Rules of Student Conduct.
- In addition, I agree to participate in _____.

I understand that I am required to treat others and myself with respect and dignity; and that my positive participation in Programs and Work Assignments will enable me to earn work time credits applicable toward my release date. I understand that racism, sexism, anti-gay/transgender/lesbian remarks, glorification of substance abuse or criminal behaviors and any other form of antisocial behavior will result in loss of privileges, extra work duty or removal from the Program Facility.

Inmate _____

Date _____

Staff Signature _____

The contract underwent permutations over the years but the intent stayed the same. It helped define the environment that we all wanted to live in, an environment that promoted the best in people rather than the worst. The contract was accompanied by a rigorous orientation process. In most correctional institutions, entering a jail was a hazing. Inmates were strip-searched and barked at and then flung into the general population to sink or swim. In our jail, civilian staff and deputized staff worked with new inmates for their first three days in the system. We went over jail rules with them, and put together a set of goals for them to pursue, which we checked on every couple of weeks. From the beginning, we set high expectations for their behavior. Leroy had signed the contract. So did everyone else in the jail.

Of course, my miserable contracts class in law school had taught me that a contract was just a piece of paper unless all parties entered into it in good faith. If we were going to expect a higher level of behavior from our inmates, we had to hold ourselves to a higher standard as well. This applied to both civilians and deputized staff. Everyone grumbled at the changes we introduced on swearing.

"No swearing? What the fuck?" Lieutenant Hunsucker yelled out from the back of one meeting, provoking laughter. Hunsucker had proved to be a thorn in all of our sides, a loose cannon of a deputy whose emotions swung in unpredictable swaths. In meetings, he'd lob rhetorical javelins like an Olympic champ, often complaining about how we were throwing money away, or about the good-for-nothing prisoners. But turned out to be a good kind of thorn because he was often the first person to say what other people were thinking.

A prohibition against swearing had been in the deputy sheriffs' manuals from ancient times, but it had been treated like "no spitting" laws in small towns, a quaint relic. We resurrected many of those rules: no swearing, no disrespect, no favoritism toward inmates, and everyone was recruited to enforce the rules. In the past, civilians wouldn't write up inmates for violations. Now, they were required to. It was a mind-set as much as a practice. My staff complained about having to play disciplinarian, but that at least put them and the deputy sheriffs on the same team. No one was allowed to say, "that isn't my job."

We also tried to break the hierarchy that existed among prisoners. This meant we did away with "trustees." Trustees, in the old system, were prisoners appointed by deputy sheriffs as their eyes and ears on the tier. The trustees received special privileges and helped manage the place. Often, the most Machiavellian figures would get the position because they could keep order. It was a bargain with the devil and encouraged corruption. We replaced the trustee system with a rotating work board so that every prisoner had the chance to be in a position of leadership.

Changing the rules inside, however, was a small part of my job. I had to make good on the promise of constructive programs, and my first big push went to getting a school in the jail.

I discovered that our neighbor to the north, just behind the razor-wire fence and a stand of trees, was Skyline Community College. I gave them the hard sell, told them our population needed their classes more than anyone else, and they'd said they would try. We were able to get state funding for the students because our inmates counted as students as much as the next person did. One of the first things the college did was help us perform a survey of our population's needs so I would know what kind of programs I should start:

- 75 percent were reading somewhere between the fourth- and sixth-grade levels.
- 90 percent never had a legal job.
- 90 percent were self-identified addicts.
- 80 percent were self-identified victims of sexual or physical violence as a child.
- 65 percent had been placed in a special-education class at some point.
- 75 percent were high school dropouts.

It was dismal. If there was ever a set of numbers that spoke more plainly to the need for some alternative to warehousing people, I hadn't seen it. Even I was surprised that 80 percent said they had been abused in the past, and I was stunned that 90 percent had never had a legal job. These were incredible obstacles. If I thought about it for too long, I got depressed. I focused instead on designing a curriculum. With Skyline's approval, we started twelve basic classes. Writing, reading and math were among the basics. I also insisted on geography because many inmates had never been out of their neighborhood except to go to jail. We offered two levels of English as a second language; basic health education (which included information about drug addiction and sexually transmitted diseases); a class called Life Skills, which taught job interview fundamentals; and another on cultural awareness (which was elementary sociology and anthropology). These joined the auto mechanic and print shop I'd inherited, which taught vocational skills. Finally, the wild-card class I brought in was physics. When I was a remedial-class dummy, I liked the experiments my boyfriend Danny got to do in his physics class, and I figured some of the men and women wanted the challenge.

Just before we got the full slate of programs up and running, I made another decision. Classes in the San Francisco jails, and in many jails and prisons across the country, had always been voluntary. But after looking at the results of our assessment, I knew this population could not afford to opt out or they would be right back in our jails within months. So we made an announcement at a staff meeting, and then in the dorms: classes would be mandatory.

Leroy led another protest. That much I expected. The inmates really got into calling us dictators. But what I didn't expect was how much resistance I received from deputy sheriffs. For them, the problem was that any change that made the prisoners unhappy also made them unhappy. A deputy sheriff's job is to keep the peace and it's harder to do when the prisoners are pissed off. Most deputies predicted there would be riots if we made the men go to classes. Deputy Powers, who had practically begged me for classes, said I was crazy to try it. Lieutenant Hunsucker made a threat every time I saw him, whether we were in a meeting or out in the hallways. "Just you wait," he'd say with a sneer. "I pray I'm not on duty when you institute this disaster."

I received resistance from my own staff. Some of them thought it was unconstitutional—that we couldn't force the inmates to learn if they didn't want to. If any argument bothered me, it was that one. It seemed horribly narrow-minded. Every day in the jails, we strip-searched people, forced them to spread their cheeks, squat and cough, while a deputy sheriff inspected their anal cavity. None of the staff complained about the constitutional rights of inmates because of *that* security measure. But we couldn't force inmates to open a book and learn to read? We could only force them to do things that were humiliating? It made no sense. Others argued that it just wouldn't work. People who didn't want to learn couldn't be forced to learn. I told them to just wait and see.

Becky and Marcum were worried about riots. Marcum, as a former inmate, knew the inmate mind-set. Any new thing that they were told to do was often one new thing too many. But to anyone who questioned the program, and this included Becky and Marcum, I made a guarantee. I guaranteed that within three months the inmates wouldn't be complaining about the classes, they would be complaining about the lack of classes, and demand more.

After two months of mandatory classes, Lieutenant Hunsucker found me in my office. Just before the class policy changed, he had switched himself to the four-to-eleven swing watch shift so he wouldn't have to deal with the programs. I braced myself for another unpleasant exchange.

"Hey, Sunny, you got a minute?"

"Sure," I said eyeing him warily. Hunsucker had been a complicated character to deal with. By his own account, he'd left blood in every jail in the county before he'd come over to County Jail 7. He had started his career on Mainline, then went to maximum security with the hard-core felons, then over to Administrative Segregation, where everyone was on lockdown. He told me he hadn't intended to become hardened and cynical, it was just a survival mechanism. You cracked heads, and locked them up and went home for the day.

"I've got to tell you, everyone on swing watch has been talking about how the day shift's horrible. They're saying there's too much activity. And you have to know that I was saying the same thing." He'd told me as much on a dozen different occasions. I began to grit my teeth. I nodded at Hunsucker but didn't interrupt.

"Last week I substituted a few days on the day shift. I was prepared to blow a fucking gasket. But ya know what? And I really hate having to tell you this but . . . it was one of the best shifts I ever had. It was much simpler than what we face before those guys go to bed. During the day, the inmates are busy! When I get them, they've got downtime. They're always asking me for shit. I get no peace until lights-out." He was looking at his shoes the whole time. "I gotta give you some credit, Sunny. In the old jail, all I did was yell and curse at people all day. Then, I would go home and sit on the couch, drink beer and not talk to anyone. Last week, I talked to my wife, if you can believe it. I had a goddamn conversation with my wife." I kept nodding, feeling smug.

"And you know what, Sunny, deputies don't live into their retirement. I just found this out during salary negotiations. The union rep told me we all keel over from a heart attack before we ever get to sixty-five. I bet that's one reason our retirement fund is so goddamn rich." He now fixed me with a rueful smile. "I can't believe I'm saying this, but it's true. If this keeps up, I'm going to live longer working here. I'm switching back to the day shift."

After a year, County Jail 7 began to work as I wanted it to. We developed training for the staff, both sworn and civilian, so that they could run programs more effectively. We had outside consultants come in to evaluate our programs, look at their effectiveness and help us to improve. We had countless staff meetings where Marcum or

Becky or I talked about turning prisoners into taxpayers. A lot of this had knocked the deputy sheriffs and civilians out of their comfort zones. We were asking them to be role models for how to act in civilized society. Some had resisted, and we had transferred a bunch of them to new assignments, but the ones who stayed with us had, for the most part, embraced the new culture. We were investing in inmates' success rather than their failure. That was more or less our motto.

After a year, I could walk into a dorm and everyone was in a class, or doing work, or taking downtime. I rarely received grievances complaining about mandatory classes. Now the most frequent petition that inmates made was about classes they thought we should implement. Staff committees planned the music and TV schedule. During television period, from four P.M. to six P.M., we might play a *National Geographic* special, or *Oprah,* or reruns of *The Cosby Show.* The radio might be playing a Beethoven symphony. One prisoner, listening to a string quartet, yelled out, "Hey, what's with the shoplifting music!?"

It wasn't paradise. Men still fought one another over absolutely nothing. On a monthly basis, we would still confiscate shanks, and drugs, and pruno. But the jail was better than it had been before.

To take an antisocial institution and try to make it human was a never-ending war. The battles I won, I won because I had Marcum and Becky fighting with me. They were nervous about some of my schemes and I couldn't blame them. Marcum especially would catch heat if something blew up. But they both said yes even when they were scared, and no if they honestly believed it was a bad idea.

Leroy Clinton made all of our lives miserable while he was with us. He was a practicing Muslim, and many of the grievances he filed had to do with our alleged failure to respect his religious beliefs. During Ramadan, he demanded his food be served to him hot after sundown, which was well after our scheduled mealtime of 4:30 P.M. That request we tried to honor, but nothing we did was ever good enough. The food wasn't hot, he said, it was lukewarm. The time and space we allotted for his daily prayers weren't acceptable. He led hunger strikes in the dorm because we were bigots. He organized protests because we were forcing them to rotate work schedules. He would write griev-ance letters about the water temperature, about not getting his mail on time, about not having a jail uniform that fit his substantial girth. Over and over, he would yell that "this is a violation of Title Fifteen and you people should know better. We may be convicts but we have our rights, too." Then, under his breath, he'd whisper, "Redneck mother-fuckers."

Some days, I boiled at the mere mention of his name. But Mar-cum, Becky and I kept faith with our mission, to hand out effective punishment. In some correctional institutions, Leroy would have been dumped in solitary confinement and forgotten, until he had grown so angry he would have taken out his rage on the next person he could get his hands on. We took each of his grievances on its own merits, and denied or honored each one after as fair a review as we could muster. On occasion, this meant doing things for the prisoners that some law-and-order types might consider coddling. For the jail uniform issue, we sent a deputy out to a paint store to pick up an XXXL orange jumpsuit.

But after Becky sat him down in the staff break room, slowly, surely, the tenor of his protests changed. When I would go into Leroy's dorm, he didn't barrel up to me. He would approach me calmly, and hand me a page of suggestions about a class he thought should be offered. We eventually allowed Leroy to organize men in his dorm to do a presentation to at-risk boys and girls who were bused to the jail. Leroy came to me afterward, excitedly proclaiming, "Sunny, Sunny, we really got at those kids, man. I touched them. I really touched them. I ain't jiving you, my hand to God. I felt something in there I ain't never felt before."

The dorm deputies began reporting that Leroy was keeping more to himself and writing. He was also getting routine visits from Rev-erend Billy Ware, a soft-spoken minister from San Francisco's Third Baptist Church, who did rounds in the jails. Reverend Ware looked out for everyone, not just the Baptists, and would gently remind us of an upcoming holiday, be it Passover, Ramadan, or even Diwali, the Hindu festival of lights. Leroy sought him out and Reverend Ware became his mentor. Ware would stop by my office periodically and tell me in a whisper, as if it were a secret, "Sunny, he's trying, and he's struggling, but you really got to him, especially Lieutenant Benoit. She got to him. I think we'll see a different Leroy when he gets out."

After about a year, Leroy came to me. He was about to be shipped off to San Quentin. His trial date had come and gone and he'd been found guilty of selling cocaine, which was no surprise to him or anyone else. He received a three-year sentence. He'd already spent over a year with us awaiting trial, and with time off for good behavior, he had only another couple of months to go. He approached me when I was doing rounds and delivered a promise I had heard many times before from other prisoners on their way out the door.

"Sunny, God bless you. I'm gonna do better. I promise you that. I ain't coming back here. My hand to God, I ain't coming back."

As a legal intern, I'd heard this promise enough to be able to recite it in my sleep. Inevitably, I would encounter the man a month or a year later, after his arrest for another drug deal, or domestic violence incident. Many days in County Jail 7 I was filled with doubt, with worry and with rage over the jail and what wasn't getting done, the deputies who fought me at every turn, the inmates who lied and lied and lied. But something in Leroy felt real to me. I had to believe he could turn his life around. I had to believe that. There was no reason to do this work if I didn't. I shook Leroy's hand, wished him luck and walked off.

Change is difficult. How many of us have set out to get more exercise, watch less TV, or lose weight, and failed to do it? Men like Leroy have to go through changes so gut-wrenching it can be like tearing off limbs. They have to change who they hang out with, how they support themselves, where they live, and most of them have to kick a habit, too (90 percent are addicted to something). It takes pulling yourself apart piece by piece, and rebuilding yourself as a new person. But I knew it could be done. I knew it. If I ever found myself doubting it, all I had to do was look at my bar exam results, or at what happened with Leroy after he got out of San Quentin.

Ten months later, Marcum, Becky and I walked into the Third Baptist Church of San Francisco for Sunday morning services. Leroy had asked us to come. By all reports, he had kept on track at San Quentin, finished his sentence, and had been released on good behavior. Leroy Clinton was now here, apprenticing to be a preacher himself. None of us knew what had happened to his Muslim faith, but anything that kept him from dealing coke and boosting cars was something we could get behind.

We found room in a pew about two-thirds of the way from the back. There had to be about three hundred people in the church. It was pulsing with energy. Kids were running around, giggling. A gospel band was noodling around, waiting for the service to start. People came and filled in around us, pushing us to the middle of the row, and I grew anxious. Ever since I was a kid, Christian services had made me uncomfortable. It was the memories of the Pulaski brothers, taunting me in the playground about killing Jesus. I turned to Becky and said, "There is no way I'm going to kneel down."

"That's the Catholic church, Sun," she whispered. "Don't freak out. These are the Baptists. You can stand up whenever you want."

The choir started up, and the congregation joined in, full-throated. Everyone was clapping, the organist took a solo, and I tried to relax. We never got to move like this in temple. I could feel the surge of joy that moved through the people, and to me it was like a sudden rainstorm in the desert. Leroy was a test case for our jail. He had been one of the first inmates admitted into the program facility, and had probably come the most distance in the program, from angry rabble-rouser to advocate. He had natural skills that should serve him well. He was a born leader, not frightened of speaking out, and possessed a stubborn streak. If he failed, if he fell on his face, then, in some ways, our program was a failure. We were trying to institute a largely untested jail philosophy—create a humane atmosphere, give criminals some opportunities, make them responsible and accountable for their behavior, and some will turn around. But if a fighter like Leroy couldn't turn around, then I would have to rethink everything I was doing.

The preacher, Pastor Amos Brown, was giving a welcoming prayer. He had a bass drum of a voice, and was getting the congregation revved up. "We've got a new man here today," he roared. "He's seen the light. He's been to prison but today he is transformed. He's going to come up and preach to us this morning."

People said "Amen" all around us. Michael, Becky and I exchanged looks. What exactly were we going to get this morning? Marcum shrugged at me as if to say, Wait and see, Schwartzy, wait and see.

Leroy bounded to the podium, his unmistakable dreadlocks still framing his face. He looked dapper, having traded in his orange uniform for a coat and tie. He pulled out some note cards, placed them on the podium and took a moment to survey the crowd. His eyes flashed with the fire I remembered. Fire I always had a hard time reading. Was he angry, or glad? He cleared his throat and began. "I want to testify today, testify to my journey, how I got here. I want to testify today about my story. I was living in hell."

Leroy talked about how he had come up on the streets. How he and his friends had started stealing cars as a way to get by. "I wanted to get ahead, you know, and I didn't know any better, my dad was gone, my mom was high all the time. I thought I could take something for myself."

He said he had started selling coke, and had pimped a little even though he'd never been convicted for that. He said he knew how to be mean and tough in order to do his drug deals, to maintain his status, to be hard. He talked about how the cocaine he'd sold had destroyed lives. I looked around. The audience was paying attention. Leroy had the preacher's touch. The voice that I remembered so well, complaining and shouting and yelling, was now raised to witness, witness his sins.

The women fanning themselves were saying, "Amen, go on brother, we're with you." I was nodding with him, knowing a little about the sin of anger, the sin of violence and something about shame.

"But I have to say that I was *saved*." Leroy landed on this last word like a hammer on a nail. "I was saved. God came and saved me. And you know God is great, don't you?"

The congregation was picking up speed. More voices were raised in affirmation. "Yes, yes. Amen, brother."

"I need to tell you how I was saved." Leroy paused again, and he started in on the next part of the story. This part was about the police.

"You know the police have never been good to us." His voice was rising. He was catching fire now. "Some white folks really hate us. They hate us, they take our children and throw them in the backs of squad cars because they're black, throw them in prison because they're black."

"Yes, yes," the congregation yelled back.

"Now, I have always thought that the police are out to get us. They destroy us, they terrorize us in our communities."

At this point he had really gotten the crowd going. I was beginning to remember the Leroy of old, the pain in the ass, staging protests to piss off as many people as he could. My heart was pounding. I wanted to crawl under a pew.

"I got a new story to tell you." Leroy was working up to a climax. "I got something to say about the Sheriff's Department, and we got three members of the Sheriff's Department here with us today. We got three of the people that ran the jail where I was held sitting with us in the congregation."

Everyone turned in their seats and stared at us. Some seemed surprised; they hadn't seen us come in. And the heat from all that attention wasn't completely friendly. I represented, after all, a symbol of so much that had gone wrong in the black community. I looked at Michael, who had a hint of a smile on his face. He met my anxious gaze, and gave me a little nod. Why the hell was he so calm?

Leroy had taken the church with him on his journey, whipped them into a frenzy, and now he was going to shock them, as he was going to shock us.

"If it wasn't for the Sheriff's Department, and those three law enforcement members who are sitting among you today, I would be dead or on death row. My world has changed. I was saved. I was saved by the loving power of Jesus Christ, but he didn't come to me directly. He was working through the Sheriff's Department and was working through Becky Benoit, Sunny Schwartz and Michael Marcum. Because without them, without them, I would be dead. I wouldn't be with my children or my wife today if it wasn't for the Sheriff's Department. I wouldn't be standing here with you and working with the youth to help them get on the right path if it weren't for the Sheriff's Department. Those three people are my family. They worked with me when I was low, when I was down with Daniel in the lion's den. They never gave up on me when everyone else had left me for dead. They are here on a Sunday morning on their day off because God worked through them, my hand to God, he was there working in them. And I tell you, this is the law I am talking about. They are here and I love them and thank them from the bottom of my heart."

People were rocking and amening and clapping and staring back at us and smiling. The air was buzzing and my heart took flight. Here was a day to celebrate a man who had pulled himself up. I knew every day would be a test for him. The habits of criminality, once learned, are hard to break. But each day that he made it, he was living a good life.

CHAPTER 11

1992

There was a Jewish woman in County Jail 7, a Jewish woman besides myself, I mean. It wasn't too often that we got a member of the tribe in the slammer. I don't know why. The old corny Jewish joke doesn't really cut it. How come there are no Jews in jail? Because they eat lox. There were plenty of black folks and white folks who came through the jails, a big population of Latinos, even some Asians. But Jews, whatever the reason, were an anomaly, and I was curious about Tanya Horowitz.

I caught sight of her on rounds in Dorm F. She was a slight woman with dyed orange hair that looked like straw. Tanya's eyes, which were ringed by large dark circles, looked blank in the way writer Annie Dillard described cows, all stew back there. I watched her wander aimlessly through the dorm for half an hour. Then, Tanya's bunkmate said something under her breath, and in an instant, she found a different gear: rage. She lashed out, calling the woman a motherfucker and yelling, "Who do you think you are?" A shoving match started and the deputy and I rushed over to intervene. But Tanya's anger had no reserves. By the time we arrived, her energy was spent, and all I could see was stew again. She had disappeared again. Tanya looked like a lost child.

I approached her after the altercation, when she'd had a few minutes to herself. She seemed shell-shocked and fidgety, a sign her withdrawal hadn't fully set in yet. In a few more days, Tanya would probably be itching at coke bugs and climbing the walls, and might have to be sent to the infirmary to detox fully. I asked her how things were going.

"I got a baby in foster care, and I'm working to get her back," she told me. Her daughter, Trudy, was four years old. "Trudy needs me, you know, I'm her mother. But I failed a drug test so it's good I'm here." Tanya was gnawing at her thumb, which she'd chewed to a bloody stump. I didn't doubt her intentions, but I knew she had no sense of the obstacles she faced. She was addicted to heroin and crack, her dealer pimped her and beat her, and she had sold drugs herself.

Tanya had a college degree and had received her master's from the University of Southern California's creative writing department. That put her light years ahead of her fellow inmates, most of whom were reading at a fifth-grade level. But she kept complaining about the deputies, and all the rules in the program dorm, and how she was worried about people hustling her for her commissary credits. These were all warning signs. When you complain about the hustle too much, you're still in it. Both physically and mentally, Tanya seemed much worse off than many of the other women, and that meant she was in trouble, because the women's dorms were a disaster.

Other staff members or deputies would always fix me with a sad stare when they heard I was going to the women's dorms. "Spending time with the heathens, huh? Hope you survive." With the women, there was always something flaring up—an argument, a fight, a confrontation with the deputies. Someone was always complaining about how she missed her man even if he hit her, or how she couldn't get a job, or, most painfully, how she missed her kids. Small fights erupted constantly. Burnout among deputies assigned there was much higher than in the men's dorms. With the men, it was just quieter. They didn't ask for attention or melt down emotionally as much as the women did.

For the longest time, I couldn't explain why this was so. It seemed counterintuitive. Men were more violent, more advanced criminals on every level, and yet the women were far more difficult to manage, especially in the direct supervision dormitories of County Jail 7.

In many respects, the male and female populations were similar. Whatever their crimes were, 80 percent were addicts, and had been forced to go cold turkey by incarceration. In addition, many were survivors of abuse (sexual abuse was higher among the women, but the majority of both populations had suffered physical and/or sexual abuse as children). Women did have an added burden most men did not. Eighty-five percent of them were the sole providers for their children. But this did not explain why working in the women's dorms was so much harder than working in the men's.

I don't think it was because the women's needs were more profound, or because the men were better adjusted. The differences, I came to believe, had to do with gender, and specifically, how men and women dealt with their emotions. The men tended to bury their feelings. There was just no socially acceptable way for them to express the shame, humiliation and fear they felt about their situation. Men who did were sissies or punks. Working with the men was like working next to a boiler that was slowly building up pressure. It could be days or weeks or months before anything went wrong, but when it did, there was an explosion. Women had fewer emotional barriers. They blew off steam constantly; their emotions were on display all the time. Even with classes, the women's dorms were difficult places to be.

I caught up with Tanya a few weeks later and her eyes were clearer, there was a spark there. She told me she had started taking classes but she was bored and didn't like all the rules. "I just want to serve my time, you know, and get out. The more time I'm in here, the less time I get to spend trying to get Trudy back."

"Tanya, what's going to stop you from getting high once you're free?" I asked. "Nothing's stopped you yet."

"C'mon, Sunny, I'll figure it out. I can't get Trudy back if I'm using. I know that."

"You knew it before," I said. Tanya didn't reply. Her thumb went back to her mouth; she looked at her shoes. Tanya was in on a possession charge, which ran out after a few months. She made it for two months on the streets, then was processed back into our dorms, a typical retread, on a charge of possession with intent to distribute. When I saw her again, she was strung out, her hair now dyed green, and she desperately needed a bath.

"Cunning, baffling, powerful." That's a catchphrase in the recovery community for the struggles of addiction. It was on posters in our jail and since nine out of ten inmates had an addiction, it applied to almost everyone. In my first couple of years in charge of programs, fighting addiction was one of my top missions.

I started with the women mostly because they needed it more. We were going to start losing deputies if the women's dorms didn't calm down. But starting a program for women was not as simple as starting one for men. On the outside, there were plenty of successful addiction programs. These were "tough-love" programs that had been developed with men and their triggers in mind. The "therapeutic community" model was one of the more popular treatment programs. Depending on who ran it, it could be very confrontational, using a military mind-set almost like boot camp. Facilitators sought to break down the participants through ridicule and hostile confrontation. The theory was you had to destroy the old addictive personality in order to replace it with something healthier.

But there were few recovery programs that had been designed specifically for women. Nationwide, women's addiction had largely been ignored as a social issue until recently. This was due, in part, to the fact that women had only had a minor role in the criminal side of the country's drug problem until the 1980s, when get-tough-on-crime programs helped cause a spike in women's incarceration rates nationwide. Treatment programs lagged well behind men's programs. But thankfully, by the time Tanya came back for her second hitch with us in 1993, we had launched a program to address her needs.

We called it the SISTER Project, for Sisters in Sober Treatment Empowered by Recovery. The model was the therapeutic community, but the SISTER Project was designed by women for women. Where men tended to respond well to military discipline, women did not. The tough love in men's treatment programs too closely resembled the way women had been treated by abusive parents or partners. There were many similarities between the SISTER Project and Roads to Recovery, the men's program we set up six months later. Sure, the SISTER Project was a disciplined place to be, but there was less of an emphasis on hierarchy and more of an emphasis on sisterhood.

Tanya did not want to be moved into the SISTER dorm. "I just want to do my time," she insisted. "I don't like sitting in a group and talking about my problems." It was a universal reaction, true for men and women. I understood. Who likes sitting down in a group of total strangers and talking about her worst memories? But Tanya responded to our prodding, and early in her second hitch with us, was processed into the dorm.

For her first week there, she was a watcher, barely saying a word. She was assigned a big sister, a woman who had been in the program longer, but Tanya didn't talk much to her, either. The women participated in groups for large parts of the day under the guidance of a counselor. They sought to understand the individual triggers that led them to seek refuge in drugs, and build defense mechanisms against them. Time was set aside for journaling and individual meetings with counselors. A typical day was:

6 A.M. Breakfast

7 A.M. Acupuncture

8 A.M. Morning dorm meeting

8:30 A.M. Morning meeting for SISTER—positive announcements, awareness games, news and so on.

9 A.M. Women attended school (adult basic education or GED classes) and/or met individually with their counselors. They were also encouraged to take care of their needs and write letters to lawyers or their children.

11 A.M. Lunch

12–3 P.M. Recovery groups and relapse prevention, which looked at various issues, including triggers for addictive behavior and creating a safe environment for women to disclose their problems. Other issues covered during these times were parenting concerns, health education and dynamics in the dorm. Individuals were pulled out for more specialized groups such as survivors of sexual abuse, or family dynamics.

3 P.M. Quiet time on bunks. The women were encouraged to write in their journal (daily narratives were mandatory and the counselors reviewed them weekly).

5 P.M. Dinner

6 P.M. Cleanup

7–9 P.M. Therapeutic groups and special events

Tanya sat at the edge of her group all day long, barely in the circle, looking bored. She stared at the ceiling. I even saw her nodding off. Her group had some strong inmate leaders, three older women, who mothered the younger ones in the group. There were also four younger black women who had bonded over their love of their children and Michael Jordan. But Tanya kept to herself.

Michelle, Tanya's counselor, was a gruff New Yorker from Queens. She told me Tanya was in a critical stage. "She could go either way right now. She's still trying to decide whether to trust this. Just gotta hope and pray that she gives in."

After lunch one day, a new member of Tanya's circle spoke up. Shantell had only been in County Jail 7 for a week. She was a fair-skinned black woman with freckles framing a round face and looked to be in her twenties. Her features were almost childlike, but her voice sounded too old for her. She talked about being raped by her father when she was five years old. She was honest and angry and hurt and talked about how she blamed herself for her father's assault and had buried that guilt in heroin and relationships with vicious men who robbed her and pimped her and raped her. She was crying so hard her voice disappeared in wracking sobs. She had snot all over her face. A woman next to her took her hand.

At the beginning of her story, Tanya had been staring at the ceiling, fidgeting with the drawstring on her pants, a vacant look in her eyes. But as Shantell spoke, Tanya's fidgeting stopped, her eyes focused. When the woman finished, Tanya was leaning forward, her chin on her hands, tears streaming down her face.

If there was anything I'd learned by that point, it was that stories could bind broken people together, and help stitch up their wounds. Every time I listened to a disclosure, I felt hints of connection, a sense that the anger I had when I yelled at Becky because I was hurt or ashamed was something many people struggled with, criminals and citizens alike. Shantell that day kicked open a door for Tanya through her story. In the days that followed, Tanya edged her way into the circle. She started voicing some of the affirmations that every inmate in the recovery dorms was taught to use. "I want to use the group" or "I need all of your support" and the women in the group would respond in unison, "You got it." It can seem mechanical, the call and response. But it serves a purpose. These women had very little support on the outside and few communication skills. They needed the basics. So we taught them how to support people in group discussions. It's a first step in accepting a program, in agreeing to join the path to recovery. Tanya started on the journey with one step, saying, "I support you." She started to answer questions and engage in class sessions. Then, one Thursday afternoon, Tanya told her story.

The group started with the elders leading the way. A stocky Latino woman with a wide smile began. "We have a new sister joining us," she said, gesturing to a mousy woman who had just made it through orientation. "We welcome her here and support her with an open heart. Why don't we introduce ourselves."

The women went around the group saying their names. Tanya was staring at her hands. She was so quiet when her turn came that someone had to ask her to try again.

With the introductions finished, Michelle, our staff counselor, opened the floor. "This is the time to speak up, let people know what's on your mind, share the struggles you're going through." Michelle was all Mother Earth, her arms falling open as if she wanted to hug everyone there. Women leaped in with quick reflections. One asked the others to pray because her grandmother, who was taking care of her kids, was sick, and she didn't know what would happen if she didn't get better. Another woman shared a poem. Then Tanya spoke: "I want to use the group." Her voice was small.

"We're here for you," said the woman sitting next to Tanya. The others echoed her.

Tanya raised her eyes. She didn't look at anyone but she took a deep breath, held it, and then the dam broke. "I'm nine, I think. I don't remember anymore if I was nine or ten. It was just before Thanksgiving, I knew, because we had just come home from school with turkeys that you make out of hands. Where you trace the outline of your hand, and your thumb is the turkey's head." Some of the other women smiled.

"I'd done three of them. One for my mom, one for my little sister and one for my dad. I'd come home so proud, wanting to put them up on the refrigerator. It was also my birthday. Of course, it's easy to remember when it happened because of that. My birthday is just a few days before Thanksgiving. No one really wants to throw a party for you. They're so busy getting ready for the holidays, and you kind of get lost in all of that . . ." Tanya trailed off and looked around. There was a glimmer of fear in her eyes. I was worried she might stop, but she didn't.

"So I brought home these three turkey pictures as presents. I was thinking maybe if I gave presents then I would get great presents on my birthday. I don't know, I guess I was a big believer in karma or something." She smiled.

"I walk in from school and I'm all excited. I guess I knew my mom and dad fought a lot. But you know, I was nine. I didn't know what 'a lot' meant. I knew that I didn't like it when they fought. I'd find my mom crying. She'd have a black eye. When I asked her what happened she wouldn't answer me. She wouldn't lie about it; she just wouldn't look at me. The funny thing is I never saw him hit her. I don't remember ever seeing him hit her. I always hid in my room with my sister. You'd hear things banging. But I tried to put pillows over my head so I wouldn't hear it. Made it feel like it wasn't happening.

"When I walk in with these turkeys, sure enough, they're yelling at each other. He's yelling about my birthday cake, of all things. My dad is screaming, calling my mom lazy, and ugly—all sorts of stuff. He's saying how he'd just worked all day and she still hadn't picked up the cake. My mom looks horrible. She's just sitting in the kitchen with her purse in her lap, she's crying but not moving. Finally my dad calls her a lazy whore and slams the door to their room."

Tanya caught herself then, and a sob broke from her. The women around her murmured, "Go on, baby. You'll be all right." Tanya fought her emotions and finally regained her breath.

"It's like she was barely there. I started walking toward her but I stopped because I was afraid. I still had those goddamn turkeys in my hand. I just stood there like an idiot. Then my mom stood up and walked out. She didn't say anything to me. She didn't look at me. I ran to my room. That was the last time I saw her. She took off going to get my birthday cake."

Tanya was shaking. When she spoke again her voice came out clear and strong.

"I hate my birthday. I've hated it since that day. I thought that if I'd never had a birthday, that she wouldn't have left. I've replayed that scene again and again, imagining my saying something and getting her to stay. I kept telling myself if I just hadn't wanted presents and a party so much, then my parents wouldn't have fought and my mom would have stayed. I really was an idiot. I blamed myself that she left. I blamed myself for when my dad began hitting us. I blamed myself for when he started going to my sister's room at night. I blamed myself saying that if I'd just said something, anything, then maybe Mom wouldn't have left."

Tanya sobbed, finally giving way to anguish for a good long minute. A couple of other women in the group were crying, too. When Tanya continued, she told the group how she started drinking when she was eleven, sneaking liquor from her dad's cabinet. How she started shoplifting when she was thirteen. How the drinking turned to drugs, how recreational use turned to addiction. How she made it through college and wanted to be a screenwriter but finally the heroin took hold. She said her life was a slow, continual, downward slide.

"When I landed in the gutter, it was like I was supposed to be there. I didn't feel like something had gone horribly wrong, it was just the logical step from where I'd been the day before. I had friends in the gutter. It wasn't like I woke up and realized I shouldn't be there. It just seemed like where I belonged. And my boyfriend!" Now she sneers. "He's the father of my child, and he's the one that keeps me high!"

Other stories flooded out of Tanya, a jumbled collection of her life today. She talked about the shame she felt over going to jail and abandoning her daughter, Trudy, just as her mother had abandoned her. Tanya talked about the men who had abused her, the men she'd lied to and stolen from. "It scares me to death to say all of this out loud. I don't want to be here. I don't want to be telling this story. I've wanted for so long for it to just go away. For this story to be someone else's. But you know what. It's my life. It's my life. It's my life."

She finally ran out of words. As she finished, she sat up straighter, tension dissolved from her face. The woman in front of me said a quiet "Amen."

I thought about Tanya for the rest of the day. How many times had I heard a story like hers. These men and women we locked up, they are supposed to be the perpetrators, not the victims. And Tanya certainly was a perpetrator. I'd come to know her record well. She'd been involved in grand theft auto, home invasion and drug dealing. Her daughter had lived through her mother's three trips to jail. She'd been dropped off countless times with relatives, lived with a junkie mother who could barely take care of herself much less a child and been shuttled in and out of foster care. When I thought of what that child had been through I wanted to lock Tanya up and throw away the key. But Tanya had a story, too, a history of damage that fueled the damage she inflicted on her child. I despaired thinking about this long line of tragedy, like someone staring into a set of mirrors that faced each other, seeing her image reflected back on itself into infinity. How could you possibly stop it?

I felt lucky. My parents hadn't molested me, they'd worked hard and had provided a roof over my head, a home for me and my brothers. They fed me and loved me the way they knew how. But there were parts of Tanya's story that resonated with me. I could tell these women of my father's overwhelming temper, how I wished my mother could have stood up for me about my brothers' bullying, and the shame I felt being sent to the dumbest of the dummy classes, and how today, I couldn't stand it when lovers didn't agree with me. How I channeled my father when I fought with Becky. I could talk about how I had learned to focus my anger to a sharp point, and jab it until I felt I'd hurt her as much as she'd hurt me. I could talk to these women of the struggles I had and how I feel at home here.

Two years later, we gave Tanya a job. Karen, the point person in my office for women's issues, had an administrative position open. Tanya had been out and clean for eight months, and had just graduated from her postrelease halfway house. She had the most education—a master's degree in creative writing meant she was overqualified—and more basic skills than any other applicant. The only reason we wouldn't have hired her was because she was an ex-con.

I ran it by the sheriff to be sure he didn't have a problem. Hennessey gave me the go-ahead, saying it was a good example of us putting our money where our mouth was. I checked with Tanya's probation officer. The job would require Tanya to have some contact with prisoners, inmates with whom she might have done time. Probation departments don't like putting felons around other felons, believing it's like an alcoholic trying to work in a bar, but her probation officer thought this was a good opportunity and that Tanya wouldn't have any problems. We hired her.

Tanya was an extremely good writer, well organized, got all her tasks done on time. At first, she had attitude problems. She could be defiant, and questioned Karen's authority. Karen allowed her no wiggle room; she knew employers on the outside had to be pushed to hire ex-offenders. If an ex-con started questioning a boss's direction and their work assignments, they could quickly find themselves looking for another job. Still, Tanya's clashes with us were short-lived. She rarely questioned the same thing twice, and she learned from her mistakes. Within weeks, Karen and I were delegating critical work to her, asking her to write letters for grant requests and interdepartmental correspondence. She exceeded my expectations.

But not everyone was as happy as I was. I knew people would grumble. Some of the hard-line deputies still complained about Marcum being put in charge of a jail. For them, ex-cons couldn't be trusted, they shouldn't get a second chance, at least not in the jails. I knew this. But I was still shocked at how angry the responses were. Soon after we hired Tanya, I got a call from Undersheriff Frank Adams. Adams handled all labor issues in the department and I had always considered him an ally. He came from the private sector, not up from the ranks of the deputized staff, and he was a singularly smart and passionate civil servant. But I sometimes thought he was too slick for his own good. I'd first met him when I was a legal intern, and he liked to question my motives. "Hey Sunny, why do you advocate for this person so much?" he'd ask me. "Is she gay or something? Jewish maybe? She related somehow?" He never could believe I was working on general principle.

When he called me, he was coy about why. "Sunny, now why do you think I'm calling?" He barked at me over the line.

"Jesus, Frank, what is this, twenty questions?"

"The Deputy Sheriffs' Association is very upset with the Tanya Horowitz hire. You couldn't guess that?" Frank was the first to review complaints from the Deputy Sheriffs' Association, or DSA. It was a powerful union, and maintaining a working relationship with them was critical to keeping the jails running smoothly. I didn't like where this was going, so I played dumb.

"I'm not sure I get you, Frank. The DSA is angry that we hired an ex-offender to do secretarial work? Why?"

"Come on, Sunny, you know why."

"No, I don't. You're gonna have to explain it to me."

"Sunny, the deputies are offended that they have to eat in the same lunchroom with a former inmate they supervised a year ago. You need to think about who you hire and bring into this department. The DSA has their code of honor, too, ya know."

I tried to explain to Frank that our sole mission with programs was to get prisoners to enter the workforce as functional citizens. "The deputies ought to know this," I said.

"Cut the crap, Sunny. It's about respect. You're telling these deputies you think they're no better than the inmates they've got locked up when you send one of them into their lunchroom to eat with them. This shouldn't be a surprise to you."

I was furious. "Frank, tell me, would you and the deputies rather have me fire Tanya Horowitz so she can collect welfare and start acting like a real ex-con? You want me to hand her a few syringes with her pink slip so she can get a head start on the whole thing? What's wrong with you? Right now, people ought to be happy for Tanya. She came in and earned herself a job from the people who locked her up. That takes guts."

"Well, don't blame me," Frank yelled back at me. "The deputy sheriffs are mad, they might file a grievance, and I would have to respond to—"

I was shaking by this point, screaming into the phone like a howler monkey. "Fuck them," I yelled. "Let them file a grievance. I'd love to read it. Nothing would expose their twisted priorities more. I would love to personally represent the department on this one if you're so worried about it!"

At that point Frank pivoted, and tried to give me an inch. "Look, here's a compromise. Let's just limit Tanya Horowitz's clearance to the administrative offices instead of giving her full access." This would mean that in addition to not being allowed into the prisoner areas, which was no big deal, she also would have been forbidden access to the staff lunchroom. The offer was insulting. It would have hung a scarlet letter on Tanya.

"Forget it, Frank, you should know better. Separate is not equal. Is this coming from the sheriff?"

"No," Frank said, which was a relief. If Hennessey didn't have my back on this, I was the one in trouble. But knowing it was just Frank, I felt okay finishing it off. "Tell the deputies to go fuck themselves and I'll see them in court!"

I called the sheriff as soon as I got off the phone with Frank. Hennessey didn't skip a beat. "Hey Sunny, you did the right thing by hiring her," he told me. "And listen, if anyone else complains, you tell them this story." Hennessey went on to tell me a parable. It was an old Russian fable. "A farmer finds a genie in a bottle," he said. "The genie offers the farmer one wish. The farmer was a poor man barely able to get by. The farmer thinks for a minute and says, 'My neighbor has a cow, and I have none. Therefore what I want you to do is kill my neighbor's cow!'"

"You think that story will work?" I laughed.

"I don't know, Sunny. It should. Say hi to Tanya for me while you're at it." I loved the man. If he had been in the room with me I'd have given him a big wet one.

The deputies never did file a grievance. I guess they realized how ugly it would look on paper. But many found other ways to send their message. Many wouldn't talk to her, wouldn't even look at her. And it turned out it wasn't just deputies who were angry. Even some of the civilian staff treated her with thinly disguised disdain. The shop manager for their union, a lifer in the department named Harold, complained to me that hiring Tanya "cheapened all of their jobs."

"Look, people are complaining," Harold told me. "These are people with master's degrees. They're professionals. You're asking them to be on the same level as an addict who just got out." I tried telling him Hennessey's story about the cow. Harold didn't get it.

One day, I was out doing rounds at County Jail 2, which was in the Hall of Justice. We were introducing some classes over there, and I was going to meet with the staff. When I walked in, a colleague of mine approached me with a concerned look on her face and placed a flyer in my hands. It had Tanya's mug shot on it and typed underneath was this message:

> *Meet your new co-worker.*
> *Employee of the month.*
> *She will deliver good tricks and treats whenever you want!*
> *Make sure to welcome her!*

"Sunny," my colleague said, "this was faxed here today. I think you ought to know about it." It was a prank, a stupid prank pulled by a bully. Then I saw that it had been faxed from the Sheriff's Work Alternative Program office, which was across the street from the Hall of Justice. I walked right over there spitting fire to find out who sent it. Alternative Program had some of the more progressive postrelease programs and staff members in the Sheriff's Department. The deputies and civilians there all functioned a little like social workers, helping inmates make the difficult transition into the world after their release. It was supposedly a place of tolerant thinking. Marcum and I, who oversaw the site, made sure to bring in deputies who enjoyed working with the inmates, who didn't believe they were trash.

If I've learned anything about bullies, whether it was bullies in my family, bullies who were inmates in the jail, or bullies who were deputies, it's that the story was never just black and white. Few people were ever just the bad guy. When I walked into the Alternative Program office, the person who had made the flyer approached me immediately to apologize. I didn't have to issue threats or do an investigation. He looked up, saw me with the flyer in my hand and came right over. He was a deputy sheriff named Jamie Perez, a quiet, gentle guy who had worked with us at County Jail 7 in the past. I'd always thought of him as a deputy who cared, who tried to do the right thing by the inmates, was tough where he needed to be, but not malicious. We went to a private room.

"Why, Jamie? I don't get it."

"I don't know, Sunny." He looked deflated. "A bunch of us were sitting around talking about Tanya Horowitz being hired and some of the deputies were really mad. I thought I'd make up something to get them to lighten up and laugh about it."

"Jamie, I'm hurt by this. Do you know how awful something like this would be to Tanya if she saw it?"

"Has she seen it?" He looked pained.

"I'm not sure, Jamie. I haven't been back to the office yet, but I sure wouldn't show it to her. I got to tell you, Tanya Horowitz is having a hard time. How do you think she feels every day coming to work with this kind of crap going around? What did she ever do to you?" Jamie started crying.

He was shook up, saying over and over, "Sunny, I don't know why I did it. I am so sorry. This is not me. I loved working with you and Marcum and Benoit. I loved working at the program facility."

I believed him, too. Deputies usually didn't cry.

"What should I do?" he asked.

"What do you want to do?" He thought for a second, then said that he wanted to take the lead and apologize to Tanya himself.

Jamie told me he had faxed the flyer to a couple of the jails in the system. Some people had probably thrown it out. I heard it had been distributed in a few places. I tried to send out the message that I wanted it destroyed, but it probably made the rounds anyway. Part of me wanted to find a way to humiliate Jamie, the same way he had tried to humiliate Tanya. But I resisted the feeling, trying to treat Jamie the way I would have treated an inmate who was trying to make amends. I didn't want to excuse his behavior, but I also wanted to try to give him a chance to make it right. I told him I'd push for a write-up in his file and he said that was fair. He told me that he would apologize to Tanya, and that he would also raise the issue with the other deputies who had egged him on to make the flyer. He accomplished the second part long before he accomplished the first. His supervisor reported to me that week that they'd had a meeting about the flyer and that Jamie had made good on his promise. His apology to Tanya took longer. He never sought her out. But he did run across her a few months later and apologized.

Tanya never saw the flyer and when we talked about it, she said she didn't want to. She told me that the day-to-day cold shoulders from the people in our office were worse than a prank from someone she didn't know.

"I feel like a marked woman some days. Like I'll never be able to live down my past no matter what I do. People won't talk to me, you know. It's like I'm back in the eighth grade and the cool kids have decided to freeze me out."

It was hard to miss the toll this was taking on her. On days when it was bad, her shoulders would slump, she would walk the halls staring at her shoes, avoiding eye contact with anyone. I would ask her to go to the lunchroom, but she'd make any excuse not to go with me. I asked her what she wanted to do and she smiled.

"Sunny, this is part of my recovery right now. I need to learn to not feel ashamed no matter what other people say or do. There are a lot of good people here. They helped pull me out of the gutter. There are assholes everywhere."

In that moment, I knew Tanya was going to make it. I just had a feeling. Two years later, after being clean and sober since her release, Tanya won back custody of her daughter, Trudy. The girl grew up to attend the University of California at Santa Barbara.

CHAPTER 12

1994

I had closed the door to my office and for a day and a half had looked through custody cards. We had one for every prisoner in County Jail 7. Each card had a photo, contact information and a list of priors. I was also going through intake interviews. In them the prisoners were asked about past crimes and past violence and often revealed incidents that weren't on their rap sheets. I was going through everything because I was stubborn. Our violence numbers had been dropping at the jail. When County Jail 7 had opened, our numbers had been about even with the other jails in the system. In those early days, we had about five violent incidents per week. After our programs got rolling, the numbers had dropped to about three violent incidents per week. I'd touted the numbers to the sheriff to show that we were on to something. But I kept hearing excuses undermining our results. People thought we were getting the easy criminals, the small-time guys who wanted to go to class and weren't violent to begin with.

"These results aren't a fair comparison," one watch commander said to me. "We have to deal with the thugs who won't go to school."

"Bullshit," I shot back. I knew we didn't select our prisoners. We did take the people who wanted programs, but about half our prisoners came to us randomly. People didn't want to admit that the programs were working. I wanted to prove them wrong.

I went through almost five hundred custody cards and intake interviews in two days. I reviewed the information we had on the current prisoners as well as any who had been released in the last six months. Marcum came in and laughed at me on the second afternoon.

"Is this really a good use of your time, Sunshine?"

I scowled. "Look." I showed him the chart I was keeping. "We're completely right. We have the same number of bad guys as the rest of the system. We've got the same number of robberies, assaults, assaults with a deadly weapon. The same number of addicts. It's all the same. It's not that we're getting the choirboys, the jail is making the difference."

Marcum looked at my pages of scribbled numbers, then back at me. "Can you stop now?"

"I dunno, Marcum, there are some things I'm seeing in here." I showed him a second page. "I started to keep a list of violent crimes. How many people are in here on a violent arrest or have a violent incident in their past."

"Okay."

"They're all men."

"Okay." He wasn't impressed. I wasn't saying anything surprising. Conventional wisdom said men perpetrated the vast majority of violent crimes.

"No, I mean, they're *all* men. Sure, occasionally you've got a woman in here who got into a fight in a bar. Or someone who was beating her children, but it's this tiny number. These women . . ." I held up a stack of custody cards for the female inmates. "It's all dealing, or prostitution, a few robberies. I've been going through this stuff and something like eighty percent of the men have some violent crime in their past—a fight, an assault, something. Who do you think they're beating up? Women mostly, their wives, people like Tanya, or their kids, who then grow up to do drugs or join gangs or—"

"Sunny," Marcum interrupted me. "This isn't exactly a headline."

"I know, Marcum. I'm just depressed, I guess. I feel like we've got this war going on. All these men are at war. They're angry and ashamed, and is getting them off drugs, or teaching them how to read really going to do anything?"

"What are you talking about, Sun?"

"How are they going to stop being violent?"

We both sat there. Neither of us had an answer.

* * *

Stevie was talking to me. Where were we? New Mexico? Somewhere in Oklahoma? All I could see out the car window was big, open, starry sky, headlight glow and blackness.

"Let's say a bear is caught in a trap, and you came across it in the forest," Stevie was saying. "This is a big, mean, angry bear. It's been there long enough to go crazy with pain. What would you do?"

"Stevie, I don't know. Listen, where are we?"

Stevie didn't answer me. It was like he was a mile away in the driver's seat. I got the impression he didn't even hear me. He repeated his question.

"If a bear is caught in a trap. And you're the only one that can free it. What would you do?"

He could be so frustrating! I needed to know where we were. It suddenly seemed incredibly important. I could see the car leaping forward into the darkness and I was afraid that the road might end in an instant, that we might pitch off a cliff, that a brick wall might materialize in front of us. The dark became more and more impenetrable until it seemed like the world disappeared.

"C'mon, Chubs, answer the question. A bear, a trap, it's up to you."

I hated it when he called me Chubs. I was annoyed that he wasn't listening to me, he wasn't worried about the road, he just wanted to know about the bear. Free the bear and risk having it turn on me, or leave it there in agony and walk away. I felt trapped.

"Damn it, Stevie, I don't know, I don't know."

"Answer it, Sun, just answer the question."

"Free the bear, I guess. I'd free the bear."

"Why?"

I racked my brain. I wanted to say something smart but I just felt dumb. Finally, I came up with something.

"Because I'd feel too guilty if I walked away."

Stevie nodded slowly. "But he might eat you if you free him. Big, mean bear, you know, how long has he been in the trap? He's hungry."

"I know, Stevie, I know. I would just feel too guilty." Stevie didn't say anything for a few seconds. Then he grinned at me.

"Good. That's a good answer." I flushed, suddenly happy. Stevie reached over to turn on the radio. For a split second the world melted. I heard a morning report. There was traffic on the Bay Bridge. A pileup near Berkeley. I pried open my eyes. My arm spastically sought the alarm clock.

Stevie. He snuck up on me sometimes. I sat up in bed. Becky was already gone, off to do a check on the morning shift. I reached over and opened the journal I kept next to my bed. I'd been writing my dreams down on orders from my therapist. Stevie didn't show up much. I felt a pang as I scribbled down the details. I remembered we'd had a conversation about a bear caught in a trap somewhere on the road between Chicago and Tucson twenty-five years ago.

It had been seven years since Stevie killed himself, and seven years since my brain sprang a leak. After Stevie's death, my family had broken—my parents clinging to each other while Jerry disappeared into his Orthodox Jewish community in Brooklyn, and I constantly disappointed them all by not doing "what I was born to do," get married and have a family. In the intervening years, my mom had been stricken with uterine cancer. She had fought it and beaten it twice, but she was a shadow of herself and so was my father, who was devastated by his wife's pain. I had tried to forge my own path, and seven years ago, changed my life. I'd walked away from being an attorney and gone back to the jails hoping to move mountains.

Five years I'd been at it, toiling away in my small corner, fighting and fighting and fighting, trying to get the money for my programs, trying to give the prisoners a chance to become better people. I'd fielded the question hundreds, maybe thousands of times: "Why do you want to help *those* people?" And my answer was always the same. I didn't want to help *those* people, or at least, not just those people. I wanted our community to be safer, I wanted to banish fear and violence, and the only way to do that, it seemed to me, was to work with the people causing the fear and violence, to try to get them to do something different.

I was proud of the changes Marcum, Becky and I had been able to make in San Francisco's jails. We had adult education and high school proficiency classes available for 362 inmates daily. We had addiction programs both in the jails and out in the communities for inmates after their release. Deputy sheriffs came up to me regularly to say that working in County Jail 7 was easier on their psyches, that they were learning something and felt better when they went home at night.

There were inmates like Leroy and Tanya who'd walked away from their demons, walked away from crime and now lived like everybody else, making a paycheck, paying taxes and contributing. But I was bone tired and frustrated. The two days I'd spent reviewing our prisoners' records had depressed me. We were making the jails better for us, and nominally better for the inmates, but increasingly I was beginning to feel like I was missing something, like there was something out in the darkness, like the cliff was coming and I was a big angry bear stuck in the passenger seat needing to escape.

There was a joke we made in the dark moments in the staff room. It happened when we were talking about a prisoner who was doing well in his classes but still fighting in the dorms, and basically a bully. "Look," someone would say, full of sarcasm, "we taught him to read. Let's put up a sign to tell him to stop beating his wife." The joke had always grated on me, but it had begun to feel like an admission of failure. Our jails were full of violent men and none of our programs confronted their violence head-on. O.J. Simpson and the murders of Nicole Simpson and Ron Goldman had just hit the news and it felt like a message. Regardless of his guilt or innocence, it was indisputable that Simpson had beaten his wife and that it had been an ongoing problem. I'd seen the pattern again and again in our inmates. I'd met thousands of these men, and no addiction prevention class or English class in any jail or prison I'd ever seen addressed the issue of a man's violence.

I was frustrated. I was frustrated at work, and also frustrated at home. Becky and I argued nonstop, and it felt connected. The violence I despaired over in the prisoners resonated with me. I wasn't physically violent, but I was an emotional bully just like my dad. When Becky didn't agree with me I could be brutal, screaming and yelling, stomping out of rooms, going completely out of control. I wasn't the same as the men I worked with, but I knew it was still a form of abuse. Becky was a fighter as well, which made for a toxic mix. She would accuse me of being a flirt, I'd accuse her of not being emotionally present. We could build these sparks into giant infernos. The programs at County Jail 7 were the only things that we didn't fight about.

The dream about Stevie distracted me. That morning, I was supposed to be packing a bag and going to Minneapolis for a conference for prison education providers. To tell the truth, I was relieved to be skipping town for a few days.

The cabbie started honking at me. When I finally got outside he glared at me and said, "I'm just about to leave. You keep me waiting so long."

I snarled back, "You want this fucking fare or not, tough guy, 'cause I can call someone else." I slammed the trunk of the car. I knew why I was having the dream. I knew why Stevie was there asking me what I would do about an angry bear. I was the bear.

The conference was one of those burned coffee, plastic pastry, bureaucratic circle jerks where you talk about what you're doing well, you complain about things that never seemed to change, you see some friends you made at the last conference, and you bill it all to the county. My mother, Frieda, would've said, "Well, they meant well," and then fallen silent.

The prison-services community was a ragtag mix of aging hippies who were still fighting the Man, clock-punchers who'd decided that the prison-industrial complex was a dependable paycheck, along with true believers, brilliant fighters and incompetent airheads. This time around, the main thing people were talking about was getting out of the conference and going over to the Mall of America. In the industry exhibits, I sidled up to a table hawking books for convicts. They looked like Dick and Jane stories and I was thinking, what self-respecting convict was going to sit and read this without getting his ass kicked? I began scheming ways to get home.

At lunch on the second day, I sat down with Shannon, a vibrant, bighearted woman who ran programs in the Contra Costa County jails just northeast of San Francisco. We compared notes sometimes. She didn't have many allies in her county. She had to fight for every last scrap and didn't have as extensive a set of programs as we did in San Francisco. But she paid attention to what was new. She asked me what workshop I had attended that morning. Between mouthfuls of rubbery chicken, I told her the guy leading the group on mandatory drug testing seemed like he had dropped two Valiums.

"I know it might sound crazy," Shannon replied, "but I really found my morning session invigorating. You should look at this stuff." Shannon handed over a packet of information. I'd never seen her so excited. I was used to her usual "this is a bunch a of bullshit" response.

"It's about this thing called 'restorative justice,'" Shannon said. "I'd never heard about it. You should read it."

The packet was titled *Understanding Restorative Justice.* The name alone piqued my interest. Nothing I'd seen in the criminal justice system had ever been in the business of "restoring" anything. I'd seen crimes committed, I'd seen people punished, lives and families ruined, but never restoration. The author of the packet (and the person who had given the presentation) was a woman named Kay Pranis. I would later learn that she was considered the mother of restorative justice and had been working to spread its principles for years. I flipped open the packet and read. "Restorative Justice recognizes that crimes hurt everyone: victim, offender and the community and it creates an obligation to make things right. The 3 principles of restorative justice are offender accountability, victim restoration and community involvement to heal the harm caused by crime."

Restorative justice didn't have many real-world examples in the United States. Some jurisdictions were supporting mediation sessions between victims and perpetrators. I'd heard about this. Studies showed that victims wanted to hear their perpetrators express authentic remorse, and just as important, wanted to let that person know how much they'd hurt them. But these kinds of confrontations were delicate and not for everyone and not solely what restorative justice was about. The goal of restorative justice was to heal the victims, for perpetrators to take responsibility for their actions and make meaningful restitution and for governments and communities to be part of the process. There were many ways these principles could be put into practice and they spoke to me on such a visceral level that I packed my bags and immediately went to the airport. I called Marcum to tell him I was coming home early. I had a new program to sell.

Most people, I think, believe that prison or jail should be a horrible experience. People don't think of it as a deterrent so much as just deserts. "They" hurt "us," therefore "we" should hurt "them." For years, politicians have won elections by promising to take away cable television and weight rooms and anything seen to make prison cushy. We have a culture where jokes about prison rape are made out in the open. The prevailing wisdom is that prisoners deserve to be treated like animals; they should fear prison and suffer while they are there. Anyone who has spent time working with prisoners knows this has largely come to pass. What most people don't realize is the consequences of making prisons a living nightmare. Most of the inmates I'd worked with, particularly when I was a law intern, felt punished, but not many of them took responsibility for their crimes, or felt any remorse. Martin Aguerro, the pedophile, the first client I had when I started in 1980, was a case in point. He complained about the squalid treatment and living conditions in jail, he felt wronged, but I never got the sense that he thought about his crimes. In fact, everything about the system of prosecution and defense is set up so that criminals get into a habit of *denying* their responsibility. Every step of the way between the arrest and the trial, people accused of crimes deny everything, or keep silent. It's what their defense attorneys tell them to do. After their trial, if they're convicted, many don't change their mind-set. Why should they? To truly confront what they've done requires confronting the shame and fear and the reality of their situation. Few people choose to do this, because it's difficult. After all, it's hard for noncriminals to take responsibility for doing the wrong thing, much less someone sitting in a prison cell. So criminals blame someone or something else—the cop who caught them, or their lousy upbringing—for their circumstances and spend their time growing angrier and angrier about being treated like an animal. They are usually full of rage when they are released, and less prepared to function as citizens; the predictable products of the monster factory.

But what if that paradigm could be shifted? Restorative justice puts a premium on getting prisoners to confront the harm they've caused, and underscores both their accountability and their potential. Was it possible to bring these principles into our jails? I started writing down ideas on the airplane.

I wanted a new program for the worst men we had locked up, the violent offenders who inflicted the most damage on our communities: the wife beaters, murderers and gangbangers. I modeled it after our SISTER Project. We would create a whole dorm of men brought together to stop their violence. I set the criteria as broadly as possible. I wanted to admit roughly 50 percent domestic violence offenders, and 50 percent random violence offenders, which mimicked the population breakdown in our jails. I didn't care if we got first-time offenders or offenders who had violence in their background, and I didn't care if they volunteered for the program or we told them they had to participate. I wanted to throw the net wide, and collect as many violent men as we could.

If I really started thinking about what I was proposing, I probably would have given up. No one wanted to begin a project with an advisory planning group made up of religious leaders, victims' rights groups, deputies, probation officers, business leaders, someone from the district attorney's office, the police department, housewives, victims of violence, perpetrators of violence, Republicans and Democrats. But that's exactly what I wanted to do. I wanted to bring the Hatfields and the McCoys together to work out their differences. But I knew that if these groups weren't on board at the beginning, then someone could object later on and sink the project.

I was in Marcum's office by the end of the day. He laughed when he saw me steam in. "I see our Sunny has really got something to tell me." I had a terrible poker face, Marcum had a good one, and he gave it to me as I told him my idea.

"Marcum, listen to me, this is it." I handed him the restorative justice handout. "This is the Kabbalah, this is the key to the criminal justice universe." I led him through the packet, the principles of restorative justice, and then to the idea, a dorm full of violent men working to stop their violence. Marcum's eyebrows shot up.

"Schwartz, Schwartz, ya got to slow down with this." I was trying to turn the pages of the packet for him. I wanted to start this yesterday. He voiced some objections, but he didn't say no. I had to hand it to the guy. Most people I knew in criminal justice would have laughed me out of the office. He brought Becky in to sound her out.

"Wow," she said when I finished. "We can do this." I knew she'd like it. It was one of the reasons we were still together. When it came to programs, we almost always saw eye to eye. Still, she was like Marcum, more pragmatic.

"Ya know, Sun," Becky said, "I think we should start with a small group of people, maybe fifteen or twenty." This was exactly what Marcum had said. "I think we should give it a chance to start. No one puts all violent offenders in a single dorm. You know that. That's a recipe for a riot."

I did know that. It was one of the cardinal rules of jail and prison management. No one put violent people together. You spread them across the general population, where you can isolate them and keep a lid on their violent tendencies. But I knew in my gut that we could do it differently. We've changed every other rule in this place, why not this one?

"Come on, Marcum, don't be a pencil dick." Marcum smirked but didn't lose his poker face. "We can't piecemeal this. We have to get the entire dorm invested in dramatic behavior change."

It went on like this, me questioning Marcum's manhood, Marcum offering cautious resistance, Becky laughing in the corner but agreeing with Marcum until finally I had worn them both down.

"Okay, okay, Sunny, I give up. Let's go after a full dorm, but first things first. We need Hennessey. An idea as nuts as this . . . and that's not to say this is a bad idea." Here he winked at me. "An idea like this needs friends. Hennessey is going to blow a gasket if we're not careful."

In order to green-light this, Hennessey was going to have to go way out on a limb. If something went wrong, there would be public outrage, which is never good for a politician who depends on the voters to keep his job.

A week later, Marcum, Hennessey, and I sat down with the sheriff at Liverpool Lil's, a classic San Francisco bar and restaurant. We sat outside, looking out over Presidio Park. A line of tall trees framed our vision, and they were gently swaying in the breeze. I was happy for the peaceful setting. I wound up to it slowly, asking Hennessey to keep an open mind (which he knew was code for "please be ready to take a really big risk"). I gave him the rundown of my experience in Minnesota, how the lightbulb came on, and I showed him the pamphlet. He looked at it for five full minutes before saying anything.

"So, Schwartz, what do you have in mind?"

"I want to start a violence prevention program, and work with violent offenders using the principles of restorative justice. I want to model it after the SISTER Project and the men's addiction program

Roads to Recovery. That means a full dorm of men committed to stopping their violence using a curriculum that we'll design."

Hennessey didn't flip out, God bless him. But he looked wary.

"Gee, Sunny, that's a little risky." He looked at Marcum and said what everyone else had said: "What about riots?"

"There won't be riots, Hennessey," I said, and crossed my fingers. "We will plan this to within an inch of its life. We won't be doing some ding-dong hippie stuff with these guys."

Hennessey asked his follow-up questions, and then fell quiet as he looked at the sky. I could tell that part of him wanted to just say no, and go back to the problems he already had. But I knew Hennessey. I knew that he wanted to shoot for the moon if he could. He wouldn't have let Marcum and me anywhere near a jail if he was just a cautious politician. He still believed in doing the right thing. After what felt like an eternity he finally responded.

"Show me a budget and a working plan when you've got it. I need to be involved in this from start to finish. Tell me again there aren't going to be riots."

"There aren't going to be riots," I replied. In the fifteen years that I'd spent in the criminal justice system, working with prisoners as an advocate, as a lawyer and as an administrator, I was never less sure of a promise I'd made, and had never been more dedicated to making it true. I could see a thin thread stretching from that restaurant overlooking the Presidio back through my life. It wove through each moment of anger and rage, through every fight I had with Becky, through Stevie's suicide, to the moment I was almost attacked in the Queens' Tank, to the first walk I took down Mainline, back through my relationships with my father and my mother and the monster Richard Speck. Violence and rage and fear had given my life its warp and woof. For the first time, it felt like I could reach out and grab that thread, and give it a tug.

That didn't mean I wasn't scared.

CHAPTER 13

1995

Marcum was pacing again. I was sure he was going to cut a groove into the rug around my desk.

"Are you sure we should invite them?" he asked. "I really don't want a war before we even begin."

"Faith, Marcum, you have to have some faith." We had the same conversation every few days. Our first planning meeting was coming up. Marcum told me I was throwing a lit match on a pile of fireworks. The issue was the guest list. I had invited everyone I could think of who had a stake in violence in our communities. This included ex-offenders: Leroy, who was still a preacher and working with at-risk youths, and a former gang member named Hussein who did similar work. Then there were Jean O'Hara and Kathy Lawrence, who were members of Survivors of Murder Victims, a group that fought for families of victims to have a bigger voice in the criminal justice process. Jean and Kathy were also mothers whose children had been murdered. I had also invited Latino activists, African-American groups, gay rights activists, deputy sheriffs, probation officers, a Baptist minister, an Orthodox rabbi and social workers who ran a battered women's shelter. I wanted everyone on the board.

"Just listen, Sunny, we have to have a plan," Marcum went on. "What if Leroy says something about how these prisoners just need a break? What if he goes on a tear about the racist prison system? How do you think the folks from the victims' rights organizations will react? If a former gangbanger says that all these 'poor kids' need is some love and a job, Jean O'Hara might walk out." I sighed. I knew these arguments. I knew I was playing with fire. But what was the alternative? I was wading into one of the most explosive political debates of the last twenty-five years. You had to take chances.

The rules change when you decide to work with violent offenders. I didn't have to be a rocket scientist to know that. I only had to look at the headlines. Back in 1993, twelve-year-old Polly Klaas was abducted from her home in Petaluma, California, and murdered by Richard Allen Davis, a repeat sexual offender who was out on parole. The case was a media event for weeks, blanketing papers across the country. A year later, in 1994, the Klaas case helped convince the California public to vote for Proposition 184, otherwise known as the "Three Strikes and You're Out" law. This law enforced strict sentencing guidelines by which offenders could receive a life sentence after a third felony (regardless of whether or not it was violent). The result was a jump in life sentences for people who had committed relatively minor crimes for their third strike, such as stealing a drill from Sears, or possessing .05 of a gram of heroin, or filling out a false DMV application. In the eighties and nineties, similar tough-on-crime laws had been enacted all across the country. There wasn't room for politicians to enact programs *for* violent offenders unless they were ready to be accused of being weak on crime.

We had been able to get the SISTER Project and Roads up and running in three months and five months, respectively, largely because they were touted as programs for addicts. But with violent offenders the stakes were higher. Sheriff Hennessey would be blamed if our program sparked a riot or if anyone got out and committed murder. In fact, politically speaking, the program was all risk. No headlines would trumpet how many crimes we might avert. But I knew in my heart we had to do it this way, and I believed that I could keep our planning committee meetings civil and successful.

I had the mothers on my side.

After getting the okay from Hennessey, I'd done my homework, searching out all restorative justice projects in the country. The concept itself was thousands of years old. Long before there were courts and laws, communities had come together to police social norms, and figure out ways to "restore" the harm done by people who had caused injury. But as laws developed, particularly in the West, crimes came to be seen as offenses against the "state" rather than the community. In the United States, restorative justice practices had only started to come into vogue in the 1970s. There weren't many places trying to use them. One of the best I'd found was in Genesee County, New York. Genesee County's Sheriff's Office had had a restorative justice program in place since 1981 under which they had pursued alternative forms of punishment besides prison. They had successfully diverted hundreds of criminals into community service, and had set up numerous mediation sessions between perpetrators and their victims.

As part of their program, Genesee County had sought advice from the community on what to do differently. One group of people they'd turned to was mothers whose children had been murdered. I was able to get my hands on a packet of the letters the mothers sent back. They came from many different kinds of women—rich and poor, black and white, college graduates and high school dropouts—but they all spoke in one clear, searing voice. Each mother was writing about the worst thing that had ever happened to her. Every letter was heartbreaking. "My son was murdered by his friend," one letter started:

> Because of that, we lost two young men to violence. My son is dead and buried and will never be here again, and his friend who killed him will forever be in prison and is dead to many. They were "goofing around" and it got out of control. What started out as a joke turned tragic and the madness will never stop until we come together to help bring peace and sanity to our community. I make a plea to the other parents: talk to your children. I make a plea to the police: intervene, set an example. I make a plea to the church: talk to your congregation. Please, we need each other and we need help. Don't let another son or daughter die by another bullet. Please, I do not want company with my tragedy. I beg of you to help.

Every single letter made a similar plea, not for vengeance but for people to come together and make it stop. I was convinced mothers would help me, help me avert a disaster. I was going to read a letter at the beginning of every meeting.

In January 1996, the night before the first meeting of the antiviolence coalition, Becky and I sat at our kitchen table. She was nervous, as Marcum was, that I was courting disaster with the kinds of people I had invited. But that night we just sat there. She wasn't going to fight me now. I smoked a cigarette and she drank a glass of whiskey for her nerves. "We have to do it, Sun. It's going to work" was about the only thing she said.

The antiviolence coalition met the next day at County Jail 7 in a large conference room. Marcum, Becky and I left our offices early to make sure everything was in place. We had coffee, pads of paper, pens and cold sweats.

"Sunny! How are you, my sister!" Leroy bellowed, his voice like a bullhorn. He was one of the first to arrive and he enveloped me in a bone-crushing hug. Soon about forty people were scattered around the room: Japanese and Latino reps from the recovery world, probation officers, cops, even a Chabad rabbi with a black hat and long beard. Deputy Drocco slunk in and gave me a nod. I'd been on him for a month to join the team.

"C'mon, Ricky, I need someone like you," I told him.

"No, babe, you know me, I'm not the meeting type." But that was precisely why I wanted him. Drocco was a natural leader who was respected by the other deputies, a hard-core law-and-order type with a volatile temper who had embraced the new programs of County Jail 7. He was like an old-fashioned coach, a Knute Rockne or Vince Lombardi kind of guy. I'd go down and watch him running a dorm. He had the place under complete control. If an inmate acted up, and it didn't happen often, he barked out, his voice gruff and direct, "Why are you being such a knucklehead? Let's get it together." As soon as the man had calmed down he'd bark out again, "There you go, babe, we all gotta live together." His dorm was calm, well run, and he left no wiggle room for complaining.

I was thrilled he was there. But I was also secretly terrified about how today would go, especially when I saw Jean O'Hara come in. She was a silver-haired grandmother from Pleasanton, California, who had experienced a horrible crime—her daughter and twenty-two-month-old grandson had been murdered by a stranger. She'd gone on to found Survivors of Murder Victims. Pleasanton was about an hour away, and she was one of the last to arrive. She walked in looking ner-

vous and took the last empty seat, which happened to be half occupied
by Leroy's bulk. Becky immediately leaned over and asked if we
should try to separate them. I shook my head.

"We have to let this play out how it will play out," I whispered back.
With that, I stood up and started the meeting.

"Some of us in this very room have lost loved ones to the most horrific violence," I said. "Some of us in this room have been perpetrators
of horrific violence and learned to take responsibility and teach others
to stop their violence. But the one thing we have in common is that we
all, I hope, want to bring safety back to our homes and our community. That's the goal I have but I know we won't be able to do anything
about it unless we stay humble, unless we open our hearts and agree
to listen. I want to start by asking all of us to listen. These are the
words of a mother."

I read one of the letters. I didn't comment on it, didn't try to put it
in context, just let her story sink in. When I finished, I asked everyone
for a moment of silence to remember those who have been struck
down by violence and to think about why we were there today. People
bowed their heads. Leroy and Jean sat quietly next to each other, lost
in their own thoughts. There was a sacred hush to the room, one I'd
felt sometimes in temple. I felt a deep yearning for connection, for
these disparate groups to find common cause and stop the suffering in
our communities. I hoped other people felt it, too.

I gave everyone a chance to introduce themselves, and say why he
or she had come. Leroy was full of love, and thanked everyone in the
Sheriff's Department for their help, but he went on too long. Drocco
made me laugh, and cringe a little. "I'm Deputy Richard Drocco, and
I'm here because Sunny told me to come. I've been working with
inmates for a long, long time. Listen, it's real simple, folks; these guys
need to be told what to do, and what they can't do. Some of them are
knuckleheads and are never going to change. Some of them I grew up
with, and they just need to get a job. These guys don't need to be cod-
dled, they need discipline. I gotta say I'm skeptical . . ." Drocco paused
and seemed to be working out what to say. "Let me just say that a lot
of these men don't want to change." He sat down. Jean O'Hara stood
up next. She looked frail but her voice had power.

"My name is Jean O'Hara. I started an organization called Survivors of Murder Victims. I'm here for my daughter Nancy, and my grandson, little two-year-old Jesse. They were both murdered. I think about them every day, and I've been working to try to honor their memories. They would want me to do this work. I am not sure if this is the place to be but I am willing to listen and see."

Later, during a break, I saw Jean and Leroy speaking softly by the coffee table. Drocco sidled up to me. "That little old lady. I could just cry."

"You okay being here, Ricky?"

"Yeah, Sunny. I wasn't sure, but seeing her . . . she's worth fighting for."

When I gathered folks back in their chairs, I saw Jean give Leroy a motherly pat on the shoulder.

This was the beginning of RSVP, the Resolve to Stop the Violence Project. Hennessey had come up with the name. He loved acronyms. For a while, I thought calling it RSVP sounded too frilly. What are we doing? Inviting the inmates to tea? But the civility implied by the name got to me and so that's what we decided to call it. The general outline of the program stayed the same from the beginning. RSVP would be started in a full dorm, with sixty-two inmates. A variety of group activities developed by the committee would keep the inmates occupied throughout the day.

We met every three weeks for over a year to plan the program. I began each session by reading a letter from a mother. These women kept us humble. Most people stuck with the process. Some did not. Kathy Lawrence, the woman who came with Jean O'Hara from the victims' rights world, never bought into what we were doing. She sat meeting after meeting with her arms crossed, her mouth set into a thin line. In the opening session, she was the first to speak when I asked for comments.

"I don't know if I like it here," Kathy volunteered. "My daughter was murdered and I don't think we should give these offenders anything. I think we should lock them up. Give them as much pain as they have given me. I don't think they can 'recover.' I think they will be lying murderers until the day they die."

I glanced quickly at Leroy, who was sitting behind her, worried he might confront her. But he stayed quiet, giving Kathy her space.

Despite her anger, I didn't see Kathy as the enemy. If anything, she was exactly the kind of person we were trying to serve. I didn't want to give any of the men in our program a free ride, either. But what I think was missing was the realization of what was actually going on in the jails. The men were suffering, sure, but they weren't learning remorse. Their suffering served no purpose except to guarantee the suffering of their next victim.

Most violent offenders got out after nine months, which was the average sentence for assault, the most common violent crime. I'd love to say that locking them up for longer stretches was a solution, but what difference would it make if, when we released them, they went out and committed more crimes? The "throw away the key" argument was never a realistic one anyway. The government couldn't afford it. State budgets across the country were strained by the population already behind bars. Start raising sentences for criminals across the boards and the budgets would collapse. I wanted their time inside to be hard time. I wanted it to be uncomfortable for them. I wanted them to suffer but not in the same way Kathy wanted them to suffer. I wanted them to suffer through remorse, and make changes in their behavior that allowed them to participate in a civilized society.

Kathy stuck with the committee until other obligations caused her to step away. Over the months and years it took to put together the RSVP curriculum, we kept a core team intact. Jean O'Hara took the lead on our victims' rights committee. Deputy sheriffs and probation officers headed up the security and safety component, coming up with the best ways to respond to fights and the dreaded possibility of a riot. Sometimes, I'd shake my head at all the things we were putting together. But the guiding principle was on softening these men rather than hardening them, getting them to feel rather than ignore the pain they'd caused. To do that, they would have to do activities easily derided as "touchy-feely" or San Francisco clichés. We were going to use theater, acupuncture, guided meditation, yoga, with the main activity being various kinds of peer education. I mean, Christ, when were we scheduling the wine and cheese?

But through it all, our diverse group of allies guided the process.

Cops, victims' rights groups and religious leaders, together with social workers, death penalty opponents and prisoner service workers, all realized that making these men truly confront their crimes would take extraordinary measures. Some of the programs looked a little goofy, but we didn't care. We had communities that had been abandoned to violence as their only legacy. We had communities where gang wars and domestic violence were a birthright. We had the men under our custody who were making these communities terrible places to live. We had a chance to change that. In the end, the coalition held together, and we prevailed in creating a program. Jean O'Hara's presence alone reminded us what was at stake. My own memories of Richard Speck and Fred Johnson, the pedophile, reminded me of what was at stake. We all made the choice to try to heal suffering rather than let it fester.

It's ironic, I suppose, that just as RSVP was about to launch, suffering would enter my life, and I too would be forced to make the choice to either try to heal it or let it grow.

I was in another meeting. RSVP was starting three weeks late. Becky was there, and Marcum, as well as a number of new staff people. It was a group with healthy disagreements. Few deputies had given up their fear that there might be riots. Becky, in particular, brought it up fairly regularly, posing the "what if" questions. What if we lost the dorm, what would we do?

In some ways it was an easy question. If we lost the dorm early on, Sheriff Hennessey could lose the next election for coddling violent criminals. I'd lose my job, and I just might lose my faith in humanity. I was certain we wouldn't lose the dorm but . . . what if? These thoughts were shooting me out of bed in the morning, full of anxiety, before the sun came up.

A deputy walked in while we were going over schedules.

"I'm sorry to interrupt, Sunny. There's a Doctor Schwartz on the phone. Says he's your brother and he needs to talk to you."

Marcum and Becky looked up. They both knew that Jerry didn't call me. We almost never spoke. Part of his embrace of Orthodox Judaism meant rejecting me. My lesbianism, my "choice" not to have a traditional family meant that I was just this side of untouchable.

My mind raced as I ran to the phone. I guess Jerry could hear the panic in my voice because the first thing he did was lie. "Everything is okay," he insisted, then quickly got to the news. "But Mom collapsed while she was in the bathroom. Dad couldn't pick her up, an ambulance came and took her to Skokie hospital."

That was all he said. I thanked him for calling and I hung up. I knew my mom was dying. I didn't move for a long time.

It was strange. Here I was in this intense work mode. I had allowed very little to intrude. I was the leader, pushing everyone, running interference at City Hall with the nervous bureaucrats who thought I was creating trouble for the sheriff. I was the one telling everyone it was going to be okay. This was going to be the culmination of my life's work. I didn't have a plan if it failed. I'd bet the house. My sense of self-worth was wrapped up in RSVP, with these violent men, and it was being rolled out in a few days. My mom and I had talked on the phone every once in a while. I talked with my father once in a blue moon, usually when my mother passed me to him. I'd gone home to help my mother the first two times the cancer had struck. Now it had returned, I was sure of it, at the moment that my life's work had reached its culmination. I had to make a choice.

I went back to the meeting, sat down with my colleagues, many of whom were now my friends. Becky reached out and touched me on the shoulder. Tears sprang to my eyes. "I'm sorry, everyone. I can't quite believe this is happening. But my mom is very sick, and I'm going to have to go to Chicago for . . . I don't know how long."

For months, we had all been steeped in the language of healing and reconciliation and restorative justice, so I couldn't have walked into a more supportive room. Marcum leaned over to give me a hug and whispered in my ear. "We've got it, Sunny, you've brought us this far. We can take it from here."

Becky followed me into the hall as I walked out. For all of our fighting, I knew she would step in front of a bullet for RSVP. We hugged and she told me not to worry. I had no fears about the staff's ability to push through the next couple of weeks. They were as dedicated as I was. But I was still afraid.

Would the men respond to the program we'd set up? At the core of everything we were doing were two very simple yet difficult concepts:

accountability and forgiveness. The men who were going to be in our program were almost all victims of trauma in their childhood, trauma that they'd never come to grips with. At the same time, they could barely name the kinds of horrors they'd perpetrated as adults. It was easier for them to feel nothing than to figure out how to own their feelings and take responsibility for what they'd done. We were going to try to teach them how to forgive themselves, and how to seek forgiveness in others. This was unmapped territory for these men, and as I packed up to go home, I realized that it was unmapped territory for me, too. I needed to forgive myself, and I needed to forgive my family and my mother, and I was glad to have every ounce of training I'd received.

I landed in Chicago and took a cab to my parents' house. My father met me at the door, looking pale. His voice kept breaking and trailing off like a weak radio signal. Stevie's suicide had almost destroyed him, and now, with his wife dying, he could barely function. I felt for him but was wary, still fearing his temper and neediness. I sat quietly with him at the kitchen table and thought of Mom. He cried and said cryptically, "Sunny, there are so many would've, should've, could'ves about you kids."

I didn't ask him what he meant. I was betting that he still wished I'd gotten married. I didn't have the stomach to go there with him now.

"Dad, you did the best you could," I told him. "I have a rich life; so do Jerry and Cindy."

I held my dad's hand. Fat tears were rolling down his cheeks, filling in his wrinkles and catching the light. I hadn't realized how old he had become.

My dad mentioned that it was Elul. Elul in the Jewish calendar is the month of repentance in preparation for the High Holidays. It builds through Rosh Hashanah, finally culminating in Yom Kippur, the day of atonement. *Elul* means "search," which felt appropriate, because we were supposed to search our hearts. Tears sprang to my eyes, too.

I didn't feel ready. I felt as if I'd been searching my whole life, trying to find the key so that I could really embrace these people, love my dad and mom and brother unconditionally, despite all our disagreements. I just didn't know if I could do it yet.

My dad had his shofar in the living room leaning against the wall.

A shofar is a hollowed-out ram's horn used in temple. His was about four feet long, made from a gazelle, twisted like a corkscrew. During the month of Elul, the shofar is blown in the temple every weekday after morning services. The sounding of the shofar is a wake-up call, rousing worshippers from their complacency and calling them to repent. When done properly, a shofar blast is a piercing sound, part foghorn and air raid siren. My dad, the jazz trumpet player, had brought a congregation to its feet with his blasts. I asked him to sound it for me. He smiled.

"Sure, Sunny, I would love to." He shuffled to get it. I closed my eyes and thought of him blowing his cornet in our Buick out in front of our house. My father's frustrations and disappointments seemed locked in place. Had I really changed so much? He put the shofar to his lips, tears still staining his checks, and blasted several short notes and a long melancholy one. I could feel his sorrow. He did the best he could. I believed that.

At the hospital, we found Jerry holding my mom's hand. He'd come straight from the airport. She looked up at me. "Hi, Dolly, what took you so long?"

As soon as she called me Dolly, I knew I was home.

My mom was extremely weak, rolling in and out of consciousness. Her cancer had returned and spread and she had days, maybe weeks, to live. Jerry, Cindy, who still lived in town, my dad and I took turns sitting with her. For days, Mom and I didn't talk about much. We just chatted. She'd always had a soft spot for a steamed Chicago Vienna Beef dog with everything and so I'd grab them for lunch. One day, while I was spreading out her dog and fries, she said, "Ya know, Sunny, you're the strong one. You know how to get things done." My heart jumped in my chest. I looked at her closely. I wanted to make sure she was really awake and lucid. She was smiling at me, her eyes shining.

Then she winked at me and said, "Jerry's a *kuni leml*." *Kuni leml* is Yiddish for fool. My mom used it affectionately. I laughed and my brother, who was sitting just outside the room, laughed as well.

At around six that day, I walked out with Jerry. He had to make a quick trip back to New York for a few days, and I walked him to the car. On the elevator, as the doors shut, I lost it. The accumulation of my mother's suffering finally wrenched my heart open and I started bawling. There was another woman on the elevator. "I'm so sorry," I told the woman. I felt compelled to explain myself. "My mom is so sick and . . ." Another wracking sob cut me short.

She looked at me kindly. "It's okay. I wish I could help. I lost my dad a few years ago." It was a generous response considering I was a train wreck. Jerry stood next to me, looking down, a little awkwardly. He and I had never been that affectionate but in his Orthodox community, physical contact with women, even sisters, was discouraged. The doors rolled open and we walked to the car. I was still crying but had regained some control. At the car, Jerry looked at his shoes. His body was tense, a steel trap. He started to stammer, "Listen, Sunny, I . . ." And then he embraced me.

Through tears he managed to say, "Ma is so special. She's a jewel. I love her so much." Then, after we had both weathered the storm, he let go. He wiped his eyes and I told him to "fly safe." Then I went upstairs to do the night shift.

In Frieda's lucid moments, we talked a little more. We talked about the work I was doing in San Francisco. We talked about the old neighborhood. I told her about going to Laverne Liberty's house to escape my brothers. I told her I wished they'd been better to me. My mother reached out and took my arm. She told me about an *Oprah* show she'd seen recently. She whispered, "Dolly, you have to listen, Oprah says 'we shouldn't hold on to bitterness, it will make us sick.'"

I grabbed my mom's hand. "You know, Ma, I know I've really disappointed you. Who I've chosen to love has disappointed you. I know that. I haven't disappointed me but . . . I just want you to know that I wasn't trying to hurt you—"

"No, Dolly," my mother interrupted, her voice little more than a whisper. Her eyes were shining, looking glassy, but her face was calm. She gave my hand a squeeze. "You didn't disappoint me. You had your wings. You had to fly."

Her words hung in the air. I wanted to dip them in amber and preserve them, hold them to my heart. But the sounds of the hospital intruded—the nurses talking out in the hall, a cart with squeaky wheels going by. My mother closed her eyes and fell asleep. For years,

I'd wanted more from my mom. I wanted her to drop her guard and embrace all of me. I wanted her to look me in the eyes and say, "Ya know, Sunny, you deserved better. I should have stood up for you. I should have insisted on you being treated better." But sitting there with her, I felt okay, maybe for the first time in my life. I smoothed the hair back from her head, and kissed her on the forehead.

Jerry had come back. It had been his night to stay with her and he'd called us at four-thirty in the morning to say it was time. When my dad and I walked in, my mom was gasping for air. I had pictured her going in her sleep, peacefully, but that gasping looked awful. We raised up her bed, which calmed her down a little. I climbed into bed and hugged her. While she struggled to breathe, I held her and told her I loved her.

Finally, she gasped and said, "I love you too, Dolly," and then there were no more breaths. Her body relaxed in my arms. A phrase kept running through my head. I don't know if someone said it or if I made it up. "Love is everything and we can't control anything."

I had finally learned how to forgive.

Shiva for my mom passed in a dream. I wore a conservative black dress, and a long-sleeved white blouse that I'd bought at Loehmann's, a costume as far as I was concerned. Jerry, my dad, Cindy and I sat on the floor. This was the Jewish way. We'd done it for Stevie, too. We were struck down by grief. The room was full of strangers to me—a group of black-suited men came from my parents' temple. Another group came from my brother's temple in Monsey, New York. They'd flown in for the day to pay their respects.

I wondered what my mother would think of all the Orthodox men who came to the house. I knew she'd be happy that Jerry took comfort from them, but she told me more than once, out of earshot from my brother and dad, that she didn't "go for all the extreme stuff." They weren't my mother's people. They wouldn't look at my sister or me. But I was filled with a spirit that was new to me, one that I attributed directly to RSVP even though I hadn't seen a single day of it yet. It was a feeling of acceptance. If these men wanted to sit Shiva for my mother, then they could sit Shiva for my mother. I said my prayers, missed my mother horribly, and, every once in a while allowed myself this thought: *There were no riots.*

The RSVP program started without me. I'd called daily to check in. It began with no fanfare, no major crisis. As I was boarding the plane to go home, I thought of Jean O'Hara, who was going to speak to the inmates in another week. She was leading a phase of the RSVP program called victim impact and she was going to be the first speaker in the dorm. If Jean could feel a shred of humanity for a convict after the loss she'd suffered, feel enough to come and speak to a roomful of them, then who was I to reject my brother and father? I needed to learn how to forgive them.

I arrived home to a San Francisco Shiva with Becky, Marcum and my friends. We sat together and I shared all the pain of losing my mom. A new week began and I vowed to keep my heart open, open to the possibility of change, open to joy and love, even in County Jail 7.

CHAPTER 14

1997

A few weeks after my mother's Shiva, I was sitting in another room of men wearing costumes. Instead of long black coats there were bright orange jumpsuits. Dreadlocks and greasy hair replaced ringlets. I was in the RSVP dorm where sixty violent men were finding their seats in a semicircle of plastic chairs at the front of the dorm.

Gang tattoos snaked up arms and peeked out of T-shirts at necks and forearms. The bigger thugs had ink invading their faces. Latino gangs, in particular, liked to proclaim their affiliations on their cheeks or foreheads. A fat gangbanger sitting a few seats away had *NORTE* written across his cheek. That was one of the more violent gangs in California, and I was hoping he was more poseur than hard-core. I looked at the staff members and the deputy sheriffs positioned around the room. The tension was palpable. We hadn't had riots, but if something were to go wrong, today would be the worst possible day for it.

Jean O'Hara was speaking to the men. She was no wilting flower. She'd given talks to kids at risk before, but this was a different crowd. These were sixty-two of the most violent prisoners in the San Francisco County jail system: gangbangers, wife beaters, pimps and murderers. Jean was giving the first victim impact statement, which we hoped would be an essential pillar of RSVP. It was one of the key additions we made to the curriculum that formed the core of the RSVP program, a curriculum called Manalive.

Manalive was the brainchild of a former community organizer named Hamish Sinclair. I'd first met Hamish in the early 1990s. He looked a little like Ernest Hemingway with an impressive white mane of hair, a booming voice and a thickly lined face. He developed the Manalive curriculum in the 1980s. Manalive was a group therapy program for men who beat their wives but we expanded it so that it applied to any violent offender. Manalive aimed at eradicating men's violent behavior through rigorous self-examination and peer education. I had found Manalive to be head and shoulders above all the other anger management classes at which I'd looked. These anger management classes focused, predictably, on "managing anger," giving men time-outs from their rage, teaching them how to avoid situations that triggered it. When Manalive was successful, men rewired their own emotional minefields, and figured out how to defuse their violent triggers.

The Manalive curriculum teaches that violent men are raised with a "male role belief system" that says they are superior to everyone around them. These male role beliefs say that feelings like shame and sadness show weakness and are to be avoided. Any time men experience these weak emotions, this is a loss of control for them, and their male role belief system insists that they reassert control by any means necessary. This could mean verbal violence or physical violence. Hamish's work in RSVP as well as victim impact has been validated by experts in the field, most notably psychiatrist James Gilligan.

Gilligan's basic theory, based on thirty years of experience working with criminals, echoes Hamish Sinclair's: shame causes violence. Men are taught that feelings of shame are not just uncomfortable, but intolerable, and any experience that produces shame or "loss of respect" must be met with a response. Ask any inmate, particularly any violent inmate, why they are in prison, or why they beat their wife, or why they got into a fight, and you are likely to get a version of this answer: "He/she/they disrespected me," which is then followed by any one of the following: "He got all up in my grill, you know, a man can only take so much." "I didn't want to beat her but what's a man supposed to do? She disrespected me." And finally, "There was no way I could let that pass. I ain't no punk."

RSVP tries to correct this kind of thinking. One of the ways we do this is by creating an environment that requires the men to confront the results of their violence through our victim impact class. Violent men have a diminished capacity to consider their victims' feelings. In fact, they resent and dismiss them. There are many reasons for this. First and foremost, their own childhoods were usually filled with pain and humiliation. This numbs them to feelings of any kind, their own or anyone else's. Then, during their trials, the offenders are kept away from the people they've hurt. This is commonsensical but it perpetuates the criminal's view that their victim is their enemy, whom they have to vanquish in court. In victim impact statements, we try to change that thinking, get the men to feel what they've done, to see that their victims are human beings just like them.

Jean O'Hara had volunteered to try to do it first.

I said a little prayer to myself that we weren't courting disaster by bringing her into this room so early in the program. RSVP had been running for just under a month. Half the men in the dorm had volunteered to enter RSVP. A few were no doubt excited to be in a program that promised to help them, but I wasn't under any illusions. I knew many had volunteered because they thought it might help knock time off their sentences, or make them look good in front of the judge or prosecutor. The Sheriff's Department intake officers had sent the other half to us against their will. Those men, especially, were not happy. Not only did they feel that they'd been sent to the "touchy-feely" jail but also they objected to being classified as violent offenders. On a daily basis, we had interventions with men who refused to participate because they insisted they should not be there. I'd sat in on one of these interventions the day before with Leon, one of our best facilitators. Leon had long hair, gentle eyes and a quiet, disarming voice. He was a former offender with a long record of drug possession, robbery and domestic violence. But he'd conquered his violence and had a razor-sharp instinct about holding other men's feet to the fire.

The inmate with the problem was Jimmy, a drug dealer who was in on a charge of possession with intent to distribute. He was covered in gang tattoos, his neck was like a cinder block, and he had a teardrop inked below his right eye, which can mean that the inmate had killed someone. His record contained no murder charge but it was full of assaults, assaults with a deadly weapon and armed robbery. Leon and I sat him down in an interview room.

"Okay, Jimmy," Leon said. "You've told me five times in group and you've told the deputy sheriff a number of times that you shouldn't be here. I got that right?"

"Man, I been telling you that all week. I got nabbed holding my buddy's coke. I didn't know he even had it. Now you got me with all these dudes talking about my feelings, and you want me to admit I'm violent? You must be crazy."

Leon opened the man's folder and handed over his rap sheet. Jimmy hesitated, scowling at Leon and me, then finally reached out and took the paper.

"That you?" Leon asked.

Jimmy looked down at the sheet for a few seconds. He looked confused. Then he turned sheepish. "Shit, man, is this all me?"

"Yeah," Leon said. "That's all you."

"Well, damn, I guess you got me."

Leon drove the point home. "Can I get an agreement from you that you are a violent man and that you do, in fact, belong here?"

Jimmy scowled again, but finally, through a clenched jaw, relented, "Yeah, I'll agree to that." Most men had never seen their own rap sheet, so Jimmy's reaction wasn't out of the ordinary. But not all men listened to reason as Jimmy had. A few days earlier, during the dorm meeting, I'd watched as half the men rolled their eyes, or sucked their teeth, or folded their arms across their chest, each act a subtle, but potent form of disrespect. It was an uphill climb for these men to get with the program. The system depended on peer support, meaning the inmates who'd been here the longest would help guide the new inmates. But no one had been here longer than three weeks, so no one was a true convert yet.

The men found their seats for Jean's talk, eyeing each other warily. A man scraped his chair up to the semicircle, slung himself into it and folded his arms across his chest, splaying his legs as wide as he could. His every gesture announced that he was annoyed. My jaw tightened. I could feel the defiance and anxiety among the men. We'd supplemented the regular deputy on duty at his post with five other deputy sheriffs. I'd asked Lieutenant Hunsucker and Deputy Drocco to be at the perimeter; both were feared and respected by the inmates. The instructions were clear. Nobody was going to put his head down or slouch in his chair during Jean's talk. No one was even going to clear his throat in a funny way.

I looked over at Becky one last time. The joy and fear of starting RSVP had pushed our own personal bullshit to the background for the time being. We were too scared and excited about RSVP to fight. She gave me a wink and I knew it was time to start.

Bianka, our victim restoration coordinator, gave the introduction. Jean was sitting back with some of the other staff members. She looked as if she had stumbled out of a Norman Rockwell painting. She had walked into the jail this morning with a classic lady's purse draped over her arm. Her hair was short and beauty-shop gray. She just looked too nice to hold the attention of these men.

Bianka wrapped up her remarks: "Jean has come here to talk to you. This is *her* talk. It is not a discussion or a conversation. You will have time to talk later. Right now, it is her time. So give her your full attention and listen." There was scattered applause. Jean stood up and slowly made her way to the center of the semicircle. She was holding a framed picture of a woman and child. She held up the picture as she spoke.

"I would like to introduce you to Nancy and Jesse, my daughter and grandson," Jean said quietly. She took the photo and handed it to the man in front of her. I got a peek at it as it went around. It was one of those drugstore portraits: a mom looking a little glazed grasping a giggly toddler. "Please pass it around the room," Jean asked. "I want everyone to get a look at it. That's a picture of my grandson and my daughter a few months before they were murdered."

The men were fidgety; there was sighing and rocking and shifting in seats. Jean ignored it.

"Early in the morning on January twentieth, nineteen eighty-seven," Jean began, "I woke up from a sound sleep. It was like someone was shaking me but no one was there. I had a terrible feeling. I felt maybe something was wrong with Jesse and my daughter. I felt maybe they needed me. Really, though, I didn't know what it was. I just sensed something was terribly wrong.

"Now, I wasn't someone who put much stock in random feelings. Maybe it was a bad dream I'd had but couldn't remember. Maybe it was an early morning chill. Who knows? I tried to shake it off as I went through the morning. But I couldn't get over the feeling so I finally decided to drop in on Nancy earlier than we'd planned."

The buzz in the room had been dropping as Jean's story began to unfurl. The men were now quieter than I'd ever heard anyone be in a jail. I was scared to breathe, afraid of interrupting. Jean's pain was right there on the surface—the look she had in her eyes, the way she stood, her voice. Most of all, you could see it in her walk. She was taking halting half steps around the circle, as if every fiber in her being resisted telling this story again. But with each short step forward, her story came out. She was mesmerizing.

"Nancy was living in Concord, California, with a man she was very excited about. His name was Paul, and he was good to her, and good to little Jesse, and she had invited her father and me over to meet him for the first time. It was a big deal for Nancy, and for us. Our daughter had never had much luck with men. But she was excited about Paul, and we were excited for her, and for Jesse. Jesse needed a father. He was almost two, and the sweetest little boy, just beginning to put sentences together.

"My husband, Jack, and I were supposed to see them for dinner, but I rushed over early. Jack was still at work, and I dropped by around noon, knocked and knocked, and I got no response. I'd tried calling and got no answer. I'd also tried calling Jesse's babysitter. She'd said that Nancy was supposed to come by that morning to drop off Jesse but she hadn't shown up. Meanwhile, the feeling I had that something was dreadfully wrong just kept growing."

Jean paused here, collecting her thoughts. Her eyes had fogged over. I could picture her standing on those porch steps, fearing what was waiting for her inside. She had stopped moving. Her lip quivered slightly. When she spoke again, she sounded far away. "I called my husband, Jack, at work. I told him to come home, something was terribly wrong with Nancy, I could feel it."

She took another break, and a deep breath, but she was finding her rhythm. Her voice picked up power as the memories tumbled from her.

"I needed to get into the house, I was sure of it. I called Jack at work, and he came home with the extra key and we went back to Nancy's. Jack had put his key in the lock and pushed the door open. We could see two people lying on the living room floor and it looked as though they were watching television, except that there was blood everywhere. A little TV was playing. Jack stepped over and touched Nancy's elbow and said to me, 'She's gone.'"

At that point, Jean turned her focus on the men sitting right in front of her. She stepped forward. Jean's move unnerved the men. They shifted uneasily. "Have any of you lost a loved one to murder?"

She raised her eyes and addressed the question to the whole group. "Has anyone lost a loved one to murder?" A sea of hands went up. Jean made eye contact with a few of the men, nodding at each one.

"Every one of you knows how I feel. I'm sure you do. There are few words to describe the shock and sorrow. I've found that sometimes words just aren't sufficient, you have to tell someone who has been through it themselves." Jean paused again and took a few more half steps back to the center of the circle. Some of my staff had raised their hands, too. My hands stayed in my lap but I was thinking of Stevie.

Jean had bound us together with her question, the criminals and deputies and the staff and the grandmother. We were all united in grief for those we had lost, all our grief now part of her grief.

"The body of my daughter's boyfriend, Paul, was laying next to my daughter. I'd never met him before and here he was dead on the floor in front of me. My husband kept his wits about him, told me to call nine-one-one. So I went straight to the phone and made the call, said get someone here quick, something horrible has happened. My husband, meanwhile, just stepped over both of them. I'm not sure how he got the courage. He ran to the back bedroom to see if he could find our grandson, twenty-two-month-old Jesse. And within probably a minute, he was back and said, 'He's gone, too.'"

Jean's voice remained quiet, but her eyes bore down on the men. "That was the beginning of a nightmare, one that did not end with the arrest of the man who had killed them, one that did not end with his trial. It's a nightmare that hasn't ended.

We would eventually find out that the killer was a man named Richard Goodfellow. He was homeless. He needed money desperately. Paul met him the afternoon before, playing pool, and Paul invited him back to the house to watch TV and have a couple of drinks. Nancy had gone to lay down after putting little Jesse to bed.

We think she was awakened by Jesse crying and heard shouts and fighting between Richard and Paul about a toolbox. We think this because that's what Richard later told the police."

I was struck that Jean called the man by his first name. It felt intimate. It fit with what I'd learned about her in the two years we'd spent on the planning committee. She was a woman of deep principles. She wasn't going to call him a "monster" or an "it." She was going to call him Richard.

"Richard was caught because after the crime, he showed up at his girlfriend's house covered in blood. She eventually turned him in. Richard told the police that Paul had no money and this made him completely lose his temper. I don't know whether he was on drugs or not, I'll never know that. It didn't come out at the trial. The only thing I can think of is that he just went totally crazy and killed Paul. Had Nancy stayed in that bedroom, I think he would have stolen Paul's toolbox, which was the only thing of worth in the apartment, and been on his way. But Jesse woke up. Nancy came out of the bedroom where she was sleeping, saw what was going on. Richard knew she could identify him, he was still in his frenzy, and so he took her. Obviously she must have put up a fight. She had been stabbed in every area of that house because her blood was found everywhere. Just horrible. So, um, and then of course with the baby, that never has made any sense to me . . . never, ever."

Jean faltered for the first time, tears started trickling down her cheeks, and I realized that silently and without any attempt to hide it, most of the men had started crying, too.

"Why Richard had to go and take baby Jesse. That never will make sense, that never will equate. I can't imagine anyone being that . . ." She stopped again and steadied herself. "He had to have had time between murdering Nancy and, we figure, trying to find her car keys, or whatever he was doing. He told the police during his confession that he went in and he slapped the kid a few times and told him to shut up. Jesse had been woken up from a nap and was crying and wouldn't shut up. Richard's answer to that problem was to take him out of his crib, take him through a doorway, where there was light, throw him down on the floor and proceed to stab him fifty-six times."

Some of the men were now shaking, holding their heads in their hands. I had tried to hold back, out of a twisted sense of professional decorum, but then I realized that the point was to feel.

Jean told the men about the trial and Richard Goodfellow's conviction. She said that she had been surprised that the conviction didn't bring her or her husband, Jack, any peace. "We felt that it would all be over with and then we could go back to our lives. And, once we went back to our lives, it would all go away. And it has not, and now we know that it never will.

"The only thing I could do is with everybody I talked to . . ." And here, one after the other, Jean took the hands of each man sitting in the front row. "'Did you hear about Nancy and Jesse?' 'Did you hear what happened to my daughter and my little grandson?' 'Did you hear what happened?'"

Jean was holding a man's hand, one from the group of men she'd approached before, but this time there was no barrier between them. Every man she'd reached out to had taken her hand willingly. Their defenses had come down. She stepped back to the center of the room.

"Gentlemen, Richard took more than three lives that night. Our one remaining daughter, Mary, went into complete denial, and when she comes to visit us, if we start to talk about Nancy, she stands up and leaves. 'I don't wanna hear it,' she says. My husband has never cried because of the loss of Nancy and Jesse. And because he's stuffed all of this pain and he's held it down and held it down and pushed it down— this year, he has had all kinds of surgeries, all kinds of health problems. My coming here and talking to you allows me to take another little piece of it and put it aside. And for that, I thank you.

"I believe that if just one of you men listens, and if one of you can have the courage to change, to give up your violence, then that means another family won't have to go through the pain that my family had to go through, and that we still go through every single day. Thank you, gentlemen, for hearing my story."

Jean O'Hara, the frail, white-haired grandma from Pleasanton, tamed the monsters of County Jail 7. After Jean left, the men were quiet and careful and respectful of one another. They were tender rather than callous and hard. They weren't putting on a show for their lawyers or the judge or the DA in that dorm. They weren't getting any breaks for participating. In that afternoon, they found the ability to share their feelings—their fears, their anger, their sadness and their sense of awe at Jean's courage and civility.

It was a start. I didn't think there would be riots.

CHAPTER 15

1998

Ben Matthews had a swastika inked into his skull. Until his hair grew, he was a walking provocation in the RSVP dorm. Ben was a wiry nineteen-year-old skinhead with a snarl etched onto his lips, not old enough yet to have a beard but he was trying. He was mandated into the RSVP dorm six months after we started. He sat at the edge of his group like a steel trap, waiting for someone to set him off. His eyes were narrow slits, and his foot bounced like a metronome. He'd been a hard-core meth and heroin addict, and he was struggling as both poisons left his system. Every time I saw him, I couldn't take my eyes off the tattoo on his head. It was like he was giving me a permanent "fuck you."

My staff and I had been watching him closely. Every afternoon we met to discuss the most troublesome inmates in the dorm and Ben often topped the list. He had beaten up someone he thought was a homosexual in the Haight, a typical skinhead hate crime. He did it while juiced on a cocktail of meth, heroin and Colt 45 malt liquor. He and a friend had been out looking for trouble. A twenty-five-year-old didn't like his tattoos, told him so, and Ben, in response, pushed him to the ground and had a "boot party" with his head while calling him a "fucking faggot." He kept assaulting him until the cops pulled him off.

Ben had screamed at Earl, RSVP's program manager, during his orientation. "I don't want to be here!" he hollered. "What the fuck is this! I'm not violent. This is war. I'm a soldier against the niggers and the homos. Just let me out of here so I can find my people." Ben made sure to repeat, in case Earl hadn't heard the first time, that he did not belong "in any dorm with niggers, kikes and homos."

Earl, a former wife beater himself, is a block of a man, the kind who looks as if he's recently been inflated, muscles straining at the skin, and largely expressionless except for his eyes. They spark and fire. He listened patiently to Ben's rant until he found an opening.

"Okay, Ben, you're not violent, huh?"

"Hell no!"

"Well, then, why don't you just sit in this dorm and listen and we'll check back with you in, let's say, three weeks and see what you think. If you still feel the same way, we'll see what we can do. Can I get an agreement from you about that?"

Ben squirmed a little. "Whatever, man, but I'm telling you, I just want to go back to a real jail to do straight time. Don't make me sit here with these fuckin' homos. I don't know what I'd do if they looked at me funny, you know."

"Hey, listen," Earl responded, his voice still calm. More than anything, it was important to stay calm with the men. "I need another agreement from you. While you're here, I need you to agree to stop being verbally violent and stop your name calling."

Ben clenched his teeth. Earl told me he thought his teeth might pop.

"Fine," Ben spit back. "That just means I'll never talk, which is fine 'cause I got nothing to say to a room full of niggers."

Earl didn't reply. He had his agreements. That was enough for now. In a normal jail, Ben would have been hooked up with the Aryan Brotherhood, the white supremacist prison gang, within a week. We had gang members in the RSVP population. But they, like everyone else, were too closely supervised to "clique up."

Three other groups of inmates were meeting around the dorm. In one, folded into a similar tough-guy stance like Ben's, was Elroy Franklin. Linebacker-sized, with a thick neck and a belly bursting over his waistband, thirty-one-year-old Elroy had been arrested and charged with assault with a deadly weapon. He'd been waiting in line for movie tickets when he attacked a man he thought was coming on to his girlfriend. The victim was Asian and Elroy had punctuated the beating with racial slurs, calling the man a "motherfucking chink." At his orientation, Elroy had announced to Earl that "I better not be put in a group with no crackers, 'cause I won't hesitate to teach a class on respect." Elroy had mashed his fist into his enormous hand. Earl had rolled his eyes.

Both Elroy and Ben exuded menace, snarling at anyone who came into their space. Elroy almost got into a fight on his second day when he informed a scraggly wife beater to "get out of my chair, honky, or I'll fuck you up." When Ben entered the dorm two weeks after Elroy made his appearance, Earl ruefully reported back to the staff that they were the "Ebony and Ivory of hate."

In six months, we'd had exactly *no* fights in the RSVP dorm. That was an enormous success, considering that everyone thought we'd have riots, and because in a normal dorm, there were, on average, three violent incidents every month. The "old-timers" in the RSVP dorm seemed to be buying into the program.

Manalive was forcing the inmates to look at their presumptions about violence, and the men, it turned out, liked this self-examination. They liked that their intelligence was being respected, liked that they finally had a way to describe their feelings of rage, anger, fear and shame. Manalive came with a specific vocabulary that most of the old-timers had embraced. Inmates were taught that in the male role belief system, they developed their own inner "hit man" who used violence to assert their control over chaotic situations and protect the men from feelings of shame and fear. Men gave their personal hit man names, like "cold-blooded killer," or "silent, impatient bully," or "raging, slick con man." They called the moment when they found themselves about to do violence "fatal peril." The theory was that fatal peril was when your male role belief system was challenged and you called upon your inner hit man to reassert control.

Some men resisted the terminology, and I admit it was esoteric and specialized, but most of the men had embraced it. They liked that they now had tools to assert some control over their violence, that there were options available to them when they felt threatened. They also liked becoming peer educators. In most jails and prisons, there is no way for men to gain respect except by becoming bigger thugs. In the

RSVP dorm, we turned that reality on its head. The more inmates gave up their violent ways, the more respect and authority they received as senior inmate advocates. All the facilitators of the program, in fact, were formerly violent men who had given up their violence. The fact that we had recognized that many of these men craved legitimate respect, socially acceptable respect, and were willing to embrace it was one of the revolutionary aspects of the program, and one of its most successful components.

Now that we'd been running for six months, no longer was every activity an experiment that had to be sold to a hostile crowd. The men knew the schedule and were actively participating. But Elroy and Ben, I believed, would test the progress we'd made. Sheriff Hennessey had been great, but if he faced banner headlines about a race riot in his program facility, our new program might disappear at the next budget meeting.

We had found that the typical initiation period for inmates was three weeks. It usually took them that long to let down their guard. Elroy started to soften somewhere around the two-and-a-half-week mark. In the late afternoon, I'd catch him laughing at the jokes of the older men. His eyes pooled once when another man in his group, a white man, talked about losing his mother to cancer when he was six years old. Elroy had wiped away the tears as soon as they came but this was how things began. Ben, however, couldn't seem to relent. At the end of his second week, he was still a hard, sharp tack.

"Ben has not said a single positive word, and more than that, he's destructive," Leon exclaimed in an afternoon meeting, throwing up his hands. "He can barely hold himself back from calling us all fairy homos for talking about our feelings all the time." Leon was normally a patient man. If he was frustrated, then I knew Ben was a problem.

"Has he actually called anyone that?" I asked.

"No, but he does say over and over that he just wants to go to a normal prison to do straight time," Leon said. "He doesn't want to talk about his feelings. I think he called it, let's see, something totally original. Yeah, I think he called it 'gay.'"

Earl snorted at the joke, then jumped in. "I'm with Leon on this one," Earl said. "Ben's physical presence by itself is a distraction. Those tattoos are awful and he's so wound up the guy is like kryptonite. He's like poison even without saying anything. I can see the other inmates react to him."

"Do you want to bounce him?" I asked. We'd only bounced four guys so far. Two were so addled on drugs they couldn't get with the program. Another went for a month without saying a single word and we ended up sending him to the psych tier. The fourth guy was a gang-banger who, I came to believe, was a true psychopath. He hadn't responded to any form of positive peer pressure, not from the inmates, and not from any of the staff. He stayed defiant, using violent language and threatening the weaker guys in his group on a regular basis. The only contribution he had made was when he talked in group about tor-turing a small dog in his neighborhood. He gave me the creeps. Let's be clear: RSVP wasn't a one-size-fits-all program. We couldn't accom-modate the most extreme monsters, the psychopaths and sociopaths, the serial killers and masochists. Our program required that the men still have some empathy left. Luckily, in my experience, that includes most offenders.

We'd probably cycled through three hundred inmates in that period, so losing four was a good track record. It'd gotten so that most men were either participating in group or staying quiet. If they started causing trouble, we confronted them, and if they couldn't get with the program by the end of week three then we would most likely bounce them. The men we bounced were sent to County Jail 3, where they sat in their cells like animals in a cage. Three of the four guys wrote me later begging to come back.

"I guess I'm not ready to bounce Ben even though I'd love to because it would be easier on my group," Leon said. "But he's not a lost cause yet, though I don't think we can live with the status quo much longer."

In the general population of County Jail 3 or in the prisons like Pel-ican Bay or Folsom, Ben would have been a success. A skinhead who hadn't caused trouble, who hadn't gotten into a fight was a win. Not here. It was not enough for men to sit quietly and stew in their anger or "manage" it. They had to join in, let down their defenses, listen and disclose, and begin to conquer their anger. That's what we expected of them.

At the end of the meeting, I suggested that we confront Ben in an interview room. I wanted a white senior advocate in with Damon, one of our African-American counselors. Senior advocates were inmates who had done enough time in the program to be able to lead discussions and be peer advisors for their fellow inmates. I thought a white inmate allied with a black staff member might shock Ben out of his stubborn stance.

It didn't go well. Damon reported that as soon as he sat down, Ben started to yell. "I am not talking in here with no nigger! Get this motherfucker away from me or I'm gonna lose it." Ben had kicked his chair over and had to be restrained by the deputy sheriff and then isolated. He had behaved like a feral animal backed into a corner.

Ben Matthews was talked about at every staff meeting well beyond his three-week probationary period. He was a riddle. There was a feeling of desperation in his episodes. I got the sense that he was growing exhausted with the effort of being defiant. I saw pain in his eyes, even when he was simmering in group. During breaks he would walk laps around the dorm, his lips moving as if he was talking to himself.

Then, Leon reported a breakthrough. "The dude smiled today, my friends. I saw his teeth. Didn't know he had 'em!"

There hadn't been any triggering event. Something in Ben just cracked. Day by day, his menacing eyes softened. His foot's steady drumbeat slowed and then stopped. I could see him begin to breathe and let down his guard as he realized he wasn't in a place where he had to watch his back every minute of the day. Here he was surrounded by tough-looking men, but they were all talking about their feelings. They were all revealing the ways they had hurt their loved ones and how bad they felt about it. They were supporting one another and challenging one another to talk about things that they were ashamed of. They were learning techniques of listening and communicating that flew in the face of every tough-guy credo he had ever learned. It's difficult to sit in that environment without being affected by it.

A day finally came when Leon reported that Ben had started talking. One minute he was silent, the next he was making agreements, using the language of the group.

"I couldn't believe what happened this morning," Leon reported. "We've got this new guy in the group, this supershort El Salvadoran kid, and he really doesn't know what's going on. He took Ben's pen, and when Ben asked for it back, the guy confronted him. 'Get your own fucking pen!' he told him. And I'm on my feet, and everyone is looking at Ben to see what he would do. And, honest to God, I could've pinched myself. Ben's hands went in front of him, palms up, just like we taught him." Leon was grinning. We taught the men to physically demonstrate the idea of "fatal peril." It was a mnemonic device. When they felt confronted, what we called a "challenge to their male-role belief system," and felt like they might turn to violence, they put their hands out in front of their faces, palms up. The action represented their choice. They could either turn their open hands into fists or put their hands down again. The action forced the men to think before they acted, to actually make the choice not to be violent.

"Ben put it all together," Leon said. "His hands went up and he tells this guy, 'Can I give you some feedback?'" This was the Manalive language, which Ben, unknown to anyone else, had memorized. Leon continued, "So this short kid looked a little stunned. He's only been in here for a day, and he doesn't know what the hell is happening, and he tells Ben, 'Sure.' And Ben, he still has his hands up, says, 'When I saw you take my pen, I was frustrated. I felt hurt. And the way you reacted made me afraid.' I could've hugged Ben right there, I felt so damn proud. Anyway, the new guy didn't know how to react, and Ben kinda lost the thread so I helped him finish. I told the new guy, 'I'd like to make an agreement with you that you respect other people's property and other people's wishes and treat them with respect.' The guy was too stunned to do anything but agree. Ben was breathing and nodding, and the men around him were all clapping him on the back and telling him 'good job.' Deep and amazing work with this kid, I tell you." Leon was laughing. "It's like the minute his hair covered that swastika some sense returned."

The next time I saw Ben, I barely recognized him. He was talking to everyone around him; a motormouth had replaced the silent angry watcher. He was relaxed, his hands rested on his knees. He reached out and touched another inmate on the shoulder, an easy intimacy that was never easy in the joint. He was engaged, eyes soft and smiling. He was a different person.

*　*　*

Leon called for a volunteer for a destruction cycle. The destruction cycle is a central activity in the Manalive curriculum that deconstructs one individual's violent act. It's intended to get men to slow down an act of violence, look at it frame by frame, to understand and, hopefully, conquer it. Often, he had someone in mind. But he was surprised when Ben, tentatively, raised his hand. Leon skeptically raised an eyebrow.

"I'm ready," Ben responded to the unexpressed question and moved his chair to the center of the circle. Two other men took their places at the blackboard behind him. On it they wrote down headings: "Verbal Violence," "Physical Violence," "Emotional Violence" and a few others. They stood at the ready with chalk in their hands.

Ben stared at the ground. The urgency he had had a few minutes earlier now deserted him. His eyes hollowed out as he sat there, his foot started bouncing. Finally, he broke his silence and his voice was like a rock rolling downhill, picking up speed as it went.

"Okay, it was a cold night. I was hanging out in the Haight with one of my boys. We were mixing speed and heroin and shooting up. I fixed myself, then I fixed my buddy."

As Ben talked, one of the men behind him started scribbling on the board, filling in categories. He wrote two entries under "Physical Violence." One was "took drugs," the other was "gave drugs to friend."

"We were bored, I was living on the streets. We decided to go trolling. I told my boy, 'Let's take down some fags.'"

The other man wrote an entry under "Verbal Violence."

"We were hanging out down on Haight Street and this guy was standing near me and noticed my tattoos. He saw the swastika I've got on my head and some of the other white-power ones I've got on my arm. I got into the whole white-power thing back when I was in juvie. I'm a small guy, and I was getting picked on by the Mexicans, they've got the Sureños gang, and they kept beating me up in jail. The only ones who would take me in were the skinheads. They were hooked into the AB [Aryan Brotherhood], and you guys know that meant protection." The men in the circle nodded their agreement. Ben wasn't unique. A minor crime had landed him in a juvenile delinquent facility, where he'd gotten hooked up with a gang, and his crimes had grown worse, eventually turning violent. Many men in the circle could tell similar stories.

"Anyway, that's how I got into it in the first place," Ben continued. "And I started to really believe in the idea of a race war, and feel like, you know, the races had to stick together, 'cause who else is going to protect me?"

There was more frantic writing on the board.

"Anyway, that's when I was living down near Los Angeles. When I got to San Francisco I was deep into it. And I'm out with my buddy and this guy, he starts talking shit to me. And I was practically programmed at that point. No one talks shit to me, and the worst kind of person was someone who was betraying their race. This guy harassing me was a traitor as far as I was concerned. Plus he looked like a fag— I mean, he looked like a homosexual to me. My thinking at the time was if someone like that talks shit to me, they're going to get a beatdown. That's just the way it was. So I pushed him. I gave him a big push, nearly knocked him over."

The two men behind Ben were working nonstop now, filling in various categories. The physical violence section was filling up. Under "Justifications for Violence" were several entries, including "threat to manhood" and "I was programmed for violence."

"So the guy is pissed. He's yelling at me saying something like 'What the hell is wrong with you?' That's when I lost it. I called him a faggot punk. I remember seeing red, my vision becoming narrowed. What do you call it? Almost like tunnel vision, and my mouth filled up with this copper taste and it's almost like I blacked out. I pushed him down and my friend and I started kicking him and kicking him more and more. We were yelling the whole time that he was a faggot punk and 'don't you ever fuck with me again.' I broke his jaw. I broke a few of his ribs. There was blood all over the sidewalk. There was blood on my boots."

Near the end of this story, Ben trailed off until the words caught in his throat. He rubbed his hands up and down on his knees obsessively, and finally found his voice again.

"Someone must have called the cops 'cause a crowd gathered and started yelling at me and pointed me out. Next thing I know I am in the back of a cop car in cuffs." Ben put his head down and slowly shook his head back and forth.

"I was so loaded," he said. "And I was so angry, about everything. I hated my life. I was ashamed of being broke all the damn time, and had been trained to hate all these people. My hit man I call the 'Ruthless Aryan Soldier,' and I was going to take down anyone who betrayed the white race. Now it seems like a dream I had once. Like it's not real."

Finally, Ben looked up. His story was finished, so it was time to move into the second section of the destruction cycle. That's when the other men talked.

"Can I give you feedback?" one inmate asked. Ben folded his arms over his chest.

"Yeah," he said, taking a deep breath.

"Well, when you said you were so loaded that sounded like blaming your violence . . . like you were blaming the drugs for your violence instead of you."

Ben's foot started to bounce. He was working hard to listen and not react. Finally, he put up his hands in supplication, the sign of fatal peril. He held them there for fifteen seconds. The rules of the destruction cycle instructed the men to "listen to feedback with undivided attention, you listen with an open mind, with an open heart, you listen for a kernel of truth, you soften and reflect on the feedback and you don't argue."

Ben gritted his teeth and said, "Thank you. You're right." His foot was still banging away like a jackhammer.

Another man asked if he too could offer feedback. Ben nodded.

"When you said 'I lost it,' that sounded like minimizing . . . like someone else took over for you, like you don't control your hit man, and you weren't in control of your actions."

Ben was getting the hang of it. He nodded vigorously this time.

"I hear you, thanks."

The destruction cycle went on for almost forty-five minutes, with Ben's peers pulling out pieces of his story and categorizing it on the board behind him. The process was painstaking. Each word and action was analyzed. Every excuse that Ben used—that he was "high" when he beat the man up, that he was doing "what he'd been taught," that he'd had to learn violence for "protection"—was talked about and assessed. Any time he tried to disassociate himself from his violence, the other men, or Leon, reminded him that he had chosen to act. It was the way the men retrained themselves to think about their violence. When men turned around and looked at the board at the end of the process, many were stunned at how many different kinds of violence they had committed, and the ways that they tried to excuse it.

There was a second side to the destruction cycle. Not only did the men learn to name their violence and own it, they were also encouraged to name their shame, and own that, too. The men embraced the pain that Ben had been through in his life. Not only had he talked about how afraid he was in juvie and how he'd accepted the protection of the Aryan Brotherhood, Ben had also talked about how his father had harassed and emotionally abused him and his mom, and that he'd never gotten over it.

"I'm so sorry that happened to you," Leon had told Ben. "That shouldn't happen to anyone. No child should have to go through that. It's not your fault, you know."

"I know, but—"

"There are no buts, Ben," Leon pressed him. "I heard you say you were sad and scared. Those are real and important emotions. It makes up our authentic self and when we understand and feel this, we can learn to intimate instead of violate, you got it?"

"Yeah," Ben exhaled. "I got it." He grabbed his chair and moved back into the larger group. The men gave it up for him, telling him "good work, man, thanks for being open." They hugged him, reached out to pat him on the back. Ben's face was flushed and his hair was wet with sweat as if he'd run a marathon, but there was nothing tense about his demeanor. He was relaxed and smiling and human. The rage I'd grown used to seeing in him, as present and acidic as the tattoos covering his body, had been put away.

While Ben went through his destruction cycle, Elroy sat in his group on the other side of the dorm. He had followed a path similar to Ben's, confronting his demons in the group, confronting the crimes he'd committed.

He went through a destruction cycle of his own, his voice disappearing in the memories of the man he'd attacked standing in line for the movies. "This dude made a gesture about my woman," Elroy told the group. "Like he wanted to hop on her or something. I walked over to him and told him that I would fuck him up if he looked my way again. This little punk ass! He told me to get out of his face. He told me that 'I was tripping' so I hauled off and cracked him. He ended up in the hospital."

Elroy had traveled the emotional gamut during his cycle. When he got angry both legs would splay out and his gigantic arms would clench. When he cried, both legs would fold underneath him, and his eyes would turn to big, bloodshot, watery pools. He was a master at minimizing, saying at first the whole thing was the other guy's fault. "Why did he have to look over at us," and he'd kept himself "controlled." "I had a knife but I didn't use it, I only used my fists!" But revelations assaulted him. He realized as he told the story that the whole reason for the attack—the fact that this guy kept making eyes at his girlfriend—was based on a misguided assumption. "I don't know what the guy was thinking," Elroy said suddenly, a look of confusion playing across his face. "I made it up, I guess. I didn't know what he wanted or what he was doing. Shit, he may not have been doing anything wrong."

"But what if he had?" Earl, who was facilitating the group, had asked. "Would that have made a difference to you."

"Yeah, it would have!" Elroy responded aggressively. But then he caught himself again. "But I guess it shouldn't have."

Once Elroy's defenses fell he, like Ben, was one of the most disciplined participants we had. He sought me out after his fourth month.

"Sunny, I gotta talk at ya for a sec. This place, I just gotta say, this place is the first time I ever had to talk about my feelings and have someone listen."

"I'm glad, Elroy."

"No, you don't get it, Sunny. I've been arrested somewhere like thirty times. I been to a hundred holding cells, had so many damn lawyers I couldn't name a single one, been processed and humiliated so many damn times. But here, this is the first place where I got to work on my problems. The first place!" I'd heard similar things from Latino gangbangers, middle-aged wife beaters and crystal meth dealers. Men like Elroy and Ben told their peers in RSVP what they had never told anyone else. In their excitement they could become euphoric, embracing the group sessions with an almost missionary zeal. It took careful managing, because what they learned on the inside could quickly disappear on the outside, back in their old environments, where they weren't surrounded by positive peer support.

We were just beginning to send our "graduates" out into the world. If we were lucky, we'd get them for six months. Four to five months was the norm. If I'd had my way, we'd get them for two years, because I believed that was how long it took for the program to take hold. This was incredibly difficult work for them, physically and mentally uncomfortable. They had grown up learning how to bury their emotions, learning, as my father and I had, to lash out rather than to feel bad. RSVP was teaching them how to feel, requiring it, and to my never-ending satisfaction, many men were trying.

After Ben and Elroy had been in the dorm for a year, Leon walked into another staff meeting with a big grin on his face. "Guess who's hanging out during their free time?"

Earl and Damon laughed. They already knew. Damon spit it out. "Ebony and Ivory, man, Ben and Elroy are like best friends. That's mighty, Sun. That's mighty."

CHAPTER 16

1999

Deputy Ricky Drocco poked his head into my office. "Sunny, these men down in the dorm are full of crap!"

"What is it this time, Ricky?" I sighed. Drocco was a reality check for me. As RSVP became institutionalized, he was both a believer and a skeptic.

"I'm in *fatal peril*, I'm in *fatal peril*," Drocco moaned, doing his best exaggeration of a prisoner in group. "I hear these guys go all sincere and boo-hooing during sessions, but you should hear them on the phones."

"What, really? Tell me."

"I just think some of these guys are pulling the wool over your eyes," Drocco said.

"C'mon, Ricky, who do you think is a problem?"

"Argh, Sun, don't worry about it. Forget it, babe, never mind."

"No, Ricky, don't do that. You can't drop a bomb like that and say forget about it. If someone is doing that, you need to call him on it. I need to call him on it. We can't just let it pass."

Drocco shared what he knew with me. I got names, which I passed to the facilitators, and Drocco intervened the next time he heard someone on the phones in the dorm swearing at his partner. It was just one of a thousand small steps. Maintaining RSVP took constant vigilance. No one could slack. The minute you did, jail culture reverted to the lowest common denominator. It reverted to the culture the men brought into the dorms.

We could depend on the criminals resisting the system. They

brought their tribes and hair-trigger tempers. They were always ready to respond to the smallest slight. That was a constant. What was less predictable was maintaining the support of the staff. Deputy sheriffs had to be recruited and trained to embrace RSVP and all the programs of County Jail 7. Rumors were always getting back to me about deputies who thought I was a pillow fluffer, who thought I was wasting my time with the liars who would never change. Becky was critical for maintaining discipline in the ranks of the deputized staff. Whatever problems Becky and I might have had at home, and they were legion, we were always allies at work. The deputies never lost their fear of her and she would bear down like a freight train on anyone who dared step out of line.

None of this was a surprise to me, however. I had come into RSVP with a distrust of deputy sheriffs. What I didn't expect was how much some of them would learn from RSVP, and how much I learned, too.

Three naval midshipmen were sent to County Jail 7. They'd had a one-day furlough to go out in San Francisco. In their twenty-four hours of freedom, they decided to go to the Castro district, beat up a gay man, and put him in the hospital. Something about the sheer stupidity of the crime enraged me and I forced myself to stay away from them. I didn't think I'd be able to keep my emotions in check.

The navy guys were processed into Dorm C, which was a regular program dorm. They were put into college or vocational classes. Because of the nature of their crime, they could have been placed in RSVP, but we didn't have the space.

In the jail we recognized any holiday we could. Many of the men and women came from such terrible educations and knew very little of cultural diversity, so most holidays we celebrated were a way for our teachers to share some history. On Cinco de Mayo, we talked about the Mexicans defeating the French. On Juneteenth, we talked about the Emancipation Proclamation, Abraham Lincoln and the end of slavery. In the last week of June, we talked about Gay Pride Day. And this is where the problems began for our new gay-bashing prisoners.

We were having ITV, Instructional TV, in which we required all prisoners to watch a video and then participate in a discussion with a facilitator. The video we chose that week was a documentary called *The Sharon Kowalski Story*. It told the tragic story of a woman, Kowalski, who was injured in a motorcycle accident and suffered severe brain damage. Kowalski had a lesbian partner whom she'd lived with for years. They'd exchanged rings, bought property together and had intertwined their lives the way any married couple would. But after Kowalski's accident, her parents, with the support of the courts, cut off access to her partner. The movie explored the legal obstacles and inequalities for lesbian and gay couples in American society.

Since the inmates didn't get much television time during the week, they would watch almost anything we put in front of them without much complaint. The navy gay bashers had been in the dorm for about three weeks at this point. They had kept quiet, not distinguishing themselves in the dorm. When the movie started, however, they stood up and turned their backs on the TV and the teachers. Some of the other prisoners followed suit, joining up in a homophobic alliance.

Lieutenant Hunsucker was the supervising officer on duty when the protest occurred. It was his job to deal with the troublemakers while the dorm deputy got everyone else back on schedule. Hunsucker came into my office with a head full of steam.

"Sun, I've got the gay bashers in an empty classroom and I'm about to read them the riot act. I know you're gonna want in on this." He then told me what they'd pulled. I'd resisted dealing with them so far but he was right. I wanted my pound of flesh.

Hunsucker had found ways to infuriate and surprise me. In staff meetings, he was still the first to complain about programs. I found some of the jokes he made to be just this side of Neanderthal. But then he'd rush in, ready to go right at the gay bashers.

He and I walked into the classroom with three sour-looking prisoners. Their haircuts were still military-style buzz cuts. Their legs were splayed, arms were crossed, faces set. Hunsucker started in with a fire-and-brimstone approach.

"This is my jail. I'm the supervisor right now, which means you are under my command. You"—he pointed menacingly at them—"are not going to run things. Now, your hate, and homophobic behavior, will not be tolerated in here and I warn you not to test me. You don't like gay people? That's your pathetic problem. The fact that you had twenty-four hours to have some fun but instead beat up a man because he is gay is stupid and chickenshit. You are not going to play those games here. We will be watching you twenty-four hours a day and one false move and you will be more sorry that you beat that boy up than you ever felt before. You are going to get a real education here. You will learn how to treat all people with respect. That means everyone."

The inmates sat up and listened. Hunsucker was a tough, burly white guy in a uniform, speaking to them like cadets, lecturing them on homophobia, of all things. He could have passed for any of their superior officers. They had to be confused. Their eyes went wide as he hammered at them, and then he turned it over to me. I was enraged. I had walked in with absolutely no sympathy, feeling as disgusted with them as I'd felt about Fred Johnson the pedophile. I wanted to humiliate them and make them squirm. One of them had the name Schwartzkoff,

"Schwartzkoff? Who's Schwartzkoff? Hey, that's similar to my name. Are you Jewish? Do you think we might be related?" I was being childish. "You think you can beat someone up because they're gay? You think your friends should beat you up because you're Jewish?" I looked over at Hunsucker, who was eyeing me skeptically, and I stopped myself. I realized, in an instant, what a remarkable thing we had going. Here was a guy I had once pegged as a homophobic fascist with a badge, trying to build a civil community. Here was Hunsucker, my enemy, doing my job better than I was. I gave up my rant. The guy I was picking on was glaring at me, looking like he wanted to attack. I took a deep breath, and pivoted. "You know, I want to make you squirm the way you made that poor man in the Castro feel fear. I, too, have to control myself to treat you like human beings. If you can't get with a jail program, you will not be able to make it out in the world, a world filled with many different people whether you like it or not. We are giving you an opportunity here to become better people." I looked back at Hunsucker, hoping he would finish it.

"This ain't *Romper Room,*" he concluded. "We aren't about third and fourth chances. We are not going to accept the hate, so you either get with the program now, or your lives get hard. I will make it hard." It was Hunsucker who made the mark with those men. I had given up my authority when I went after one of them. It was that easy to lose it.

The men went back into their dorm. I went back to my office, profoundly thankful. This was becoming a healthier community. These damaged people we brought inside the walls had a chance to take control of their lives and change. They had the chance. Some of them would take it. And they weren't the only ones learning to control their damage. I was learning. Hunsucker was learning. We were all learning each day to make our lives a little richer, a little better. There was a quote I had posted on my wall that I sometimes forgot was there. It was from Egon Bittner, a groundbreaking sociologist who studied the relationship between police and society. He wrote, "The consideration extended to the seemingly undeserving person is not intended for his or her personal benefit, but expresses the moral integrity of the one who extends it. It enhances the dignity of human life, especially in situations where extending it appears to be hopelessly misspent."

Nine months later, the gay bashers were released. I hadn't followed their progress but I recognized them as I drove up to the gate. New releases had the option to take the bus into the city or to walk out the front door. They were walking down the road as I pulled into the parking lot. One of them saw me and walked up to my car. I was a little wary but he smiled nervously and waved. "Ms. Schwartz," he said. "I want you to know, I really learned a lot here and thank you."

I wished him luck and he almost skipped away to the car that was waiting for him.

CHAPTER 17

2000

The deputy flipped the switch. The heavy metal door slid open. I slipped through to soft murmuring. Men were gathered into four groups in front of dry-erase boards. They were talking in hushed tones, and a few were scribbling furiously on the board. Men waited their turn to join the conversation. Except for the county-issue orange, I could be in church, or a lecture hall, anywhere but a jail.

I thought of my first day on Mainline, which is just a random cross-section of criminals, not nearly as hardened as the group we brought together in RSVP. RSVP had the worst our system had to offer. But the difference between Mainline and the RSVP dorm was the difference between chaos and calm. In short, it was the difference between a place where the thugs controlled the culture, and a place that was controlled by all of our better instincts. They might as well have been two different planets.

Each group in RSVP was overseen by a facilitator. Most of the day, veteran inmates led the discussions, and helped control the flow of the day. Ben was facilitating one of the groups, his small, wiry frame folded into a chair off to my left. Elroy was facilitating a group to my right, his bulk engulfing a chair, his hands doing half his talking as he made a point to his group. Both men had been reborn in RSVP and were among our greatest success stories. Ben had spent a year in a postrelease residential treatment center for drug abuse and joined us, after twelve months of training, as a peer educator and facilitator. Elroy had taken a similar journey.

They had ended up becoming dear friends. Ben's mother died

recently and Elroy went with him down to Orange County as he wrapped up his family affairs. I watched them both work for a few minutes. At thirty-two, Elroy was almost ten years older than most of the prisoners, and his imposing physique was offset by a kind face and soothing voice. It rumbled but didn't roar. His size conferred instant respect, and he was also one of our most focused facilitators, never letting standards slip in his group. Ben's nervous energy had moderated. His toe still tapped when he was thinking. He still fidgeted, but it was passion, not anger, that drove him.

A new prisoner was going through a destruction cycle in Ben's group. The man, José, a short Mexican with a long braid down his back, was laughing a little as he told his story.

"So, me and my boys we hang at the corner of Mission and Twenty-second. Oh man, we drink too much." Here he smiled nervously. "We smoke too much, too. For like six months, I don't think I go a day without getting high. And this one night, I go home to get my car keys so we could cruise the hood but my old lady she snatched the car keys outta my hand. So I tell her, 'Bitch, you better not mess with me tonight, I am in no mood for this bullshit.' I was drinking too much and she wouldn't give up the keys. She was like, you know, fighting me for the keys. And I was drunk and I fought back. I was loaded. I barely remember what happened." José wound to a close and looked up.

"What does that mean? You beat her up. What exactly did you do?" Ben asked.

"Man, I dunno, I was pretty wasted," José replied.

"You chose to drink, didn't you?"

"Well, yeah, but . . ."

"You knew you were more violent when you were loaded, right?"

"Sure, man, but everybody I hung out with was drinking." The guy looked put-upon.

"Hey, I'm not picking on you," Ben's tone softened. "But it's important and I want you to recognize the way we talk about our actions, right? The way we talk about them is the way we understand them. Everything we do, at some point, we made a choice to do. If you know you're violent when you drink, then if you drink, you've chosen to be violent, right?"

The men around Ben voiced their agreement. The inmate on the hot seat nodded slowly, letting the idea sink in.

"So tell me what happened after she took your keys," Ben said.

Now the man really began to squirm. "Man, why you want to play me? I just don't remember much, you know."

Ben stayed on him. "Look, that's not gonna fly here. Can I get an agreement from you right now? Can I get an agreement that you will listen as much as you can with an open heart and disclose everything you do remember and know that all of us are violent men. This is the important stuff. You may not remember every detail. But you saw the aftermath, right?" Ben looked at José until he slowly nodded his agreement. "You saw the ambulance come, right? People told you what happened, right? So you tell us that. Tell us the damage that you did. Saying you don't remember is a way we use to avoid responsibility for our actions. If you truly don't remember, you better go learn what you did. The hospital reports will be in your defense attorney's file. There's no excuse for not knowing. Can I get an agreement about that?"

I looked back at the inmate. He was steaming, his eyes were blank, his shoulders tight. But he couldn't escape. His hands slowly came up to show fatal peril. He would have to confront his crimes either today or soon.

On the other side of the room, Elroy was doing the same work in his group. The groups went on all day. RSVP had helped these men. In the first years of the program the evidence had been anecdotal. Men I'd seen come through the jails numerous times I'd realize weren't there anymore. They'd done a hitch in RSVP and I'd hear they had gotten a job driving a bus, or working in an office. But then we got proof that the anecdotes added up to a larger reality. We had sought out Dr. James Gilligan, the violence expert then at Harvard, and he'd agreed to do an evaluation of the program. His study looked at recidivism rates for the RSVP men, and the results were impressive. The simple takeaway from his study was that the more time inmates spent in RSVP, the less likely they were to be rearrested for violent crimes.

Inmates who had participated in RSVP for at least 8 weeks had a rate of arrests for violent crimes per day in the community during their first year

*after release from jail that were 46.3% lower than those of the 101 mem-
bers of the control group (p 0.05). For those in RSVP for 12 weeks or
more, the violent crime rearrest rate was 53.1% lower (p 0.05); and those
in for at least 16 weeks had a violent rearrest rate 82.6% lower (p 0.05).
In each of the three pairs of group comparisons, the members of the experimental group who were rearrested spent significantly less time in custody,
and significantly more days in the community before their first arrest (for
either a violent or nonviolent crime), than did those in the control group.**

Gilligan did find that many RSVP graduates were still being sent
back to jail, but most of that was for drug possession instead of violent
crimes. Many men who had gone through RSVP had stopped their
violence. The men who spent longer in RSVP were doing better than
the men who had spent less time. RSVP was helping these men. I had
the hard proof. And, I'm happy to say, RSVP was helping me, too.

After nine years together, after hundreds of fights on old battle-
grounds, Becky and I found something new to fight about—she began
staying out late. She'd never had many of her own friends. She'd
always been a loner. But she'd finally, after many years, made a new
one of her own. The woman was a nurse and had just gone through a
bad breakup after catching her lover in bed with someone else. I
invited her over for Shabbos dinner and she and Becky had hit it off.

Then, over time, Becky slowly grew irritable with me, impatient,
lost behind a newspaper, in front of the television, or just out. She
began going out and not coming home until past midnight. I tried
confronting her. "Come on, Becky, just tell me what's going on."

"There's nothing going on," she'd tell me. "You're imagining it. I
can't believe you would want to start a fight over the first friend I've
had."

When she finally admitted to me that she was having an affair,
some four months after the fact, my heart crumbled. I could not see
straight. I'd been wrecked before, by Stevie, by other women, by my

---

*James Gilligan and Bandy Lee, *The Resolve to Stop the Violence Project: Reducing Violence
through a Jail-Based Initiative*, commissioned report, December 2000.

mother's death, but something about Becky's betrayal brought me to my knees.

In the midst of this, I went to sit in on a Manalive class that we helped run out in the community. Many of our facilitators at County Jail 7 participated in these groups, since they were former violent men themselves. I went to one that Earl facilitated in the basement of San Francisco's Third Baptist Church.

I took my seat as part of the circle. I was the only woman there, and many people knew I was the big mama of RSVP. Some of these men had been inmates in the program. Earl was checking in, going man to man, asking the traditional questions at the beginning of meetings. What's your name? How do you feel? Have you had any moments of fatal peril?

He reached a guy with the build of a construction worker who couldn't answer. He couldn't speak; he put his hands to his face and started breathing hard. Finally, he regained his composure, said his name was Dennis and said he had to talk about what he'd done. His voice was clipped, as if he'd had to bind it in order to make it intelligible.

"My wife is six months pregnant," Dennis said. "She has been cold to me, lately, not talking or giving me anything. I suspected she was cheating on me for a while, but she denied it when I asked her. 'You're fucked up,' she'd say. Once, I was on her for so long she started screaming, 'Get out of my house.' I kept at her, though, more and more. I was calling her a fuckin' whore, telling her she was a piece of dirt, every day I was at her until finally she snapped back.

"She said, 'That's right. I am a whore. I'm sleeping with Roger.' Roger is this asshole she grew up with. My wife, she was real cold. She said, 'Fuck you, and for all I know, it's his baby.' Man . . ." At that moment Dennis's hands went up, indicating fatal peril. Tears were streaming down his face.

"I lost it. I hit her. I knocked her to the ground and kicked her." Dennis started sobbing but kept trying to talk. "I was wrong. I hurt her bad. I might have hurt the baby. I would do anything to turn back time and . . ." He finally couldn't speak anymore. There was a dead silence in the room punctuated by Dennis's sobs.

While Dennis was telling the story, my heart and guts rebelled. I hated him for doing what he had done. I couldn't stop picturing it—a pregnant woman being knocked down, cowering, defenseless, with this big brute standing over her. I hated him. And yet, I felt a shred of pity for the pain he had felt, his feeling of betrayal, and then, all of a sudden, I was overwhelmed. Tears were streaming down my face. I was trying, and failing, to hold back sobs. Before Becky had confessed everything to me, I had felt like the biggest intrusion in her life, like I was a speck on her shoulder that she kept flicking away. I felt like he did. His shame was my shame.

When it came to my turn to speak, I couldn't get the words out. Earl just looked at me with sweet, serious eyes. He wasn't going to bail me out or insist on me talking. He patiently waited until I was ready. Finally, I composed myself enough to look at Dennis and say "Man, I hate you so much for doing that to your wife. And I appreciate that you are trying to look at yourself and working at it so this never happens again. But I hate you for what you did." Dennis looked at me and nodded his head and said nothing. We were both wrecks.

Dennis had reminded me, in the most powerful way possible, that if I didn't figure out how to be okay with what had happened with Becky, I was going down his path. I could either embrace the shame, embarrassment and humiliation, or I could turn it to rage, which would mean I'd never have to deal with these raw feelings.

For once in my life, I had every "justified" reason to go crazy. I wanted to scream, throw Becky's things into the street, slash her tires, lose my marbles. I'd done it to lovers in the past with women who had done nothing wrong. But with Becky, amazingly, I kept the rage in check. I let grief overtake me, and never let it spin out of control. Dennis and RSVP and my own therapy kept reminding me to stay with the hurt but not let it turn violent.

Every morning I would wake up in a puddle, sobbing on my bedroom floor. I felt like I did when my father's temper filled the room, blotting me out. I felt like I did when my mother couldn't stand up for me, when she let my father rage and call me a dreck lesbian. I felt like I did when my brothers left me behind to go play baseball, Stevie yelling, "Get lost, Chubs, no one wants you around." I felt like I did failing the remedial classes, a hopeless loser who didn't deserve love, or happiness. I felt it all. In fact, the only being capable of getting me off the floor was Towby, my beagle, who would drown me in sloppy kisses until I sat up laughing, my misery pushed aside for a minute. I'd pull myself up from my knees, throw coffee down my throat and wander into work a zombie. By the end of the day I'd be alive again. I'd listen to the men of RSVP who would confess to horrible crimes, and admit to shame, and fears and hurts that they had carried for their whole lives, and pledge to do things differently, pledge to get on a better path.

They all were struggling with far greater injuries than mine. Ben's father had abandoned him when he was nine, and rarely reached out to him again. His uncle had molested him. Elroy's mother had been a heroin addict. He'd been abandoned to the foster system when he was twelve. Each of the men they worked with discovered similar shame in their own past and they confronted the pain they caused in their victims. They felt it all together, and I felt it with them.

CHAPTER 18

2000

There was no magic we performed on Ben or the rest of the men in RSVP. There was nothing we did to them that can't be replicated in any other prison or jail. We didn't create new therapeutic techniques. We didn't reinvent the wheel. The list of things we provided for the men was revolutionary simply because almost no one had done what we did in a correctional setting. RSVP can be re-created. It can be re-created in every jail and prison in the country. And it can also fail.

As part of RSVP, we had a program for the victims of RSVP men, which offered counseling and other practical services. It was a core part of our program but we were always scrambling to keep it funded. We let victims know we existed. We did not, as a rule, try to convince them to participate, or try to set up reconciliation meetings between our RSVP men and the victims. It was simply too delicate and depended entirely on the needs and desires of the victim. If a perpetrator wasn't far enough along, if he tried to minimize what he'd done, or excuse it, we risked hurting the victim all over again. We also didn't have the money to do more than we already were. It was a small but important part of the larger program, which ran smoothly until just before Halloween, 2000.

It was Friday morning. Jack-o'-lanterns dotted the halls in the administration wing of County Jail 7. Halloween decorations always gave me the creeps in jail. Demons and ghouls bore too much resemblance to some of the monsters who came through our doors. Before I made it to my office, Leah, one of our administrative assistants, rushed up. Her face was ashen. Leah worked with Bianka in the victims' outreach program, which offered counseling and other help to the victims of RSVP men. Leah could barely speak but managed to say that one of their clients, a domestic violence victim, had been murdered the night before. Neighbors had seen her abusive ex-boyfriend, a man named Tari Ramirez, running from the house with a bloody knife.

"Sunny," Leah said, "Ramirez just spent four months in the RSVP dorm. He was released about three months ago." Her bottom lip was quivering. "What do we do, Sunny, what do we do?"

I lost my balance for a second and sat down heavily in a chair.

I couldn't believe it. Didn't want to believe it. It may sound stupid but I had never prepared for this. We had grown so used to working with the worst monsters the monster factory could produce. I'd grown used to their feeling remorse, taking responsibility for their violence. So many had walked out in better shape than when they'd walked in. This was a sucker punch.

"Leah, what do we know? Are we sure it was one of our guys?"

"Sunny, there were multiple eyewitnesses. People are sure he's the one. I went to get the file as soon as the call came in this morning. Ramirez came to us on a DV charge against Claire Tempongko." *DV* was shorthand for domestic violence. "He was in the RSVP dorm until August, and then was released. He attended the postrelease Manalive classes as well."

"Claire Tempongko, she's the one who was killed?" I asked.

"Yeah." Leah sighed. "They say that last night, Ramirez broke into her home, waited for her and attacked her with a kitchen knife when she came in. Her two kids were right there."

"Oh Jesus, Leah, how old are they?"

"Five and ten."

Later in the morning, I called the entire staff to my office. Everyone knew already. Ben came in looking like he'd been sick to his stomach. The other men who worked in the dorm—Leon, Elroy, Earl and Damon—looked tired. Bianka, Delia and Marcela, our victims' coordinators, had red eyes. There was a feeling of defeat in the room. We'd had only two fights in three years, and each fight was a push and a shove. At the time, that had freaked us out.

"I don't know what to say," I said. "I am devastated like you are. I don't have a speech prepared. I think people should just talk."

There was silence for a long time. Then Ben spoke. "Tari was in my group, I, um, I'm . . . I don't know how I am . . ." Ben's voice trailed off. He was the one who had most recently worked with Ramirez. Ben was running the postrelease Manalive classes for graduates of RSVP. "Ramirez, the guy was like a Boy Scout. He was helpful, he had all the lingo down. He seemed really interested in getting with the program. I guess I missed it."

"Hey," Leon interjected. "You can't blame yourself here. You're doing good work, you know."

"I know Leon, I know," Ben agonized. "But I just can't help but feel this is my fault. I should have known. I'm supposed to be able to see when these guys aren't being straight. I didn't pick it up with this guy at all. What the hell are we doing? Does any of this make sense?" People reached out to support Ben, but we all felt some version of what he was saying.

We went around the room, sharing what we knew, sharing regrets. Earl had had Ramirez in his group in the RSVP dorm. "Ben's right, man. The guy was polite, obedient really. I mean he started out all jacked up, like Ben did, or like me even. You know. He had the 'What the fuck is this? You can't force me to be here' attitude. But he snapped to it real quick."

"Yeah, he did," Ben confirmed. "He used the language. He called other people on their bullshit. I'd sit and wonder sometimes, you know, the subtle clues weren't always right. He seemed like he was parroting the language sometimes. But he was a good liar. I bought it."

Bianka had her own regrets to add. She said she was out in the neighborhoods working with victims. Claire Tempongko had been on her list of clients. "We had an appointment with Claire last week but she canceled. She said she wasn't feeling well. It's not the first time she'd canceled on me but it felt to me like something was wrong. I tried to follow up with her but I never got her on the phone."

Delia remembered meeting Claire from a women's group we had sponsored for survivors of violence. "She sat in the front row. Leon had given a presentation, saying what they were doing with the men. Claire had raised her hand to complain: 'This stuff doesn't work. Tari doesn't take responsibility! He accuses me of being violent!' At the end of the session, I tried to tell her about services, but she'd shrugged them off."

There was only so much to say. My greatest fear had come true. Tari Ramirez had taken the hope of RSVP and subverted it. He had played the system, resisted the peer leadership, and went right back to his abusive ways when he hit the streets. I tried to encourage the staff, telling them we had done what we could to try to help Ramirez and Claire. After Ramirez stopped attending Manalive classes, Ben had done the right thing and called Ramirez's probation officer. Failure to appear was a probation violation, and the PO could have sent Ramirez back to prison, but he didn't.

"You know, we opened the door to a better life for this monster," I said. "Many men have walked through that door. He chose not to."

But the words didn't satisfy. Not even me. We learned more details as the day went on. It turned out that Claire had called the police numerous times after Ramirez was released from our custody to report that he was stalking her. This should have set off alarm bells and sent Ramirez back to prison but the system had failed. Police reports didn't make it to the probation officer. The ones that did weren't followed up on. Claire was murdered. And Tari Ramirez escaped. After two days, he still hadn't been captured.

I called Sheriff Hennessey the day of the murder. I knew it was going to hit the papers.

"Yeah, I heard about it. Killed in front of her children. Just terrible," he said.

"Hennessey, I got to tell you. He spent some time in RSVP. About four months."

"Oh that's terrible, Sunny. You guys all right over there?"

"Yeah, we're shook up, but we're okay."

"Did we do all we could? We make any mistakes?"

"No, Sheriff. He stopped attending classes after his release. We reported him, but he disappeared off of our radar."

He didn't say anything right away. I knew he was relieved to hear it wasn't our fault. I was relieved it wasn't our fault, too. But I was still heartsick and wondering what he would say.

Hennessey finally responded. "Listen, this is a high-risk business. We're not working with altar boys. We're working with violent men. This is a horrible thing that happened, but we have to remember that this is just one of the crimes we weren't able to stop."

There was finger-pointing in the media, a "crisis of conscience," and the blame fell on the police and probation departments. Not on us. There were reforms in the aftermath, overhauls that were long overdue to improve communication between the agencies. Those were good results. But the murder had exposed one of the central problems buried in our criminal justice system, one that my work hasn't begun to touch. There are too many teams working at cross purposes in criminal justice. I was relieved that we weren't to blame for Claire's murder, but just thinking that missed the point. Eighteen years earlier, when I'd tried to find a solution for the release of Fred Johnson, I'd met with a common response from everyone I'd talked to. "It's not my job. You can't save everyone."

I have two responses to that. The first is that the person truly at fault is the perpetrator. Blame ultimately starts and ends there. And so it's a true statement to say that "it's not my fault that this happened." But the second response is that we are either part of a solution or we're not. We either share in its success or failure, or we don't. If we are going to play a role in the life and crime of a community, then all of us, from police to prosecutor to jail worker to ordinary citizen, have to take some stock of what happened to Claire, and what happened to her two children. So the questions, I believe, fall on all of us to answer. How do we stop more children from becoming orphans? How do we stop this cycle of crime? How do we draw a line in the sand and say no more? Men got out of RSVP and renounced their violence but men also got out of RSVP, hit the streets, scored a speedball and went back to sticking up convenience stores. Even an 80 percent reduction in violent rearrests meant that 20 percent were still untouched by what we did. The program "fails" every single day. But that doesn't mean that I didn't get up each day, go into work and search for new ways to make it better, that I didn't fight to make sure no one fell through the cracks, that we wouldn't take our best shot with every single person who came through our doors. This was high risk. After Tari Ramirez killed Claire Tempongko, in RSVP we learned to look at every survivor we worked with as as if they were in a pine box. That was what was at stake.

I talked regularly with our RSVP staff, especially the men who had been violent, about being active in their restorative justice work. What had they done recently to restore the community they'd harmed? In one meeting, I mentioned that I'd received a call from Temple Sinai over in Oakland. They had invited me to come talk to the congregation about our work during their "Peace Seder" on Passover. I wondered whether any of the men wanted to come with me. I asked them to think about it, then we went on to other business.

Ben sought me out in my office a day later.

"Hey, Sunny." He was rubbing his hands together nervously. Usually, he liked to shoot the shit, but today he was like a laser. "Listen, I have something I need to ask you. I've been thinking more and more about what you said in the meeting yesterday about what we can do to give back to the community. I couldn't sleep last night thinking about the synagogue; it seemed right for me and my crimes. But it scares me so much to think about going. What do you think?"

I'd been hoping Ben would think about it. "It's going to be a difficult crowd," I told him. "I've been there a few times and they are a mixed group, a lot of young, active, progressive folks and older folks, too, and some of them are Holocaust survivors. There are going to be a lot of people in that crowd who absolutely despise skinheads, even former ones."

Ben was coiled in the seat across from me. "Sounds scary and good," he told me. "If you think it won't be a problem for the congregation, I am for it, one hundred percent."

I talked to the woman who invited me. She was moved by Ben's story and thought it was worth the risk to have him speak. A month later, on a warm afternoon, Ben and I drove over the Bay Bridge to Temple Sinai in Oakland. Sinai is one of the oldest congregations in the Bay Area. Founded in 1875, it sits in Berkeley's orbit, and for years had been out front putting reading programs in Oakland schools, protesting the war in Vietnam and leading the charge on feminist issues. It is a liberal reform congregation, but that didn't mean I thought Ben would get a loving welcome. I was terrified of how the day would go.

As we drove, Ben was quiet, his hand beating out a rhythm on the armrest. He confessed to me as we parked, "Sunny, I'm scared shit-less." I looked at him. His hair was covering the swastika on his head, and he was wearing a long-sleeve shirt that covered the tattoos on his arms. But how would they see him inside? I'd never been involved in something like this before.

There were about thirty round tables in Temple Sinai's large audi-torium, set and ready for the Passover Seder. I introduced ourselves to the organizer and we found a table with about ten other people. I led the conversation, telling the people what we did, getting the usual oohs and aahs of support. Working with prisoners was a good conver-sation starter. Most people want to know what it's like behind bars. Ben was fidgeting and quiet. Soon the service started.

We drank the wine (Ben abstained) and gave thanks for deliverance from Egypt. The questions were asked—"Why is this night different from every other night?"—by a cute moppet with ringlets tied into ponytails behind her head. Ben's head stayed bowed. We were memo-rializing the Jews' deliverance from slavery to freedom and I was thinking of my deliverance from my relationship with Becky. I imag-ined Ben was thinking of his own victories. He was clean and sober, and had rejected the hate that was suffocating him. I was proud of him, and also worried for him. Sitting at the next table was an elderly cou-ple. I saw tattooed numbers crawling up their arms.

The Seder was nearly over and there was a pause in the service when Temple Sinai's director, a middle-aged woman with a peace but-ton on her lapel, stood for announcements and to introduce us.

I kept my talk short. I told the congregation a little bit about the jails and RSVP and the work we were trying to do. Then I introduced Ben.

"One of my colleagues from the jail who works in the RSVP dorm has come with me, and I want to turn the floor over to him. Some of the things he is going to disclose today are going to be personal, and may be difficult for you to hear. When he's done I want to make sure you know that we will take questions, and take all feedback with an open heart." With that I sat down. Ben sprang from his seat. He was sweating and though he was used to talking in front of crowds, and did it every day in the jails, he fumbled over his words.

"Thank you for having me here," he finally managed to say. He coughed. "I, um, as you might be able to tell, I am very nervous talking to you. Everything I want to share with you is said with a full heart. I work with the men of RSVP as a facilitator. That means I run groups for violent men, directing their conversations, helping with the peer-led therapy, and work one-on-one with them to try to get them to stop their violence. But I also need to share that I was one of them a little over a year ago. Most facilitators in the RSVP dorm were violent men themselves at one time. I was in jail and everything I have done is my fault and my responsibility. I have done some very bad things. For many years, I was a heroin and meth addict, a member of a racist skinhead gang and a thug. I want to share some of my journey with you and will not blame you for hating me." My heart was racing as I watched him turn the corner in his story. I looked around. There was a wariness to the crowd; concerned looks showed themselves at many of the tables. Behind me, someone whispered, "I can't believe they let someone like that in here." My heart skipped.

Ben continued. "I was raised in Orange County. I was a very lonely kid and always wanted to be a part of something. I made some stupid decisions and hooked up with people I thought would look after me. They took me in as part of their family. They were skinheads, and they ate, drank and slept hatred all day long and soon I was doing the same. They made me feel like I was somebody. It was twisted thinking on my part. This skinhead group thought the white race was superior and everyone, especially blacks and Jews, were inferior, thought they were not worth living. Soon I believed it, too. I started believing horrible things about Jewish people, even though my first name, Benjamin, is Jewish. I fueled my hatred with drugs and I became a monster. I hurt a lot of people. I beat up black people, gays and Jewish people in the streets of Van Nuys where I grew up and up here. I was arrested in San Francisco for beating up a random stranger on the street." There were quiet responses all around me. Deep sighs racked the older couple I had noticed earlier. Some of the women I saw looked visibly pained. I checked for the nearest exit in case things turned ugly. I quickly ticked through the ways I

could interject to calm an angry crowd. "Come on, folks, let's listen
to this man who is now committed to making sure this does not happen again" or "Come on, let's be mensches" or "Yell at me, I invited
him" or, worst-case scenario, "Hey, look over there" and then high-
tail it out the back. But Ben soldiered on.

"But then I was arrested and I never thought I would feel this but
it was the best thing to be arrested in San Francisco. I'd been arrested
maybe twenty times before but here in San Francisco, they made me
go into a dorm, the RSVP dorm, where they taught me how to stop my
violence. In RSVP, I was forced to look in the mirror and I didn't like
what I saw. I hated what I saw in me. I was ashamed. But RSVP helped
me to name it, to accept my shame rather than run from it. Rather
than let my shame fuel my violence, I learned to let it be. The work in
RSVP helped me be the real man I am today." Ben started tearing up.
"I want to tell you how sorry I am for saying horrible things about
Jewish people. I want to tell you how sorry I am for trashing a synagogue in San Diego, for yelling out hateful things to people in your
community, for assaulting people because I thought they might be
Jewish. Part of my recovery process is to try to make restoration to the
communities that I've hurt and I want to apologize to you today and
say that I will do anything to give back to your community." By this
time Ben had lost it. I went over to him and stood next to him. He
looked done so I finished for him.

"I want to thank all of you for listening to us and want to open the
floor to questions or concerns—" I had more to say but I was interrupted. The congregation began clapping, and they stood up, and
started to crowd around Ben and me.

An old man with a thick Eastern European accent took Ben's hand
and didn't let go for about five minutes, until he finally said, "I never
thought I'd ever see the day when someone who identified with Nazis
would say 'I'm sorry.'"

Ben sat down finally, with tears staining his cheeks. The rabbi said
the final recitation. I flushed and gave silent thanks and thought of my
family. I thought of my mother, my grandmother Bubba, Uncle
Henry and Stevie, all dead now. I thought of the raucous Passover
meals we had. My father always led the prayers. It was tradition. But
my mother always knew the order of events better, always whispered

along, filling in the gaps where my father faltered. Someone was read-ing in the large, echoing room at Temple Sinai, but it was the whisper of my mother I heard.

> *And the Lord brought us forth out of Egypt with a strong arm and an outstretched hand, and by great terror, and with signs, and with wonders.*

EPILOGUE

The work in County Jail 7 eventually grew beyond it. And there are many other programs of which I am proud.

We started a charter school for the inmate population, the first of its kind in the country. It was Sheriff Hennessey's idea and I worked with the Republicans in the California leadership to help bring this about. The issue really isn't partisan. I haven't met a Democrat or Republican who hasn't responded to the idea that what we need to do with prisoners is get them to hold a mirror up to their behavior and their lives, not get them to kneel on pebbles. The first step in holding up that mirror is getting the prisoners a basic education.

I'm proud of getting to walk out onto the San Francisco Giants' diamond every year for Strike Out Violence Day. Back in 1996, I received a call from the new general manager of the team, Brian Sabean. At first I thought it was a prank call from a buddy who was as big a baseball nut as I was. But after a few embarrassing minutes, I finally started to listen. Brian said he'd heard about RSVP. His team had a policy of 100 percent player participation in a community cause, and he was wondering if the Giants could get involved in our work. Later, in his office, as I tried hard not to revert to teenybop questions about players' personal habits, I told him about sitting in the bleachers of Wrigley Field as a teenager, marveling at the combined energy of the fans. I wondered what would happen if we could get those fans thinking about violence in their homes and community. The sheriff, Larry Baer, Brian Sabean and I agreed to devote a day at the ballpark to raising awareness, and a year later, Strike Out Violence Day was born.

The event was the first of its kind in the country, where a major-league sports team, a law enforcement agency and a national domestic violence agency collaborated to educate fans on resources to stop violence. It included a pregame ceremony where ex-offenders, victims of violence and community leaders stood together to promote a peaceful society. To date we are in our tenth year, and close to 500,000 fans later, we have successfully married a compelling public awareness day with America's favorite pastime—baseball.

I'm also proud of being Trisha Meili's pitching coach. Trisha Meili became notorious as the Central Park jogger who was beaten, raped and left for dead in New York in 1989. In 2003, she wrote a book about her attack and recovery and revealed her identity. That year I invited her to throw out the first pitch at Strike Out Violence Day. Trisha also agreed to give a victim impact statement to the men of RSVP. We stood in the parking lot of County Jail 7 practicing her fastball. She had a pretty good arm.

Her presentation to the men of RSVP was phenomenal. She talked about her recovery, how she felt blessed not to remember the details of the attack, how she had to learn how to be a person again: how to speak, how to write, how to add and subtract. It was the first time she'd met with violent offenders. It was the first time she'd come close to the kind of men who had hurt her.

One of our inmates stood up during her question-and-answer period and confessed that he had raped someone. He said it was the first time he had ever told anyone this and that he would never have the opportunity to say he was sorry to his victim but that he was sorry for what had been done to Trisha. Trisha blanched as the man spoke, her face a riot of emotions. But when he was through she accepted his apology. On the ride to the ballpark she told me she was heartened. She felt that if just one of the men were changed by what she'd said, then she had hope. At the ballpark, she threw a fastball down the middle into the catcher's mitt while the crowd roared.

On the flip side of all that hope, of course, is the reality facing many of the people we are working with. The inmates in the San Francisco jails are the dregs of society, and disappointment and failure are our daily companions. Tari Ramirez was on the run for five years before he was apprehended in Mexico. He was extradited in 2006. Some people in my office went to his first evidentiary hearing. Claire Tempongko's family was there, their faces drawn and tight, having to see, just like everyone else in that room, the bloody evidence photos, the gruesome record of Claire's last moments. As I write this, Tari Ramirez is preparing to go on trial. I fully expect him to be convicted and do time, but nothing that happens now will undo the damage he has done. He will always be an example of the limits of our program. Anyone in the RSVP dorm has the potential to be like Tari Ramirez. Every year we have men leave the program whose transformations feel profound but who revert to their old ways when they hit the streets. The only test for men in RSVP is whether they can carry their transformation to the streets, and resist the pull of their old culture, their old habits, and become good men. Even some of our greatest success stories have fallen.

Ben faltered. He got lost in alcohol and had to step away from the jails, found a job managing a café and got back on track. Elroy, sadly, didn't make it. One day, we found out he was a deadbeat dad, not making his child support payments. Soon I heard from people on the street that he was using. His eyes narrowed when I called him to my office and asked him if he'd been smoking weed. His face became hard like his old convict mug shot—blank, tough, a look of provocation. He asked if I was going to fire him. I asked him if he would agree to take a drug test.

"Sunny, there's gonna be no trouble. *No trouble,* I tell you, because I'm clean as a whistle. I promise you that."

Elroy tested positive for marijuana. His job was to teach other men to be honest and accountable and he had stopped making payments to his child, and he lied to me. I had to fire him. I called him every few weeks to check up on him, but he slipped away, consumed by shame, never able to be honest with me. In 2006 he came back to the jails, this time as a prisoner on a drug possession charge. I took some solace in the fact that it wasn't for a violent offense.

The kind of men who come to RSVP are the reason so many people are sickened by the criminal justice system. They are the reason the American people have institutionalized a no-tolerance policy toward criminals. These men are the dirtbags who beat their wives, who start the gang wars, who shoot innocent children in the street over turf, who are addicted to drugs and rob and beat up people to support their habit, and keep coming back to jail over and over again. You have to know that you will often fail.

The word I use most with my staff is *humility*. I remind us all to stay humble, to know that the men we work with often come from the second, third and fourth generation of incarcerated men. Those men have inherited violence, substance abuse and the absence of personal responsibility like a birthright. We know how profoundly difficult it is to break these patterns, and that failure with some of the men is not just a possibility, it is a daily expectation that carries the promise of profound tragedy. I also know, having had to struggle to maintain the programs every year, how hard it is to convince lawmakers, and voters, that the betterment of criminals is worth spending money on. Voters have been happy to spend money on jails and prisons, but not on anything to keep these men out of jail.

I haven't talked much about money yet. The fights I've had to try to get each of our programs funded could fill their own book, though I'm not sure anyone would read it. They are mind-numbing tales of bureaucratic logjams and Solomonic decision making. I have often been given the choice: Do you want reading or domestic violence prevention this year? You've only got money for one. Programs usually are the last thought in a perpetually cash-strapped criminal justice system. My approach has always been not to make the choice. We find the money for the programs elsewhere—from grants, from local funders, from wherever we can get it. But money is only part of the battle. Programs are about leadership. If the leadership wants a workout room for correctional officers rather than a parenting class then that's what happens. In San Francisco County, I've been lucky to work with Sheriff Michael Hennessey. His even-keeled approach and dedication to the principle of programs has been steadfast. He knows that these men and women will be making a round-trip to prison after their release if we don't do something.

But the challenge is for all of us, not just for me or for Sheriff Hennessey in our small corner of San Francisco. What if all the juvenile and adult correctional facilities in the country were set up to address the problems and deficiencies of our criminal class from day one of lock up? What kind of society would we be if we made sure each prisoner received the therapy, education and peer pressure pushing him to do the right thing so that when he's released, he can grow up and get a job and stop terrorizing us. If that happened we could stop the violence and stop building prisons. I believe violent people have to be taken out of circulation. But it need not be a permanent removal if we stop sending them to monster factories and instead direct them to places that invest in their success.

The approach and principles I have described are biblical. You hurt someone, you take responsibility. You give back to the person and community that you harmed. There is nothing innovative about that idea. This is basic human decency, what I call being tough *and* smart on crime. And it works. Former Harvard professor and violence expert Dr. James Gilligan, who studied our program, found dramatic reductions in violent rearrests after just four months in RSVP. Four months can change behavior! This is revolutionary, and it didn't take an arm and a leg to do it. A healthy budget for RSVP, which includes postrelease programs such as job training, therapy, life skills and housing (critical to the program's effectiveness) is forty-four dollars per prisoner per day on top of the ninety-six dollars we now spend in San Francisco County to house and feed them. The money actually saved by society in court costs and medical bills and everything related to crime, not to mention the reduction of trauma for generations, would be astronomical. This isn't a money issue; it's a perception issue. What is needed is leadership.

In 2008, Westchester County in New York initiated RSVP East. County Executive Andrew Spano, his right-hand man Larry Schwartz and Commissioner Rocco Pozzi, like Sheriff Hennessey, took the risk of importing the full RSVP program into their jails, the only other institution in the country to do so. In Valhalla Jail, as in County Jail 7, they have a dorm filled with violent offenders. I was on the floor the first week of the program with forty-four monsters, who were tough, tattooed and snarling. Within days they had abandoned their hard exteriors and started to learn how to be accountable for their actions, and talk with their hearts and their minds. When it began, the Westchester folks had the same reservations we'd had in San Francisco: Does it work? Can we keep correctional workers safe? Is it worth it? How do we pay for it? But they committed to the program seeing the need to stop the cycle of violence.

We've won awards for RSVP. The most notable is probably the

Innovations in American Government Awards from Harvard University. They call it the Oscars for government public service. But while it's wonderful to be recognized, it pains me that our approach should be considered innovative. I think it should be as common as court time. If I've done my job right, after reading this book, hopefully you will think so, too.

I have a two-year-old named Ella. There is too much to tell about how I came to be a mother in a loving relationship with a beautiful, brilliant woman whom I adore, who is tough on me, and kind and generous. Recovery from the habits of my childhood is an everyday activity, but my partner, Lauren, keeps me honest. I promised Ella, our daughter, when she was born that wherever she went, I would always be there for her. And I asked only two things of her: that she please love baseball and never vote for bullies. So far, she's embraced our season tickets to the Giants, and she has another sixteen years before she can vote.

Jerry called me the other day. He invited Lauren, Ella and me to come for a visit. His sixteen-year-old daughter got on the phone and said, "Ella is my cousin, so when can we meet her?" I was delightfully floored. His four children are all grown. I have met them all, and they are sweet and beautiful. It's taken twenty-five years for my brother and me to get to this point, but we aren't locked into the roles we had as children. He has broken from his shell, and I have broken from mine. People can change, hard-core criminals, aloof older brothers and loud-mouthed sisters alike. Looking back now, I can see he was struggling with the challenge our family posed, same as I was. He had his own way of dealing, which sometimes left me out. My child, I hope, will know what it is to have a loving extended family and to understand the true meaning of being a mensch.

Lauren and I take turns taking care of Ella during the week. On one of my days with her, we were at the park and she took off running. Before I could stop her she'd run right up to a homeless guy splayed on a bench. My stomach clenched. Primal fear took over as my little girl approached a guy who was unkempt and smelly and damp and was probably mentally ill. Ella's hand went to his knee. She smiled, gurgled out a Hi. I finally caught up and put my arms around her. "I'm sorry," I blurted. The man looked at me and smiled. "That's okay. It's not every day I'm touched by an angel."

Here I was about to snatch my kid away without a second thought after spending twenty-five years convincing others not to judge people at face value. And he surprised me with his humanity! And you know what? I get it. I completely understand the objections and utter impatience people have with criminals. They have hurt us, our pocketbooks, our souls. I too can fall into a fearful us-versus-them mind-set, and feel I would want to kill anyone who hurt my child. I get it.

But what do we want to do about that anger? We spend more than 10 billion dollars a year in California, thirty-four thousand dollars per inmate per year to incarcerate criminals. California has about 312,000 people behind bars. Around 280,000 of them will eventually be released. Across the country, there are over 2 million criminals in jails or prisons. This year alone, 650,000 criminals will be released nationwide. Most of the places where these men and women are held are monster factories. The prisoners have nothing to do, they stew and rage and whine until they are released. I've sometimes been called a radical and a prison abolitionist. In some ways, it's true. I am both of those things. I do want to abolish *traditional* incarceration, but not all incarceration. I want to expect more of the men and women who are supposedly repaying their debt to society. The only way to do this is to challenge them to learn, to strive, to become better citizens. I also firmly believe there are some people who are beyond our help who should probably never again see the light of day. Tari Ramirez is probably one of them. But the 650,000 people who aren't psychopathic killers and will be released into our communities this year need something better than monster factories, and so do we.

I still have dreams as I wander the halls of the jails I've patrolled for a quarter of a century. These prisoners are different from the ones I first met here in the 1980s. They seem more violent, less capable of empathy. But their stories of desperation, of failure, of violence, are the same. So is their potential. Whether we want to admit it or not, our fate is tied to them because, like it or not, they will be released into our communities at some point. We have the tools to help them join us as partners, as allies, as citizens, and not enemies. In my dreams, we start to use these tools, bring them into every prison in the country, not just into my jail in San Francisco. In my dreams, we remake the monster factories into engines of accountability rather than instruments of retribution and despair. And I know in my heart that we can make these dreams real, if only we have the courage to dream them together.

ACKNOWLEDGMENTS

My gratitude is boundless.

I want to first thank Michael Hennessey, our sheriff, the mensch, who for over twenty-eight years has given me the freedom to grow and create and take wonderful chances for the citizens of San Francisco. If every sheriff was like Hennessey, the world would be a safer and more decent place.

This book is about my life and in no way do I want to convey that I did this work alone. On the contrary, many people are responsible for the programs described in this book. I want to acknowledge the contributions of those individuals who were instrumental in conceiving and running these programs. To Leo Bruen, Erik Camberos, Muin Daly, Deputy Richard Drocco, Tijanna Eaton, Marcela Espino, Lieutenant Desiree Felix, Deputy Sheila Frazier, Delia Ginorio, Elyse Graham, Sergeant Dean Gross, Siddiq Jihad, Floyd Johnson, Lazanius Johnson, Dr. Martin Jones, George Jurand, Bhavani Kludt, Maureen Lees, Karen Levine, Leslie Levitas, Lieutenant Robby Limacher, Ramona Massey, Joanne McAllister, Jean O'Hara, Ron Perez, Bianka Ramirez, Captain Tom Redmond, Lieutenant Richard Ridgeway, Jerry Scoggins, Roberto Varea, Reverend Billy Ware and countless other deputy sheriffs and civilian staff. They have renewed my faith in humanity and have given the San Francisco Sheriff's Department the ability to turn a small corner of the monster factory into a place of change, hope and accountability. To the Honorable Leslie Katz, for being the first elected official to get RSVP funded.

To Becky Benoit and Michael Marcum for your gutsy leadership. Without you RSVP would have remained just a good idea.

To Hamish Sinclair, who pioneered Manalive and has trained

thousands of men to unlearn the male-role belief system that fuels their violence.

To Ruth Morgan and Community Works West for not taking no for an answer and insisting that expressive arts be part of RSVP. She recognized that men develop empathy through theater exercises and group work, things that also give survivors and victims a dignified voice.

To those who came before me in this work, especially Ray Towbis, who is the pioneer of prisoner programs in San Francisco. He was the first civilian allowed in the San Francisco jails to work with convicts. He taught us how to question authority. He redefined the word *chutzpah*. Thank you, Ray. May you always watch over the castaways.

To the survivors of violence, may you always walk with your heads held high and continue to gain the courage to love and to live as fully integrated and self-determined human beings.

To the ex-offenders who have had the courage to look at themselves in the mirror and say, "I was wrong, I am accountable, I am sorry; I will stop my violence for your sake, for my sake, and for the sake of our communities."

To Deborah Mitchell and Mark Rosenthal for smart and compassionate therapy.

To my amazing agent, Priscilla Gilman, who never ceases to astound me with her heartfelt intelligence, empathy and advocacy for what is right and just. I remain amazed at your ability to immediately understand the importance of this work.

To Alexis Gargagliano, our gracious and phenomenal editor who understands matters of the heart and mind. Thank you for your skills in getting this "call to action book" edited so people truly understand.

To David Boodell, my co-writer, who must be a lesbian Jew trapped inside a heterosexual Catholic man's body. You have transformed my words and life into something that has exceeded my dreams. Liesl, thank you for supporting such a beautiful and talented man.

To my family: Cindy, who taught me the power of sharing and the beauty of art and music; Jerry, who made me popcorn and watched *Gunsmoke* with me on Saturday nights; my mother, Frieda, who saw the goodness in everyone; my father, Seymour, who brought crazy, passionate music and spontaneity into my life.

To Stevie, even though I still ache for you, I forgive you for leaving without saying good-bye. I am so sorry for your pain. Thank you for teaching me about survival and that mean curveball.

To Steve and Merilee Obstbaum, who have taught me the true meaning of family. I am forever grateful for your generosity, care and advocacy. Papa Steve, I will always remember your serious talks, urging me to write about my work. You set this off!

To my beloved Lauren, your beauty, honesty and brilliance knock me off my feet daily. Reality with you is the best fantasy I have ever had. No joke, this book would not be possible if not for you.

Finally, to our Ella Frieda, whose extraordinary spirit already shines brightly everywhere she goes. May our work make the world a safer and more compassionate place to live for you and all children. Beautiful Ella, may you always walk tall and be proud of who you are.

Here's to the peaceful revolution.

RESOURCES

The resources and books listed below are either directly related to and provided guidance for the programs described in this book or are national resources to get help.

Al-Anon
www.al-anon.org

Alcoholics Anonymous
www. alcoholics-anonymous.org

Community Works West
www.community-works-ca.org/

Family Violence Prevention Fund
www.endabuse.org

San Francisco Sheriff's Department Five Keys Charter School
www.fivekeyscharter.org

Manalive
www.manaliveinternational.org

Narcotics Anonymous
www.na.org

Restorative Justice Online
www.restorativejustice.org

University of Minnesota Restorative Justice
at the School of Social Work
     www.rjp.umn.edu

San Francisco Sheriff's Department
Resolve to Stop the Violence Project (RSVP)
     www.resolvetostoptheviolence.org

Bazemore, Gordon and Mara Schiff. *Juvenile Justice Reform and Restorative Justice: Building Theory and Policy from Practice*. Portland, Oregon: Willan Publishing, 2005.

Gilligan, James, MD. *Preventing Violence*. New York: Thames & Hudson, 2001.

Gilligan, James, MD. *Violence: Reflections on a National Epidemic*. New York: Vintage, 1997.

Pranis, Kay. *The Little Book of Circle Processes: A New/Old Approach to Peacemaking*. Intercourse, Pennsylvania: Good Books, 2005.

Zehr, Howard. *The Little Book of Restorative Justice*. Intercourse, Pennsylvania: Good Books, 2002.

ABOUT THE AUTHORS

Sunny Schwartz is a nationally recognized expert in criminal justice reform and a twenty-seven-year veteran of the criminal justice system who has devoted her career to reforming traditional incarceration, well characterized by the stereotype of "idle and wasted downtime." Ms. Schwartz speaks nationally about the establishment of the Resolve to Stop the Violence Project (RSVP), an internationally recognized, award-winning restorative justice program that brings together traditionally opposing groups in order to confront comprehensively the costs of violence. Ms. Schwartz and the RSVP method of stopping crime have been featured on national television, including *The Oprah Winfrey Show,* the Discovery Channel, PBS and *Larry King Live,* and earned the prestigious Innovations in American Government Award, sponsored by the Ash Institute at Harvard University's Kennedy School of Government.

David Boodell is a writer and documentary filmmaker living in Los Angeles. Like Sunny, he grew up in Chicago, but while she was at Wrigley, he was in the Comiskey Park bleachers rooting for the White Sox. He got his start with National Public Radio working for a Chicago arts and current affairs show and then began working in television as a writer, producer and supervising producer for nonfiction television on A&E, the History Channel, Discovery and other networks. His most recent film is *Facing Life: The Retrial of Evan Zimmerman.* This is his first book.

AN INTERVIEW WITH SUNNY SCHWARTZ

Q: Is our prison system in crisis?
A: Yes. The bad news is that there are more than 2 million people incarcerated right now and our hard-earned taxpayer money is being thrown in the garbage because 650,000 people are released every year from jails and prisons, only to have close to 70 percent return within one to three years. And what are they doing while they are in prison is a travesty and an insult to taxpayers. They're sitting there doing nothing except stewing in their violence, their denial and their lack of accountability. They are being trained to be monsters.

Q: Who is in our jails?
A: I see the grandchildren of men and women I worked with as a law student in 1980. That means that in my tenure at the Sheriff's Department, I'm seeing the third generation of incarcerated people.

Seventy-five percent of inmates are high school dropouts. Eighty percent disclosed that they are victims of child abuse and/or sexual abuse. Eighty percent reported that they've been perpetrators of violence. Ninety percent reported that they are addicts. The average reading level is fourth to seventh grade. Race is also a big issue—nationally, one black man in nine between the ages of twenty and thirty-four is incarcerated, a rate six times higher than for whites in the same age group. That is not to say that white youths are not lawbreakers, as they, too, carry and use drugs just as often as blacks, but they seldom get caught, and if they do, they are more likely to get off with a warning. In one study, 60 to 75 percent of black teenagers in Baltimore and Chicago said the police routinely harassed them.

Q: How do you measure the success of RSVP?
A: Dr. James Gilligan, who started the Center for the Study of Violence at Harvard Medical School, measured the men in RSVP compared to other violent offenders. Over several years, men in RSVP had an 80 percent reduction in violent rearrests if they were in our program for four months or more.

Q: What do you attribute it to?
A: Opportunity to change. The vast majority of violence is learned, and it can be unlearned. That is our motto. This is not therapy; it's education.

Q: Where do you hope to be in five years?
A: My dream is that every jail and prison will be a place where we create and provide no-nonsense programs that invest in people's success and our public safety. These programs must be comprehensive and must focus on changing the attitudes, beliefs and behaviors that fuel violence; they must also help prisoners' reentry into our communities, including providing continuing education and programming through our probation departments, churches, synagogues and chambers of commerce. We must invest in people's success.

Q: What new programs are you working on?
A: We are currently planning to create RSVP for Veterans. There are more than 100,000 veterans who live in or will be returning to California. The majority of those deployed will be coming home within the next three years. Approximately 15 percent of those veterans will be arrested—primarily for domestic violence, substance abuse and possession of narcotics. We must be poised to intelligently and humanely address their problems.

We are also exploring ways to address the horrible and unspeakable violence toward children. This is only in the discussion phase, but given the reality that sex offenders are released back into our communities, we think it's unconscionable to ignore them while they are incarcerated; rather, we should look at no-nonsense initiatives that will protect our children once sex offenders are released.

Q: What should people do to try and bring similar programs to their local jails?

A: I think the best way to begin is with a conversation. Begin having community meetings that include all criminal-justice stakeholders, such as probation and parole officers, court officials, public health administrators, domestic-violence service providers, faith community leaders, survivors of violence and ex-offenders who are accountable and wanting to restore their community.

Q: Neither crime nor prison reform have been at the forefront of the political discussion recently. Why is it essential that this topic be addressed now?

A: Crime affects absolutely everyone. Everyone either knows someone who has been victimized or knows someone who has committed a crime. The recent Pew study reports that one in thirty-one people in our country have either been in prison, arrested, on parole or on probation. This staggering statistic doesn't even include the millions of family and friends of victims of crime.

Depending on the jurisdiction, it costs $35,000 to $80,000 to incarcerate one person for a year. And what do we have to show for that? A 70 to 75 percent failure rate. We're making progress in San Francisco, but we and the rest of the country need to do more. We have no choice. We spend more than $50 billion a year for a 70 percent failure rate. If we continue with these same failed approaches, the prison budget will outpace state funds for health, education and infrastructure.

DISCUSSION QUESTIONS

1. Discuss the many ways that crime affects a community. Why is it important for community members to care about how our criminal justice system works?
2. The Resolve to Stop the Violence Project (RSVP) is based on the principals of restorative justice. Discuss this philosophy and the ways the principles of restorative justice are applied in the RSVP program. Can these same principles be applied in your life?
3. What's the difference between rehabilitation and restorative justice? What are the benefits and pitfalls of each?
4. How can a restorative justice approach work within our current system?
5. The RSVP program operates on the belief that people can change. Do you believe that violence is a learned behavior that can be corrected? Do you think people really can change? Why do you think people are resistant to change?
6. What happens when criminals return to their communities? How can we change the system to make their transition back to our society more successful?
7. Do you think the current way of incarcerating people keeps us safe, and if so, how? If not, why not?
8. Discuss the benefits and liabilities of RSVP. How are different people in the criminal justice system—the staff, the wardens, the prisoners, the victims, the outside community—affected by the program? How do you think defense attorneys and prosecutors are reacting to the program?
9. Is there a cost advantage to this program? Are there creative

ways to integrate these programs into our criminal justice system without costing the community too much?

10. An integral part of the RSVP program is restoration to the community. Discuss the importance of this. What are some ways offenders can give back to communities and people they have harmed?

11. Often people do not want criminals released into their communities. For example, "Not in my backyard" is heard when there is a move to have residential drug treatment homes in different neighborhoods. Why is there a fear of such treatment facilities in your community, and how can we make this happen while ensuring safety?

12. Many of the ideas behind RSVP—accountability, forgiveness, restoration—can be applied in the lives of everyday people. Sunny herself struggled with anger for many years and the program helped her have healthier relationships. Did anything in the book resonate for you on a personal level?

13. What is forgiveness? Have you done something you want to be forgiven for? What stops you from asking for forgiveness? Conversely, have you ever had to forgive someone for something?

14. Sunny Schwartz writes about being a young law student working in the jails and how she had to deal with a pedophile who was about to be released and who said that he would molest again. What does that story tell you about how our criminal justice system works? How do you think the system can be improved? What would you have done had you been in that situation?

15. Discuss the ways Sunny has stood up for people over the course of her career. Have you ever had an experience where you wanted to defend someone who was being treated unjustly? Did you stand up for that person? Why or why not?

16. If you or your loved ones have been the victims of a crime, what was most helpful or difficult about the criminal justice process? How would you change the process to benefit victims and their loved ones and to create a more humane and just system?